Making Sense of
New Labour

Making Sense of New Labour

Alan Finlayson

Lawrence & Wishart
LONDON 2003

Lawrence and Wishart Limited
99a Wallis Road
London
E9 5LN

First published 2003

British Library Cataloguing in Publication Data.
A catalogue record for this book is available from the British Library

ISBN 0 85315 956 4

Text setting E-type, Liverpool
Printed and bound by Bookcraft, Trowbridge

Contents

Introduction

Over the few years of its existence, both critics and enthusiasts have advanced various themes or ideas as central to the 'project' of New Labour. Some have focused on constitutional reform and the possibilities for an enhanced democracy,[1] others on the illiberal nature of the government's social authoritarianism.[2] Where some see a radical and bold agenda others find only vacuity and sloganeering. Still others point to a perceived capitulation to the exigencies of the global capitalist market,[3] the abandonment of substantive commitments to equality[4] and the extent to which the government emulates Thatcherism in its refusal to take on corporations and force them to be more responsible in the long-term.[5] Theorists have pointed up the affinities between New Labour and the New Liberalism of the turn of the century, to which Blair has made his allegiance explicit,[6] or the ways in which New Labour ideology involves a fusion and re-articulation of elements of the liberal, socialist and conservative traditions.[7] Still others think they detect in New Labour the adaptation of a Rawlsian approach to redistributive social justice.[8]

This list of interpretations could proliferate. Their extent and variety is indicative of the apparent fluidity of contemporary politics as well as of the specific character of New Labour. The 'project' of this government will always be in development because it is concerned with the changing nature of society and the consequent inauguration of a 'permanent revolution' (a term Blair uses in his pamphlet on The Third Way). This makes it difficult to pin down exactly what is going on with New Labour if our focus is restricted to the government and the Labour Party. To understand it we have to make sense of how it makes sense of social changes. Then the analyst can understand this open-ended activity in terms of the larger strategy of which it is a part. It is for day-by-day commentators to get carried away by whatever 'scandal' or 'initiative' is dominating the headlines of the moment. The serious analyst has to look past the froth in order to discern what the intended strategy of the government might be. Central to understanding such a strategy is making sense of what those formulating it think they are doing. If we want to know how someone is playing a particular game we have first to try and understand what sort of game they think they are playing. This too means that the focus cannot be restricted to the government and its personnel since what they think they are doing is shaped by events, processes, phenomena and ideas that are independent of them.

A serious analysis thus requires that we take New Labour seriously even when we are not taking them at face value. For New Labour the point of being in government is to stay there and to stay popular – but only so that they can continue in their historic mission of creating what Blair has called, on several occasions, a 'twenty-first century model nation'.[9] Blairism is concerned, like so many of its predecessors, to transform the British state and economy in order to meet perceived challenges brought about by wider, perhaps even epochal, transformations. New Labour is thus redefining the modes through which government takes place, but it is also part of a larger process of the redefinition of government itself, the scope of which far exceeds the narrower interests and perceptions of this particular government or its particular members. This also means that whatever is distinctive about New Labour is to be found not in their attempts to change British politics or society but in their particular way of interpreting and trying to legitimate such change.

For these reasons it is entirely insufficient, as some critics might like, simply to dismiss the government as charlatans, manipulating us through media, obsessed with maintaining power, tailoring themselves to whatever focus groups demand and motivated only by a desire for power. Nor can we simply assert that New Labour lacks the courage to take on 'Middle England' and institute the taxation policies needed to deal with decline in public services. Impugning the character or motivations of individual political actors makes good copy for columnists and has short-term political gain for party hacks. It is also often true. But it is less useful as a tool for serious explanation. New Labour did not come to power because Peter Mandelson is skilled in the 'black arts' of media manipulation or because Alastair Campbell annoyed some lobby correspondents. While facile populism certainly forms a part of New Labour (and could there be a serious government that was not concerned to have 'the people' behind it?), this is because it is a rational strategy suggested by the Labour Party's own analysis of the social, economic and political climate in which it operates. But that analysis (and the form of rationality it introduces) is itself shaped by wider presuppositions that give form to our 'political culture'. These presuppositions have been a long time in the making. They have roots that extend back into British political and cultural history, and to the intellectual history of political science, political economy and political theory – not only in the UK but in Europe and, especially, in the US. The ideas that come from this complex mixture are widely propagated not only by politicians but by academics, journalists, members of think tanks and a range of 'public intellectuals' and opinion formers. To make sense of New Labour we thus have to make sense of three things: these presuppositions themselves; the wider context that has made them seem like truths opposed only by the wildly out of touch; and the way New Labour has adapted and employed them in its own political thinking and political action.

Famously, New Labour has declared itself beyond Left and Right: the product of a post-ideological, 'anti-political' age interested in pragmatic perspectives, in what works rather than what is dogmatically right. This may be a merely vacuous rhetorical claim. But there is a sense in which New Labour is correct to see itself as transcending old political dualisms and oppositions. For New Labour cannot be understood if its ideology is simply mapped somewhere along a continuum of political philosophies structured by the differing stresses laid on oppositional terms such as public/private, civil society/state, freedom/authority, capital/labour and so forth. Basing itself on the premise that these oppositions mean less now than they have done in the past, New Labour has attempted to rework them. To understand this we shouldn't simply dissolve their pretensions back into the true dualisms on which they really stand; rather, we should attempt to understand *how* New Labour became possible, what configuration of concepts and what social and political conjuncture made this sort of thing thinkable (and attractive). The substantive political theories and strategies commonly identified as the constituent elements of New Labour are drawn from its 'conscious' ideology – the doctrines and dogma to which it itself attributes the formulation and justification of its policy and outlook. But we need also to look to its 'spontaneous' ideology, that clutch of taken-for-granted assumptions and prioritisations that inform its decisions and assessments. For New Labour also formulates its political and policy claims on the basis of certain beliefs about current social, economic and cultural conditions, from which are derived generalisations about the way society needs to be re-ordered.

Thus this is a book about ideas. But it is not concerned only with the surface level of such ideas. Making sense of New Labour through its ideas is not simply a matter of restating in more clear terms the propositions put forward in a pamphlet by Tony Blair, speech from Gordon Brown or book by Anthony Giddens. For one thing these do not usually amount to a coherent or identifiable 'philosophy'. Indeed, in trying to establish what the underlying political theory of New Labour might be we have to engage in a kind of conceptual 'backwards-engineering' because, despite numerous attempts to put across a particular theory of society and politics, New Labour is as much guided by spontaneous and unconsidered presumptions (of which it may not be aware) as it is by explicit reflections or immediate strategic necessities. In working out how New Labour makes sense of the world, we are establishing how it formulates a particular political practice out of the raw materials bequeathed to it by the traditions on the basis of which it operates. These raw materials are, to be sure, ideas but they are not philosophies. They are a clutch of opinions and arguments touching on the nature and purpose of the state, the ways in which politics can and should be conducted, the correct aspirations of individuals, the workings of the economy and so forth. This underlying 'doxa' not only shapes New Labour's attempts to establish what the truth about society and politics might be, but also predetermines, to a degree, what will count for it as a truth; it is that which is not thought out by New Labour because it makes the New Labour way of thinking possible.

In trying to specify some of the elements of this 'doxa' and examining how it affects aspects of policy, we will have to 'historicise' New Labour thinking – which is to say we will have to put it into a context that helps us understand the ways in which it has been shaped by the traditions of British politics, the structures of the political system, and the history of the Labour Party itself; but we also need to understand New Labour in terms of the 'traditions' of the 'now' – the currently predominant and fashionable ways of making sense of our world. When we examine the ideas of New Labour, suggesting that these explain what it is doing, we do so because such ideas have consequences. They lead us in certain directions, and may set us on paths of which we are not aware. They have come from somewhere, travelling to us loaded down with the baggage, souvenirs and memories picked up along the way. As Weber argued: 'very frequently the "world images" that have been created by "ideas" have, like switchmen, determined the tracks along which action has been pushed by the dynamic of interest'. What New Labour's ideas are, where they come from, how they work, how they define interests, and the way in which they relate to, and tell us about, the present political conjuncture, is the subject of this book.

In examining New Labour through essays on its approach to media, concept of modernisation, idea of politics, attitude towards the subject-citizen and theory of the state, I have deliberately included a certain amount of repetition. Readers will find that an argument made in one chapter is repeated in the different context of another. This (hopefully) has a number of effects. It rhetorically reinforces the argument and shows that there is to New Labour a consistency and coherence across 'policy areas' that is not always noticed by a pundit culture looking to make cheap digs rather than broader analyses. At the same time the way in which themes repeat themselves is also indicative of New Labour's tendency to justify a diverse range of actions through an unstable rhetorical trope such as 'modernisation'. While there is an aspect of coherence and 'big thinking' to New Labour this is also a multi-faceted and contradictory government. Such are the times. This means that developing a single theory or single perspective on New Labour is probably a mistake. It seemed to me, therefore, in trying to make sense of New Labour, that one option was to approach it from a number of different angles, trying to place each into a context greater than this government and this particular time. That meant acknowledging that themes and styles were repeated in differing contexts – such repetitions are part of New Labour. But, in the very moment of their repetition, they also become different, giving the party a degree of mobility and fluidity that is an important part of the way in which it governs, and of the way in which it convinces itself of its 'holism' or 'joined-up' nature.

There are, of course, some common threads to my arguments. Much as I have tried to pretend to be (in a loose sense) objective, I am aware that my critical (though also sometimes ambivalent) stance with regard to this government is hardly hidden. I suppose one of the things I wanted to make sense of was what it is that I do not like about New Labour, even when I find them to be (as they are on occasion) convincing. It seems to me now that my problem lies in the fact that I truly like politics, and think it matters more than anything else. It follows, naturally I think, that I believe politics is only very partially (though still significantly) about the government and political parties. Politics is an essential and undeniable aspect of all social relations, which is to say that any situation in which there is more than one person around has an aspect of the political embedded in it. I do not mean by this that everything is political all of the time. What I do mean is that social relations (the ways in which people organise their lives with, or without, regard to each other) always involve a constant nego-tiation (or conflict) as to the way in which those social relations should be organised and experienced. This could be a very bad thing, for it implies a permanent struggle for domination, a Hobbesian world of eternal conflict. But it can also be understood as a good thing in that it implies the permanent possibility of the social world being reordered by those who live in it, as long as they are able to act politically, to behave in concert, having pooled their power and resources, in order to achieve a common aim, constantly relating with each other and dealing with the problems and disputes that arise. In this sense politics is the energy within society, the name we give to the forces that make, unmake and remake it. It can be a destructive force, but it can also be a creative one. What it cannot be is ignored.

But New Labour does not like politics very much and certainly doesn't like it to happen outside of its purview. It would prefer to imagine a permanent consensus under its permanent management. It sometimes seems to be dreaming of a world of pure individuals, permanently innovating new products and managing social relations through the terms and practices of trade. Economic rather than political exchange becomes understood as the basis of community and its freest expression is the private market not the public meeting. This is not only intellectually objectionable; it is also an ideological trap. Thinking itself in tune with (and in charge of) the real movement of people, the world and history, New Labour is not really able to grasp the conditions of its own emergence or the context within which it operates. It is thus unclear about how to affect change. For this reason I think it is also important to see the strange pathos of New Labour. They really really want to change things, and think they know how to, but have no real understanding of how change happens and so find themselves frustrated, becoming more inward-looking, zealous and increasingly buffeted by 'events'. They are, in the end, the victim of circumstances they feel are beyond their control. This makes them rather contemporary and gives them something in common with the rest of us.

At the risk of sounding old fashioned it seems to me still the case that human beings live at the mercy of conditions that are of their own making. We are alienated from our own activity and do not see how we can ever begin to direct it in the ways we want. To some extent this is probably a good thing, because we don't really know what we want and a world in which we did control everything would be intolerable. But that does not invalidate the effort to make sense of and act on our world – an activity that can only ever be done collectively and which rests on our realising that we are social beings before we are individuals and so are always already thrown into a world that requires us to be political – ready and willing to take each other on in both senses of that phrase. I suspect that this is all I wanted to say.

The structure of the book is as follows.

Though I am not especially concerned with the methodology of political science, some very general conceptual issues are addressed in Chapter One. Here it is argued that New Labour needs to be understood primarily as a symptom of society rather than as a cause of anything (including itself). This claim is advanced through a consideration of transformations to the relationship between politics and communication. The movement and management of communication within a polity are fundamental to politics and, as the nature of what is and what can be communicated changes, so too does the shape of society and the distribution of powers within it.

Chapter Two, 'The Pitch: Media and Marketing', examines in more detail the ways in which New Labour has sold itself. Putting this 'political marketing' into a general context, it looks at manifestos and election broadcasts from 1997 and 2001, making sense of them in ways that open up the politics of the party.

Chapter Three examines the term 'modernisation'. It argues that this fulfils a key function in the rhetoric of New Labour and structures their political thinking in significant ways. 'Making sense' of modernisation is both what New Labour does and sees itself as for. But modernisation is also a form of governance. Thus this chapter tries to show how the practice as well as rhetoric of modernisation are central to New Labour.

Chapter Four, 'Politics: The Third Way', examines the concept of the third way in terms of how it implicitly structures New Labour's conception of politics. It puts the third way into the context of some recent and relevant political and intellectual history, but focuses primarily on aspects which, I argue, have most bearing on the government's notion of the political. This too leads us to consider the ways in which New Labour understands government as having to take place.

Chapter Five, 'The Subject, Citizenship and Welfare', utilises recent theories concerning the 'constitution' of subjectivity to explicate the ways in which New Labour imagines (and its policies create) the ideal subject of the new economy and society, paying particular attention to the organisation of welfare.

This builds up to Chapter Six, 'Culture and the State', which looks at the way in which New Labour uses and operates the state. The chapter draws attention to the way in which New Labour is developing a form of governance centred on 'culture'.

The book then concludes with a review of these arguments and seeks to extend them into something more reconstructive and proactive (though only in a very general manner). The conclusion begins an argument about the ways in which the 'principle of the political' could usefully be applied across a range of governmental (and ultimately social) activities.

Debts that can never be repaid are always incurred in a project such as this and the dispersed nature of the original work which formed the basis of some of the essays in this book has increased these greatly. Firstly the editors of the various journals that saw fit to publish the essays that got me started on this study. Doreen Massey, Mike Rustin and Stuart Hall at *Soundings*; Paul Thompson at *Renewal* and Andrew Gamble and Tony Wright at *Political Quarterly*. Also the editors of books in which my essays appeared (and who were in part responsible for encouraging me to dwell on this): Timothy Bewes and Jeremy Gilbert (editors of *Cultural Capitalism*, London, Lawrence and Wishart, 2000) and Wendy Wheeler, (editor of *The Political Subject*, London, Lawrence and Wishart, 2000). In addition to all the helpful comments derived from these editors I have also benefited from conversations over an extended period with James Martin, Ben Levitas, Jeremy Gilbert (again) and Jeremy Valentine. Sally Davison at Lawrence and Wishart took the task of editing to be an intellectual as well as technical activity (a rare recognition in the profit-hungry world of publishing) and in so doing contributed greatly to whatever clarity this book may have. Numerous conversations with Keri Finlayson have also shaped my perspective immensely. Final dedication must go to Luke and Jake for putting up with my hogging the computer when they (quite properly) wanted to play games. I hope this has affected their entry into the new knowledge economy.

Notes

1. See for example Stewart Wood (1999) 'Constitutional Reform – living with the consequences' *Renewal*, 7 (3), pp1-10.
2. See for example, Ralf Dahrendorf (1999) Whatever Happened to Liberty, *New Statesman*, 6 September, pp25-27.
3. See for example, David Held (1998) 'The Timid Tendency', *Marxism Today*, pp24-27; Doreen Massey (1998) 'Editorial', *Soundings* 7.
4. See for example, Roy Hattersley, 'Why I'm no Longer Loyal to Labour', *Guardian*, 26.7.97.
5. Amongst others see Colin Hay (1999) *The Political Economy of New Labour*, Manchester, Manchester University Press.
6. Andrew Vincent (1998) 'New Ideologies for Old?' *Political Quarterly*, 69, No. 1, pp48-58. See also Tony Blair, *Let Us Face the Future*, London, Fabian Society 1995.
7. Michael Freeden (1999) 'The Ideology of New Labour', *Political Quarterly*, Vol. 69, No.2.
8. Steve Buckler and David P. Dolowitz (2000) 'Theorizing the Third Way: New Labour and Social Justice', *Journal of Political Ideologies*, Vol. 5, No. 3, pp301-320. See also the critical response: Marcel Wissenburg (2001), 'The Third Way and Social Justice', *Journal of Political Ideologies*, Vol. 6, No. 2, pp231-235.
9. See Tony Blair (1998) *Speech to Labour Party Conference*; (1999) *Speech to Labour Party Conference*.

CHAPTER ONE

Making Sense of the New Labour Symptom

Introduction

A central thesis of this book is that New Labour is not so much a cause as an effect; a symptom more than a source of what ails the body politic. A good doctor should not treat only the symptoms a patient experiences (much as immediate relief is desirable) but, on the basis of the symptoms with which that patient presents, try to determine the underlying cause of disease. But this search for the underlying reality (of which the symptoms are merely visible signs or expressions) doesn't mean that one can ignore the symptoms themselves. After all, they are no less real and the only evidence placed before us.

Were we psychoanalysts (rather than medical doctors) we might say that the hysterical symptoms with which a neurotic patient presents have a degree of rationality about them. Just as an allergic reaction is indicative of the body trying too hard to cure something it perceives as a threat, so the hysterical symptom may be the manifestation of an attempt to work round or through some original traumatic event that cannot be grasped directly. By paying careful attention to what the patient does and says (to the ways in which the symptoms manifest themselves), the analyst hopes to be able to work out what event those symptoms refer to.

Tempting though it may be, the suggestion that politics is the realm in which the hysterical symptoms of society are expressed is not being made here. Nor is the political analyst like the medical doctor taking on the job of relieving unsightly swelling. But there are traditions of political analysis that try to do something like this. Marxism, for example, teaches us that political events and expressions can be understood by reference back to the traumatic class struggle on which capitalist society is based, and which is a fundamental source of conflict that cannot be openly expressed lest it lead to revolutionary collapse.

Conservative philosophies argue that social 'pathologies' (teenage pregnancy, welfare dependency, crime, etc) are an expression of the moral collapse brought about by a rejection of traditional authority, the original crime of social parricide to which liberal individualism cannot admit.

We too want to understand contemporary politics, as manifested by New Labour, as a symptomatic expression of underlying contradictions and conflicts. But where Marxism, Conservatism or psychoanalysis usually begin with some certainty as to the primary cause of all trauma (class conflict, the rejection of tradition or the oedipal complex), we do not start out with such a certain diagnosis. Instead we will have to pay careful attention to the way our symptom (New Labour) is expressed, in order to refer back to its causes and to the contradictions from which it may derive. A number of these (though not all of them) are fairly apparent: a fixation on media management; a desperate need continually to evaluate poll data; demands for a 'big idea' followed by its proud declaration then almost immediate disavowal (as with 'stake-holding' or the 'third way'); a refusal to identify enemies combined with sudden lashings out at a variety of perceived combatants ('consensus' politics in which anything that questions modernisation is 'old' Labour or a 'force of conservatism'); the dissemination of power (to regions, devolved assemblies, local authorities, boards of school governors) and the simultaneous imposition of centrally devised regulations (or candidates). These symptoms are not unique to New Labour or to British politics. That this is so suggests that New Labour is itself the symptom of underlying problems in the general organisation and enacting of politics in Britain.

To interpret or make sense of New Labour we have to begin by acknowledging that (because of its symptomatic nature) New Labour cannot be understood on its own terms, since these terms can only be understood by reference back to that of which they are the symptom. However, at the same time we can only make sense of New Labour if we pay attention to the very terms it uses and actions it takes, since these are where it manifests the symptoms. That is why, in this book, the primary source is what New Labour actually says.

Because words are so important to this study we need, in setting the scene for our 'diagnosis', first to think a little about political language; to clarify some things about the relationships between communication, words and politics; to begin exposing some of the ways in which these relationships have been transformed thus affecting the way New Labour functions. As a result the rest of this chapter is a little more abstract than the rest, but essential nevertheless.

Politics, words and ideas

Politics is very much a matter of words expressed in certain ways, in certain formats or locations, in order to achieve certain effects. This is not everything to do with politics, but we do need to give proper account of the symbolic and communicative aspect of politics, as well as those political moments concerned with rational or transparent negotiation and deliberation, stitch-ups managed by elites or the exercise of domination, be it economic or physical/military. At the very least we have to acknowledge that politics under democratic constitutions is about some people trying to persuade the rest of us of their virtues or the virtues of their political position. To do so, they employ rhetoric intended to illustrate the ways in which their political programme will be good for us by, for example, associating it with positive ends and characteristics. Anyone who has had any involvement in a political organisation or campaign knows that a central aspect of such activity is the strategic one of trying to find ways in which to connect with the wider public through various images, modes of speech and so forth. The power of the US presidency may be only 'the power to persuade' as Neustadt put it,[1] but that is an important power, dependent on the capacity of the occupant of that office to transmit a persuasive presence based on the embodiment of a particular type or set of values that can legitimate a political programme or campaign.

As a British example consider the behaviour of Tony Blair when, in his first term of office, Princess Diana was killed. At the time the press and other commentators all remarked on the Prime Minister's ability to be in tune with, and so shape, the popular mood. As Norman Fairclough has pointed out, Blair's words after the death managed to combine the articulation of a collective expression (what 'we' were all feeling) with a personalised and informal manner of talking.[2] He began by speaking about his own feelings before shifting to how we, the nation, felt. Mixed in with a formal statement were vernacular terms – he spoke of being 'utterly devastated' (perhaps a phrase we more usually hear uttered by defeated footballers on cup-final day) and said, 'Our thoughts and prayers are with Princess Diana's family – in particular her two sons, two boys – our hearts going out to them', the inclusion of the term 'two boys' incorporating the intimate into the formal. Through such linguistic mechanisms Blair simultaneously displayed formal authority and an ordinary 'blokeishness' that is central to his style.

This symbolic or stylistic aspect of politics cannot simply be discounted as irrelevant, superficial or only for the benefit of stupid people. It is part of what lends legitimacy to the office of Prime Minister or President (if not to the actual incumbent), and gives it, automatically, the charisma that Weber identified as one of the sources of authority. It is also one of the central 'powers' of politics. Giving definition to certain events or phenomena is not only about pulling the wool over the eyes of a gullible public. It is a fundamental social activity: one that increases in importance as society becomes more complex and differentiated.

This activity of giving definition and making sense is particularly important in the post-Enlightenment world. For, despite the pleasing caricature portrait of 'modernity' as bringer of order and reason to the social universe, it now looks much more like the introduction of systematic disruption and contingency. A world ordered from the top down in the name of an absolute God, manifested through an established church, gave way to one forged only in the name of man, in which the free thought of the individual was taken to be paramount. This collapse of an absolute authority able to declare the objectivity of itself was substituted by a subjective principle, threatening to lead to the permanent clash of opinion that Hobbes feared: the war of all against all. At the same time stable social roles derived from traditional hierarchies, and the general immobility of people, began to give way to the endless opportunities of trade and commerce and, eventually, the boundless possibilities of democracy – in which, as Plato warned, everyone arranges their life as pleases them the most, where the 'diversity of characters, like the different colours in a patterned dress, make it look very attractive'. For Plato the democratic character is always shifting, variable and lacking in the solid foundations that can only come from a rigorous (and restrictive) philosophical search for the truth.[3] In such a context sophists become powerful. They purvey pretty words whose function is to organise our ways of looking at the world and give to them the semblance of unified sense. But sophists will do whatever they are paid to do, and produce conceptions that please rather than are true. In the modern democratic world, grateful to be shorn of despotisms, sophists came to be called 'ideologists', providing solid ground to a world that defied the principle of having a ground, and that was hiding from itself the truth that it was the source of its own institution and much declared objectivity.[4]

Sophists become popular because, standing on the shifting ground of a complex and varied society, in which rules are unreliable and social position can seem a matter of chance (even when it is nothing of the sort), we modern democrats find ourselves faced with the horrific task of having always actively to grasp the nature of our social existence and to make sense of it for ourselves. Sociologists – such as Anthony Giddens – tell us that we recreate habits and routines in order to establish security and stability; and Goffman suggested that we adopt roles and read from ready-made scripts in the hope of giving to social inter-action the regularity of a daily performance.[5] Others seek out a stable promontory from which they can exercise judgement: the certainty of experimental method, of felt religious truth, of the always rational choice of individual wills, the mathematical precision of econometrics, the structured explanations of psychologists or evolutionary theorists. Phenomenologists turn to the ways in which we orient ourselves to the things, the tools, of the world into which we are thrown; structuralists and functionalists (like all metaphysicians) look to the underlying regularities that produce what only appears as variety and transforma-tion, while a new kind of social critic (made possible by that same enlightened modernity) shows how we establish certainty through clinging to the unity and closure afforded by ideologies or the simple somatic satisfactions of the commodities served up by the culture industries.

Social life and solidarity (as nineteenth-century sociologists found in the midst of their anomie) turn on the generation of meaning and the making of sense in common. While anthropologists observed the unconscious generation of such commonality in the rituals of 'primi-tive' peoples, for modern societies it became a conscious activity and, by extension, a political one. From Marx to Arnold, Sorelian mythology to Parsonian functionalism, the creation or management of consciousness became a primary concern. In our 'late-modern', 'post-modern' or 'hyper-modern' societies, the making of sense is now not only a conscious activity and object for scholastic investigation. It is an industry, usually called advertising, public relations or marketing: a social necessity turned into a commercial opportunity.

Human beings live in worlds shaped by metaphor. For us a rose is never just a rose – it is a token of love, a charming young beauty, a brand image for a political party. In complex, capitalistic, democratic societies, where we always jostle alongside each other, it is through sharing in meaning and metaphor that some semblance of community and consensus can be attained (or won). We are all making sense as we go along – but not alone, for there is always someone there offering it to us. As Zygmunt Bauman points out, citing Ernest Becker, 'Society is a living myth of the significance of human life, a defiant creation of meaning ... All societies are factories of meaning ... the nurseries of meaningful life'.[6] We seek, however, a transcendent meaning, a touch of immortality to lift us out of our frighteningly finite nature. As a primary form of social power, this creation of meanings, especially of apparently transcendent ones, is of the most fundamental importance for politics. Indeed, politics, we might say, has often involved the establishment of these shared delusions: it can be a supremely creative activity.

Governing, meanwhile, is concerned with the management and defence of such shared delusions, an activity not necessarily, any longer, carried out exclusively by governments (who face stiff competition in the 'market' for social delusion). Understanding this process requires us to investigate how those with power have attempted to dominate our understandings and interpretations – how they have made sense of things for us. Domination is not only a matter of instilling fear into people. As any reader of Machiavelli knows, it is far better to make the people love you, believe in you and want to follow you.

But the meanings any of us make (whatever our power) do not emerge from a vacuum. They are dependent on prior meanings and interpretations, the innumerable forms and modes of representation with which we are surrounded. In making sense of something, we draw on sources, themes and influences that shape us consciously and unconsciously. Thus, investigation must also focus on how those with power come to forge their own understandings and on what shaped their illusions. We are not simply looking at what 'they' are doing to 'us', but at what we, all of us, do to ourselves.

A political project can be thought of as an attempt to be the determining centre of this network – to be in charge of it, direct it and determine what sense can and cannot be made out of it. Part of what political movements, parties and governments are up to is making sense of things on our behalf. They interpret the world for us and then ask us to believe in their interpretation. But they too are caught within wider networks of 'sense-making'. Consider, for example, those landmark texts that achieve such a hold on the ways we make sense to ourselves and each other that they introduce new terms even concepts into our vocabulary. These range from the obvious and incontrovertible, such as readings of the Judeo-Christian bible that shape pretty much everything around us in the West, to more minor but not insignificant works such as a novel like Mary Shelley's *Frankenstein*, which brought to the world not only a good story but a new term that is often used to help us conceptualise science, mankind, the creation of life and (latterly) the food industry.

Communication is *always* prone to this sort of surplus, and to the tendency to exceed the intentions of all parties. The authors of the sexual code prevalent in parts of Bronze Age Palestine were not intending to provide a justification for discriminatory policies in the southern states of the contemporary USA. Mary Shelley presumably did not hold a firm opinion on the genetic modification of soya. But their expressions were meaningful because of their place within an already existing set of (possibly inexhaustible) meanings to which they were added, becoming tools for further acts of sense making. This is not a process with much finality. Acts of communication or meaning-making 'well up', as it were, from the reservoir of potential communications or meanings. They bring with them some of their prior associations and are reshaped and reiterated (in certain ways) before passing on.

So it is that the words of any politician are never quite their own. As the Marxist literary critic Terry Eagleton points out (in a very different context and with reference to Jonathan Culler), to say to someone 'I love you' is always in part to offer up a quotation. Love itself is inde-finable and only expressible because we are referred back to its prior expressions. This citation carries the weight of our feelings when we try to make them known. But this means that '... in its very moment of absolute, original value, the self stumbles across nothing but other people's lines, finds itself handed a meticulously detailed script to which it must slavishly conform'.[7] As in love so in politics. When any politician speaks of 'freedom', 'choice' or 'justice', he or she is, inevitably, referring back to and drawing upon an entire tradition of political theory, argument, rhetoric and practice. These concepts may well be, as Gallie argued, 'essentially contestable'.[8] But the politician aims to 'de-contest' them and so provide them with a solid meaning and foundation (the better to put forward a programme that appears convincing and legitimate). And it is not just these core political concepts that are expressed in the form of quotation or citation. We can add more recent and ambiguous terms, such as 'modernisation', 'knowledge economy' or 'globalisation', which acquire much of their meaning and force from the way they are used. But they are never empty terms prior to their use, and bring to political speech their own interests (as it were) and elements of their previous usage.

It is with this background in mind that we can assess the sympto-matic statements of New Labour. In so doing we must place those statements into three interlinked contexts. Firstly, the immediate linguistic context in which we read not only what is said but how it is said, since the style and means of expression shapes their meaning and may even be part of it. Secondly, we have to put this into the broader historical context that has given political words and phrases their meanings. This includes the range of arguments, claims and policy positions that have been advanced within the British labour move-ment, and the international and intellectual left, as well as the counter-arguments that, particularly over the last twenty years, have been advanced by the conservative and neo-liberal right. Thirdly, we need to consider the context provided by the structures and institu-tions that shape the terrain on which political actions in the UK take place. This includes obvious things (but not so obvious they should be ignored), such as the fact that British politics takes the form of representative parliamentary democracy in which governmental office is secured only through popular election, or that the economy of the UK is capitalistic in form and is structured by the need continually to produce profit that can be distributed to shareholders or owners of corporations and firms. We need, then, to refer to specific features of the British state form, especially as shaped by recent political interventions such as Thatcherism, an earlier rewriting of the script of British politics, which changed the nature of the play being performed. In this sense an analysis of New Labour has to understand the kind of play New Labour believes itself to be adapting, and the stage on which it is forced to perform.

Political scientists can argue endlessly about the hierarchy of such contexts. Half of them prefer to make the institutions and structures the primary concern and to understand political actions as derived from them. The other half choose to push such institutions to the background the better to focus on the rational choices political actors make. Here, we reject both these options. Structures, to re-use an old phrase, do not march in the streets, and they do not often enunciate political statements. Political actors do that, but they do so in circumstances not of their own choosing, and conditioned by those structures, including linguistic and philosophical ones. True political skill consists in finding ways of doing and saying political things that, just as they come from such structures, supplement and transform them. If this could not be done there would be no history. But if we could do anything we please there would be no politics, only permanently shifting individual preferences, the rationality of which would be intelligible to nobody but those whose preferences they were.

Our focus here is determined by the object of study: it is New Labour (and not political science) that we want to understand. For us that means we have to examine the ways in which New Labour makes sense of the range of ideological or political positions that predominate in the political discourse of the west and how, in making sense of them in particular ways, it believes itself to be transforming them. To be sure, to truly understand everything of what New Labour is up to we would have to take note not only of the ongoing development of British and international capitalism, but also the changing nature of social and cultural life in the West and the history that has shaped this – which is to say that making sense of New Labour ultimately requires making sense of everything else. A project of such scope is impossible. For this reason we will limit the focus of our analysis to the words and ideas of New Labour and the ways these have worked themselves into government and affected the ways in which it takes place. Other matters will be referred to in the course of our study, but they cannot be the primary focus.

There is a certain tradition found within the social sciences generally, but of particular importance for the left, that tends to subordinate ideas to what it believes to be material reality. For this tradition ideas are to be understood as the reflections of social structures. In as much as such a view challenges the naïve supposition that society or history can be explained by reference to ideas presumed to have been independently generated in the minds of particular individuals and then simply applied to the real world, it has great virtue. But in as much as it reduces thought itself to the mere expression of social conditions this is a highly problematic approach (and one that nobody really believes). Conversely, in analysing the political ideas of New Labour we are not restricted to the explication of the books and pamphlets from and in which New Labour has tried to develop philosophy and policy (as if our project was only to give coherence to what previously lacked it). Ideas take on a concrete reality when they are operationalised. The mechanism by which ideas are operationalised is communication. It is only through communication that ideas are able to be manifested either as ideological programmes or policy prescriptions. In communicating (to a public, to its supporters, to its employees or to itself), a government or political party is engaging in a specific form of social and political action undertaken in order to motivate. This action is not reducible to the social, structural or historical context within which the action takes place. It is not even reducible to the systems or structures of communication (much as that matters). It is its own element articulated with all these others. It is part of that context, and that context also includes among its elements the forms of communication employed within and upon it. The rest of this chapter will (in order to explicate this a little further) investigate politics, communication and New Labour in some more detail. It will show that it is worthwhile, when trying to 'make sense' of New Labour, to refuse to ignore its 'style' and presentation and instead to make this a part of the analysis. Indeed, it is necessary to do this because that style is itself part of New Labour's policy and of its way of trying to govern us. These are not 'merely' cultural or ideological elements, although they do not exhaust all that there is to politics. Communicative power is not independent from coercive or economic power. But then these are, by the same token, not isolable from communicative power. Nor are the cultural, symbolic or ideological elements of a political project something that the leaders of New Labour or any other political movement are able (through sheer skill and will) simply to seize on and manipulate in order to gain power – although, as we have seen, this is certainly a part of the art of politics. Let us turn then to an example from New Labour's General Election campaign. A fuller discussion of New Labour's media presentation makes up Chapter Two. For now we are interested in illustrating only abstract themes.

(Not so) smart propaganda
As far as I was concerned the 2001 General Election campaign began on Sunday 18 March when, for the first time, I saw the billboard poster released by the Labour Party the previous day. It was a film poster:

> The Tories Present: ECONOMIC DISASTER II. Coming to a home, hospital, school and business near you.

It 'starred' the only two Tory front-benchers (other than Anne Widdecombe) that (at that time) most of us could immediately identify: 'Michael Portillo as Mr Boom' and 'William Hague as Mr Bust'.

The immediate message of the poster was obvious. In the top right-hand corner, where on normal film posters we would find the BBFC age certification, was the label '15%', the interest rate after disaster befell the Major government's Exchange Rate Mechanism policy in 1992. In the bottom right, where the poster was identified as a Labour Party product, was the slogan that could sum up the whole 2001 Labour campaign: 'Don't go back'. Judging by this poster it is indeed all a question of 'the economy, stupid', and the central selling point of Labour's campaign was that the Tories were simultaneously rubbish and frightening.

This was a smart, if gimmicky, poster, both crudely obvious and rather subtle. It lacked the immediate transparency of the rival Tory poster campaign that took the form 'You paid the tax ... so where are the teachers/police/nurses'. The film-poster style made it less obviously a political advertisement. It might have made some of us look at it more closely than we otherwise would, thinking it a real film. It was a poster that needed to be interpreted to be understood. We had to spend time letting the image occupy our mind (and the competition for access to that part of our 'private' space is indeed intense).

The poster did not seek to advance a substantive policy proposal or an ideological argument. It did not even make a direct statement, seeking only to establish a connection, or connotation: the Tory party equals economic disaster. They had brought it about before and would bring it about again if elected. The photograph of Portillo made him appear smug – all grin and jowls. Hague, eyes half-closed, the corners of his mouth turned down, appeared both resigned and ineffectual. This is how propaganda works. It establishes a connection between something positive or negative and that which the propagandist wants to promote or denigrate. Here, Portillo and Hague were shown to be destructive, consumed by their own disastrous economic implosion. The advert did not invite dialogue but sought to create an image of truth.

At one level this is not particularly new or interesting. The techniques of advertising have been employed in the service of political campaigning many times before (see Chapter Two, below). In 1979 the advertising agency Saatchi and Saatchi produced the Conservative Party election advertising campaign, including the subsequently famous poster showing a long queue of the unemployed accompanied by the slogan 'Labour Isn't Working'. Certainly this was propaganda – and effective too. It condensed a particular view of the state of the country, and of who was responsible for it, into a single image and a memorable three-word slogan. But, while the Saatchi and Saatchi poster employed some of the tricks or skills of advertising – its double pun leading to an intriguingly paradoxical statement – it still very clearly belonged to what we might call the genre of political sloganeering. It may not have been as historic and successfully inspirational as Lenin's 'Peace, Bread, Land', but, despite being negative in orientation, it aimed to work in essentially the same sort of way, deploying advertising techniques in the service of the tradition of political campaigning and propaganda, conveying a specific message. But is this still the case with Labour's film-poster advertising campaign twenty-two years later?

The style of the Hollywood blockbuster advert would probably have been unconsciously obvious to many people – especially to those who regularly go to the movies (by and large younger voters and those not yet eligible to exercise that democratic privilege). The orange and red explosion out of which the words 'Economic Disaster II' seemed to emerge was reminiscent of the wave of spectacular action-adventure films with which Hollywood plied us during the 1990s – a science-fiction flick such as *Armageddon* (1998) or a more straightforward disaster picture like *Volcano* (1997). Was the poster trying to make us feel that the Tories are like a bad movie? The reference to Portillo and Hague as Mr Boom and Mr Bust (deliberate usage of a charge previously made against Labour governments by the Tory party), connected not only to a critique of their economic competence, but also to 'cool' films like Tarantino's 1992 *Reservoir Dogs* (with a *dramatis personae* all referred to as Mr ...), or to *Lock, Stock and Two Smoking Barrels*, which was populated by fictional gangsters bearing monikers such as Barry the Baptist, Bacon and Hatchet Harry.

The poster appealed to our appreciation of these references; and to

the young and fashionable, for whom such movies are the very definition of film art. It announced a self-conscious 'postmodernism' – a
deliberate and knowing fusion of otherwise disparate styles or genres
of popular cultural address and discourse. Perhaps, at this level, the
poster was also 'for' the people who made it – the advertising executives and the style-conscious Millbank minions for whom it was
probably much more impressive and clever than anything the Tories
could ever come up with. For these adverts the medium was the
message. The style of their expression was as important as the content.
This told us that the adverts were made by people who regard themselves as in control of a particular medium; that they are not only style
conscious, but also consider it necessary to link into our popular
culture consciousness in order to put across their message. Part of that
message was that the producers know all about popular culture. Not
only do they know about Hollywood movies, they also know that
these are something spoofed, joked about and used to make references
or put across points. They know how such things are a meaningful part
of the everyday cultural landscape most of us have little choice but to
inhabit. The adverts did not only use a style to put across a point – their
style was part of the point. In making the Tories look stupid and like
bad movies the adverts also put their makers above this, as, by implication, savvy and sophisticated consumers and users of contemporary
culture. As one commentator said of a Labour Party broadcast from
the 1997 election, rapid jump-cuts and a zippy style were 'more about
conveying an impression of newness, change and youth to Generation
X voters than about communicating formal content'.[9]

The campaign continued once the General Election was properly
underway. Towards the end of May, Labour unveiled two more posters
in the same vein. The 'U' certificate 'Towering Interest Rates': 'A Tory
Production' about 'Millions of people trapped by two men's incompetence'. The accompanying image was of a grand looking skyscraper, in
the shape of the magic number 15%, flames shooting out and
surrounded by helicopters. In the foreground were Hague and Portillo,
described respectively as 'the builder' and 'the architect'. It was a solid
enough pastiche of the 1970s disaster movie poster, most obviously of
Towering Inferno (1974), which, like most of this genre, combined a
hackneyed story line with a thin moral message about hubris.
Accompanying this poster was another, 'The Return of ... The
Repossessed', in which the prospect of a Tory government shifted from
naff disaster movie to cult 1950s drive-in exploitation flick. This time
Hague and Portillo were a couple of zombies and the tag line was 'No
home is safe from spiralling interest rates'. Together the posters rein-
forced the message that the Tories are economically incompetent and

that we must remember the disaster of negative equity. But, once again, they did not advance this message in the form of a simple and memorable slogan as direct as 'Labour isn't Working'. Rather than being couched in the terms of 'traditional' political advertising it took on the contemporary parodic style prevalent in advertising more generally.

These posters were brought together in the second of Labour's television election broadcasts. Beginning with a mock-up of the BBFC certificate that accompanies all cinema releases (this time for 'Tory Policies Will Hurt'), the voice-over delivered the classic line: 'Just when you thought it was safe again ... they're back'; this was followed by: 'from the people that brought you *Economic Disaster: The Tory Years*, comes a series of sequels, even more terrifying'. The broadcast also sought to remind us of the disaster of the Tory years and the threat that they represented to the stability of our economy. It harped on that rise in interest rates, the incompetence of the Tory administration, the loss of homes and the threat to public service spending. Once again the advert sought to appeal at the connotative level rather than through stating any general case.

However, this broadcast while slick and in some ways an accurate pastiche, did not work. I do not mean that it didn't convince people – this is hardly the function of the under-watched and doomed Party Election Broadcast. Rather, it didn't work on its own terms. The internal narrative of the broadcast was undermined by a tension between the form and the content. It was a parody of an advertisement, the kind that tries to convince you that you want to go and see an exciting, scary movie. It thus ran close to presenting the Tories as, in some way, worth going to see: a spectacle, an exciting if scarily bizarre phenomenon. As a result, half-way through, the advert had to change tack. In a scene reminiscent of the 1996 film *Independence Day* (in which giant alien space ships hover over Earth's major cities), we saw a darkening shadow fall over ordinary street scenes and heard how: 'You gasped in horror as the Tory shadow of disaster fell across the nation ... no city, town or home was safe. People ran to avoid being caught in its devastating path yet it was still to unleash the full force of its fiscal fury'. Then the voice dropped a register, leaving behind the dramatic tempo of a sales pitch and intoned: 'It would have been funny if hadn't been so tragic ...'. The advert then turned into a more straightforward reminder of how the Tory years threatened homes and jobs before returning at the end to Mr Boom and Mr Bust.

This hiatus or break was revealing. The parodic register simply clashed with that of political product placement. The manifest content of the broadcast was that Tories are bad for you – run away from them. But this could not be expressed fully in the context of a parody of adverts for exciting and successful Hollywood movies. Parody neces-sarily involves identification with the object of mockery and makes the viewpoint of that which is parodied also the viewpoint of the performer. As Judith Butler argues: 'it is impossible to perform a convincing parody ... without having a prior affiliation with what one parodies, without having and wanting an intimacy with the position one takes in or on as the object of parody'. Parody 'troubles the voice, the bearing ... the audience or reader does not quite know where to stand, whether you have gone over to the other side, whether you remain on your side, whether you can rehearse that other position without falling prey to it in the midst of the performance'.[10] In straying into the genre of parody, New Labour's election strategists ran this risk of having their own voice overtaken by that which they were mocking. Now, this seems to be a more general problem with New Labour. It is never clear in what voice they speak, or in what register. Ministers and back-benchers seem robbed of their own voices, afraid of angering the Gods of Millbank by chanting the wrong incantation, or of bringing hellfire down upon their heads by giving our relentless media too much information or too much space. The parodic voice might therefore seem attractive, since it enables one to make a point without actually committing to anything. But the risk is that our voice becomes lost to the parody and we become speakers of another language. In this case New Labour risked becoming not Tories but Hollywood film producers.

It may appear that politics has become subordinate to the entertain-ment industry or, worse, that New Labour treats the public as if they can only understand things expressed in the terms of popular (rather than political) culture. The posters and the broadcast were not simply using the language of the entertainment industry; they were using it to say the sort of things we say about that entertainment industry; and they were relying on its language in order to be able to express some-thing. They were not simply drawing on the lessons that can be learnt from successful marketing (though they certainly did do that). In this campaign, New Labour were speaking their political truth in and through the language of popular culture – primarily American popular culture – and in the ironic fashion which is central to it. The political claim was not totally subsumed into popular media culture; but, equally, it was not using it solely as a vehicle. It is not that the Labour Party simply gave into popular culture and dispensed with all political point-scoring of a normal sort. The posters were still political posters in an old style – mocking the intended target, trying to undermine them. Electoral campaigning has not turned into a mere showbiz spec-tacular where we choose the troupe that entertains us most. Rather, this aspect of the campaign indicates that, in some way, political language and the language of popular culture and entertainment are inextricably interwoven. Advertisers produce TV adverts that are often visually better than many films. Films are directed by advertisers and draw on its techniques. Propaganda has almost always been a part of Hollywood movies, and politics speaks to us in terms derived from the movies. All draw on the same set of resources.

New Labour presents itself as just like everything else we encounter in a world dominated and defined by mass culture and advertising. But rather than showing New Labour as sucked in by a form of communication more common to mass and popular media than to political discourse, or as simply exploiting that media, these adverts suggest that both moments (that of political communication and 'ironic' entertainment) are contained within the same process. It is as if it is no longer possible to think of the discourse of politics and that of entertainment as discrete entities. The possibility of an authoritative distinction between a political statement and something said as entertainment is slipping away. The authorisation of politicians to make statements of a political kind has collapsed. We might find more sense and meaning, a better comment on our condition, in a Hollywood film or a late-night sitcom than in a House of Commons debate (but then, there may well be better jokes made in a late-night commons debate than in anything so strained as a British situation comedy). Rooted in an increasingly pervasive condition, the adverts are best understood as symptomatic. It is to this condition that we now turn.

Communicating politics

Communication is absolutely fundamental to politics. This was the claim made by Aristotle when he argued that our capacity for speech differentiated us from other animals and made it possible for people to come to a common view of what was just or unjust. For Aristotle it is because we are the animal that speaks that we can be the political animal also. Communication is constitutive of politics and polities because through it disagreements can be manifested and agreements about what is just or unjust reached. Aristotle's teacher, Plato, also understood this and made his philosophical-political project that of separating politics from all forms of speech (poetry or rhetoric for example) except for philosophy which alone searched for the truth. Classical political theory in general devoted itself to the study of particular forms or modes of communication and to the explication of their practice. For the inhabitants of democratic Athens the art of speech, or rhetoric, was central to the exercise of power or influence. Politics was about speaking well in the proper arenas and winning people over. It had its own language, its own rhetoric, with its own modes that, some believed, could be taught and learnt.

Medieval societies also specified forms of, and locations for talk, from courtly speech and religious liturgy to the telling of tales, and through this they divided society and persons, each communicative form being linked to social groups with specific forms of power (monarchical, religious, cultural). In modern societies communication (in the form of free speech) has become a central pillar of the liberal democratic vision. It is the conduit and expression of freedom and rationality. In contemporary political philosophy many now argue that the space of communication is the one in which rationality can be grounded: a mutually enriching form of spoken argumentation provides the ethical context and ontological basis for the securing of political reason.[11] Simultaneously, futurist visions of cyberspace as a smooth and equal space of free and open communication seem, to some, to make possible a concrete manifestation of such an ideal.[12] States face insistent demands for clarity, and politicians have come to speak in more demotic modes of discourse (because nobody must be 'talked down' to). Politicians (or intellectuals) who do not adopt such modes of speech can easily find themselves accused of breaching the liberal ethic of 'equality'.

All this has helped to make democratic societies complex and hard to manage from any central location. The numbers of people allowed to speak in formally public spaces, and the mechanisms that allow them to do so or that create such formally public spaces, have increased dramatically. The court room is one of the only spaces left where people still mostly believe they need a professional person to speak the correct language on their behalf (it is also, not coincidentally, one of few public spaces not to be made visible through live television). But the more people have been allowed to speak in public in this way, the more each specialised role within the division of labour has sought to produce its own distinctive form of speech. These are our ubiquitous professional idioms, many of which are developed and deployed in professional or trade publications. In the past the state in western societies took on the role of managing the translations between different groups in society. It has co-ordinated discrete spheres such as the legal, military, cultural and economic, or has claimed explicitly to be able to mediate between, say, capital and labour. But as the demand for absolute transparency and openness at all levels becomes ever more shrill (all hospital and educational records must be published, all minutes of every political meeting made available), the privileged position from which society can be managed shrinks and political speech comes to appear as just another professional idiom.

If politics is to be able to perform the task of mediating between component parts of a society then it must necessarily be clearly authorised to do so. In the past, in the British political system, this was achieved through the sorts of regulations that, in the name of openness, are no longer permitted: restrictions on the repeating of things said in Parliament; guarantees that certain statements would be made there first; deference to politicians and the way they were talked about in the public arena.

Contestation of the boundaries that hedged off political speech from other sorts of speech has been central to democratic politics. At first this took the form of contesting who could speak. Demands were made (and eventually satisfied) that working men and then women be acknowledged as able to speak politically. But latterly this has extended into a general challenge to the distinctiveness of political communication. It is no longer a case of demanding that certain previously excluded people be able to enter the properly constituted locations and to speak politically once there. What counts as a political statement or expression has also been subject to challenge such that any form of communication can be regarded as political. This has been one of the central political claims of Cultural Studies in the UK and USA. Conjoined with some versions of both feminism and 'multiculturalism' this has turned into the demand that people be regarded as speaking politically without their having to speak in a particular way. They must be able to so in their 'own voice', since one of the ways in which 'minorities' can be excluded is through the demand that they match up to a particular form or standard of speaking (identified as one that is white and male).

Such a demand appears as the logical outcome of the democratisation of communication. After all, governments rarely do ensure transparency, and the art of politics is understood by many to be the art of communicative obfuscation and exclusion. Certainly the demand that one be recognised as having something to say, the insistence that the voice of the hitherto voiceless be heeded, is a supremely political demand, even the most political.[13] But the collapse of any viable authority over the specification of what is and is not political communication is *not* the same as its liberation, and may even lead to the undermining of the very possibility of anything at all being political. Insistence on the loosening of linguistic conventions and the full-scale deployment of the demotic in political discourse *is* a form of regulation. When any statement can be understood as a properly political statement, then by the same token no statement is really properly political. States or governments are forced to compete for recognition of their having political import along with everybody else. Everything collapses into incommensurable forms of micro-politics, while the authority to assess what is a political claim of import to the whole of a given political community passes to – who knows where? For Marx the first ideologists were the priests, deriving their power from their superior position in the division of mental and manual labour and taking on the role of managing consciousness.[14] The first form of social power was that of classifying the world into sacred and profane. Now the power of priests has passed to those with power over the means of communication and it is they, the high priests of consciousness management found in all our communication industries, who have the power to decide what counts as a form of political speech and who will be allowed to speak it.

So, for fear of authoritarianism or totalitarianism, the activity of sense-making and of political communication, the reproduction of the symbolic systems that enable us to live together, passes from any recognisable legally constituted democratic authority to diverse forms of media maker, whether those in charge of professional bodies that define occupational codes, the 'experts' in every area of policy or social experience that can get themselves air time, the industries and corporate organisations that put into play numerous codes or images through their products or their strategies for securing competitive advantage in the market place, and to the communications or 'creative' workers themselves. Communicative power flattens out and runs throughout the social body, shaping the activities of government, entertainment and economic exchange alike. In this world the makers of the 'knowledge' economy reign supreme.

As Alain Touraine writes:

> Power used to be in the hands of princes, oligarchies, and ruling elites; it was defined as the capacity to impose one's will on others, modifying their behaviour. This image of power does not fit with our reality any longer. Power is everywhere and nowhere: it is in mass production, in financial flows, in lifestyles, in the hospital, in the school, in television, in images, in technologies ...'.[15]

If you want to make a point about how society should be run you do not now go to your MP, nor do you join a political party. You put out a press release, hire a Public Relations executive or, if you have the money, buy a newspaper chain. This is a profound alteration in the structures of power within western, democratic and capitalist societies.

It is this backdrop that New Labour's election posters and broadcasts reveal. They are indicative not only of what New Labour is trying to do but of what New Labour has to do; of a power to which they too must submit: not simply the power of the communications corporations, but also the power of the language, or forms of symbolic communication, that they produce – and which they too can be subject to. One cannot simply blame government and politicians for 'dumbing down' political discourse. There is no systematic or observable division between roles and functions, no marking off of areas of activity. Religion draws on the language and style of entertainment, and entertainment draws on what were once the unique practices of religion (it promises salvation, gifts and prizes from heaven, immortality, community and to always be there for us). 'Gurus' in the business world practice cultic techniques of 'motivation', while art exploits the language and style of commerce, which in turn makes as much use of art as it can. New Labour, as a party and as a government, is not able to occupy a seat of power from which it can attempt to direct society. It is instead forced to play along with everything else, and thus it is a symptom, an expression, of a more general condition in which everyone has lost their voice somewhere in the melee and the shouting.

Disorganising sense

What we see hinted at in New Labour's broadcasts is the way in which the act of making sense has become dispersed. The meanings they try to mobilise are already deeply embedded in other dense networks of meaning. These networks help to make the acts or expressions possible in the first place – without them all expressions would be unintelligible. If an election poster fails to connect properly with other points of reference it will be unsuccessful and useless. But election posters and broadcasts, governmental acts and statements, are not just passive results of this system. They are attempts actively to organise, even institutionalise it, in particular ways. In so doing they organise us and attempt to organise our making of sense. They construct a symbolic network and attempt to place us within it, so fixing or limiting our apprehension. As such, they must necessarily fit in with other ways in which our being is organised. Just as *Frankenstein* was composed in the context of genres of gothic storytelling and contemporaneous cultural anxieties, so a political project must act on and out of the context of the conjuncture of which it is part. But we are now subjected to so much communication that acts of political communication lose their specificity and become lost amidst the plethora of images and mediated experiences. Government competes with other organisers of sense and other practitioners of governance.

When Kant, that key figure in the self-understanding of modern liberalism, argued that political activity in a good republic was based on the presence of public reason, he presumed that a reasoning public could deliberate on matters of moral or political concern and subject claims to the tribunal of reasonable people having reasonable discussions. That public was also a reading public, literate and informed and so able to form a reasoning public sphere. These days, in Habermas's terms, we have shifted from a 'culture debating' to a 'culture consuming' public.[16] But we should note that these days there is so much more to read than there ever was for Kant. We have to read everything. Not just treatises and newspapers, but clothes, haircuts, furniture, postal codes, and 'lifestyles' – if we are to negotiate our way through the 'gaily coloured' variety of contemporary life. In this condition the capacity of the state to be the location of the conscious direction of our social efforts is seriously weakened. On the one hand, this allows the flowering of some forms of individual liberty, since everyone reads – increasingly – alone. But it also initiates the collapse of forms of freedom based on any kind of collective social determination. This situation is exhilarating and terrifying in equal measure.

It was from this world of nervous individualisation, social anxiety shared between strangers, permanent and competitive judgement, mass media distraction, fear of collective activity and constant search for leadership, that New Labour was born. Our condition is that of a simultaneous proliferation of meanings and a downscaling of their meaningfulness. Everything needs to be read but nothing is really worth reading. Meanings proliferate because of the extension of our means of communication and contact, which opens up all things to scrutiny and contest. But they are downscaled because our acts of meaning-making have become individualised. We can tailor-make our exposure by sticking to the niche markets created for us, and in which we are confined. We no longer partake of collective meanings, only of partial and barely substantiated individual ones. For part of the twentieth century psychology and psychoanalysis taught us to live out and live through the meanings of the past, rectifying the errors and closing down the traumas of our scarred personal history. Then we began to live in a permanent present, encouraged to live for the now, in the moment, maximising our individual pleasures in order to be sure that we really were purposefully alive. Now, we live not in the future but in a permanently recreated future anterior – clinging onto the idea of what we will have been when we have achieved the next thing, passed the next stage, completed another test, always trying to catch up with our projected image of ourselves, and seeking assistance from the consumable objects and practices around us, each of which promises to make us into who or what we think we ought to have been.

If we are to re-imagine our social and civic ties, we need to remind ourselves how to read each other not only as individuals, but also as a social group, a collective. To be a reasoning public, engaging in deliberation concerning the nature, value and justification of our public affairs, we need to be able to 'read' and make sense of the symbolic systems that constitute that social or public world and make us what we are (and enable us to be what we will). This is one way in which we may pull ourselves out of what Kant called 'our self-incurred immaturity'.

But the contemporary process of governance (which does not necessarily have a lot to do with government) does not solely entail a limitation of competing readings (as happened, say, with the Catholic Church at the time of the Inquisition, or with the censorship of Fascist and Communist dictatorships); nor is it simply a process of managing between competing interpretations or readings (as we might like to think is the case in a democracy, where the state acts as a neutral guarantor of our right to dissent). Rather, our readings are increasingly governed in the moment of their expression. In order to communicate, to put across a point, to say something political, we find ourselves (all of us – citizens, consumers, media managers, politicians and advertisers) drawing on a language that is as much a part of commerce and entertainment as it is of politics. It is rational for us to do this, because people will, we believe, understand that language and get the point. We want to speak with those people, address them in the way they address each other. This is not patronising: it makes sense to speak to people about the world in the way they themselves speak about it. But this means that each of our statements, as well as expressing itself, also reproduces that general underlying structure. It may feel as if we are taking a superior position to that culture (we understand it sufficiently well to mock and turn it to our advantage), but in truth we are only legitimating it. Such forms of talk are the Latin of the high church of globalisation, effective because they do not deny our ways of speaking and thinking, but make them possible.

In drawing on this culture to advance its anti-Tory message, New Labour revealed to us something about what it is and how it works. It cannot simply speak about and 'do' politics in 'traditional' ways. It is engaged in a process of 'making sense'. It is trying to open up or forge new ways of approaching political problems and issues. It presents one way of understanding present conditions (social, economic, cultural and political) and of responding to them. But its way of making sense of them is already conditioned by them. We might say that government cannot any longer act on society because it is now just a part of the social, alongside everything else.

The Labour Party billboard advertisement is illustrative of how the party relates to the wider context of our culture and society. Blairism displays a kind of self-consciousness of our time. It speaks out of and to the context of its own emergence. But this self-consciousness is itself typical of the present context. Precisely because it is so much of its time, Blairism cannot really grasp that time. It is aware that it is oper-ating at a particular historical moment to which it must be sensitive, but is not aware of the extent to which it is itself just a part of that moment. As such it contributes not to the transformation of the moment but to its reproduction. New Labour is merely an expression of what already is, yet it mistakes itself for a true and critical conscious-ness of the times. It is, we might say, its own transcendental illusion, the source of its own mythos. This is a very 'now' way to be.

Democratic political discussion can only proceed from the fact of disagreement. If there were no disagreement, if we agreed on every-thing, then there would be no need for politics. Society might still require administration; but this would be a simple matter of applying to the levers of state exactly the amount of pressure that everyone had already agreed upon. There would be no need to call the administrators to account (except in cases of incompetence or negligence, which would be easy to judge, since it would simply be a question of proving whether or not the administrators had done what everyone knew they should do). But, in the real world, there is disagreement, not only as to *how* things should be done, but also as to *what* should be done. Such disagreements about the policies to be enacted emerge from even larger-scale disputes about the *reasons why* things should be done, the criteria by which such formulations and judgements are made, and the very principles that organise our understanding and evaluation of social and individual life.

In politics such fundamental philosophies are always in play, under-lying the reasoning given to justify or explain any particular policy, and central to the evaluation of the activities undertaken by politicians and governments. These fundamental philosophies, or ideologies, are projected as public in their nature. In a democratic polity the attempt to secure support for a particular perspective on the conception and organisation of society requires the successful extension of that posi-tion to the public – a kind of universal – level. That is why it will, of necessity, have to connect with the ways in which people already see and understand things, and will have to mobilise languages, concepts and image styles with which we, the public, are already familiar.

But this process of connecting and universalising has become divorced from the practice of politics in its sense of mobilising for a particular philosophy or ideology. Everything is oriented towards preventing disagreement, 'healing' society and flattening dispute (elim-inating debate as part of the process). If there is some sort of generalised consensus about the ways in which public discourse can be carried out, political talk can narrow down to matters of pragmatic policy. Historically, states have operated to generate this sort of consensus – to make possible a more uniform, and implicitly universal, code of communication enabling a polity to talk with itself. Now a 'universal' code is already in place in large parts of the world, and increasingly we all partake of a 'global' language of exchange, rights, duties, historical and cultural references. When we look into the field of politics we find that this widespread consensus is not generated from there. It is created elsewhere through mass media, commercial production, mechanisms of personnel management and so forth. Politics is left without a role.

We see this reflected in the dream of a digital utopia peddled by Bill Gates, Tony Blair and a thousand IT pundits. It is a dream of an absolutely transparent and conflict – free space in which all communications are equal and connected to all others. In such a utopia consensus will be an automatic outcome of being on the network. It will be an immanent feature, not something to be won out of struggle and contest. But this is not a truly free space, since acquiescence in its world of meanings is the precondition of participation. As we enter, we are already being inveigled into belief in its myths. Within it, the nature of politics and of resistance is transformed. Opposition used to be manifested by those wishing to develop and impose a new or different language upon the social. This new language would embody an alternative principle for the unification of the polity, and for the shaping of the ways in which it would address itself. We could think, for example, of those who want to place our worker identity and productive capacity at the centre of things; those who stress (their version of) our universal humanity; or those for whom nationhood or race provides the framework within and through which the polity would be made to speak. But in the contemporary global utopia, no such comprehensive alternative can be expressed in this way. Opposition to what is does not come from great alternative blocs or ideologies. It crops up in a 'molecular' fashion when single cells or small clusters of parts of the social organism suddenly turn out to be working against the unity and harmony of the social fabric: truckers feeling threatened by the price of petrol, farmers faced with declining incomes, anti-capitalists and environmentalists could all be regarded in this way, but so too could the apathetic, indifferent, indigent and criminal (truants from the compulsory schooling of contemporary culture). These casualties of the extension of a uniform regime of power across the social field are best understood as a kind of fallout; as problems against which the state deploys the forces of uniform communication and order. Rather than propose an alternative political language, such movements simply manifest hostility and display minimal interest in universalising their claims (often quite deliberately celebrating their minority and conspiratorial nature). Thus they appear to powers of governance as simple errors in software rather than the expression of hardware faults that present a challenge to the very structure of society. They burst forth periodically and then fade away, unable and uninterested in being part of a larger putatively hegemonic movement.

This is the backdrop: a shifting mode of governance, and a relocating or reorganising of politics; and this must also be the horizon of our attempts to make sense of what is happening to us. Into this steps New Labour, bold and brave, shiny and new, ready to take on and transform the world so it can make us match up to the promise of deregulated utopia, unaware that with every gesture and every breath drawn in to make some statement it reproduces the dominant language created and adjudicated from elsewhere. Thus New Labour plays its part in adjusting us all to the beautiful liberty of a world in which nothing is anything any more because everything must always be essentially the same after the 'end' of ideology (which is a synonym for the almost absolute triumph of ideology). This is a world of permanent movement and flux in which we are always running to keep up and yet one in which nothing ever really changes. The more trade is made open and free, the more wealth flows to the parts of the world that already had most of it; the more labour is made mobile the more rigid becomes occupational mobility; the more the equal right of all to compete in the market is asserted the greater becomes inequality. As our 'runaway world' gets faster, the present state of things becomes ever more immobile, and the power of contemporary machines for the production of the sophistry that reconciles us to the world in the name of necessity grows stronger. Those machines include the think-tankers, academics with 'big-ideas', media organisations and the opinion formers they sponsor. Their ultimate expression, the symptom they produce, is New Labour.

Notes

1. See Richard E. Neustadt (1960) *Presidential Power: The Politics of Leadership*, New York, Wiley.
2. Norman Fairclough (2000) *New Labour, New Language?*, London, Routledge, p7.
3. Plato, *Republic*, 555b-562a.
4. See Claude Lefort (1986) *The Political Forms of Modern Society: Bureaucracy, Democracy, Totalitarianism* (edited and introduced by John B. Thompson), Cambridge, Polity.

5. Anthony Giddens (1984) *The Constitution of Society*, Cambridge, Polity; Erving Goffman (1969), *The Presentation of Self in Everyday Life*, Harmondsworth, Penguin.
6. Zygmunt Bauman (2001) *The Individualised Society*, Cambridge, Polity, p2.
7. Terry Eagleton (1986) *William Shakespeare*, Oxford, Blackwell, p19.
8. W.B. Gallie (1956) 'Essentially Contested Concepts', *Proceedings of the Aristotelian Society*, 56, pp167-198.
9. Martin Harrison (1992) 'Politics on the Air', in David Butler and Dennis Kavanagh (eds.), *The British General Election of 1992*, Basingstoke, Macmillan.
10. Judith Butler (1998) 'Merely Cultural', *New Left Review*, 227, Jan/Feb, pp34-5.
11. See, for example, Jurgen Habermas (1997) *Between Facts and Norms*, Cambridge, Polity.
12. See, for example, Bill Gates (1995) *The Road Ahead*, London, *Viking*
13. See Jacques Ranciere (1998) *Disagreement: Politics and Philosophy*, Minneapolis, University of Minnesota Press.
14. Or rather contradictions intrinsic to the division of labour. See 'The German Ideology', in David McClellan (ed.) (1977) *Karl Marx: Selected Writings*, Oxford, Oxford University Press, p168.
15. Alain Touraine, cited in Manuel Castells, *The Power of Identity*, Oxford, Blackwell, 1997, p309.
16. See Jurgen Habermas (1992) *The Structural Transformation of the Public Sphere: An Inquiry into a Category of Bourgeois Society*, Cambridge, Polity.

CHAPTER TWO

The Pitch: Media and Marketing

Introduction

One way of making sense of New Labour is to treat it as utterly cynical. Here is a party prepared to shed anything and get up in any new costume if it thinks this will help in the securing of power; through focus group and opinion poll, news management and image manipulation it will attempt always to appear as all things to everyone, ever-ready to sacrifice a principle for a polling point.

This is an appealing description. Such denunciations of New Labour make their claimants seem all the more powerful – able to slay the self-serving dragons of hypocrisy and defend principle to the death. Furthermore, regarding all politicians as lying, scheming bastards is really rather comforting. It relieves us of the burden of having to make any sense of what is going on in our political culture. But that culture, even in the most flaccid and feckless of democracies such as ours, cannot develop without the blessing (however tacit) of the population at large, or the direct influence of opinion leaders (such as the same media professionals that make the charge). The accusation of cynicism grants to our politicians a certain rationality. The self-serving at least know what they are doing, and it can be known by us. How much less frightening this is than the thought that our politicians really believe most of what they say and are committed to the ideology they dispense, or that we have a responsibility for the people who end up taking office.

With New Labour the cynicism charge has an even greater weakness: it isn't true. Underneath their obvious (and, contrary to received media-opinion, usually rather ham-fisted) attempts to manipulate their media image, the apparatchiks of New Labour are astonishingly consistent. The day-to-day appearance may be that of flux and adaptation to the prevailing winds, and like all major political parties they will back off from anything that seems to be going too much against the popular mood. But, over a longer time period, what is most clear about New Labour, and especially about Tony Blair, is that they have been saying the same thing all along, and saying it, usually, in pretty much the same way. When, for example, did Tony Blair say that the Labour Party must be the 'party of new economic opportunity, not engaged in a battle for territory between private and public sector ... ensuring social action assists individual responsibility and is not substituted for it in areas like crime ...'? (This attitude clearly informs the policy of the second Blair government, particularly as it applies to public services.) This view was expressed in an article for *Fabian Review* back in 1993.[1] Perhaps pundits don't notice this continuity because our fast-turnover media culture has a limited attention span – or perhaps to admit it would require them to own up to the fact that there isn't too much mystery to New Labour (which would not make good copy).

In contrast, this chapter takes seriously what New Labour says and how it says it. It looks, primarily, at New Labour's election broadcasts and manifestos, using these as a way into an analysis of their ideology, and of the party as a contemporary phenomenon. In analysing these forms of political communication it is not enough to treat them simply as manipulative texts, interested solely in selling something. Of course they are that, but this is not, in itself, a cause for despair. Politics is in large part about the art of communicative persuasion. A party or move-ment has to make itself known to a public, and it has to put across its message. In democracies one of the most crucial dynamics is that between a party platform and the public to which it is addressed. There is a reciprocal relation between the two – the platform is necessarily reshaped in order to secure victory, but at the same time the party tries to bring people on side with its views. Thus, taking this kind of 'marketing' seriously can tell us something about the current state of our political culture.

There is also a subtler conceptual reason for taking the marketing of New Labour seriously. The charge of cynicism, so often made against New Labour, implies a distance between appearance and reality. It suggests that what we see is definitely not what we get; that the image is a misleading front designed to obscure or hide the true intentions and real policies of the party. But with New Labour (as we will see), the image is a central part of what we get. There is no great distance between the appearance and the reality. This is symptomatic of the contemporary culture of politics more generally, but of New Labour in particular. In order to get elected (to make itself electable), New Labour set a premium on appearing electable. Its capacity to create a well-managed party was part of the way in which it put itself forward as able to manage the country. Demonstrating that it had made 'the mental leap that says that aspiring to the middle class is positive ... people want more money, a decent house, a good car'[2] entailed appearing like a party of successfully aspirational people with money, good houses and cars. This helped to ensure that the party could put up a good campaign and make itself seem professional, in the same way that corporations and charities make themselves seem worthwhile by presenting themselves in a way presumed to be skilful.

New Labour is concerned to make its appearance match its ideological or policy commitments. In order to advocate 'modernisation' the party must itself appear 'modernised', its own transformation thus heralding the transformation of the country as a whole. Its form, therefore, is also the content; and it is part of its 'pitch' to the electorate. As we saw in Chapter One, the way in which New Labour communicates is part of what it wants to communicate. An ability to communicate in a way that is 'of the moment' would confirm that it really is 'of the moment' (in distinction to opponents who are represented as relics or dinosaurs).

For these reasons, an analysis of New Labour's marketing is one way into an analysis of New Labour as a whole. But this aspect of New Labour is not simply the outcome of the cunning and insight of its campaign managers. It is a reflection, a symptom, of the kind of media and marketing culture that occupies a position of dominance in contemporary capitalist democracies. Here, as elsewhere, New Labour is less 'on top' or in charge of things than passively moulded by what is going on in the world. We will therefore begin this chapter with a more general and contextual consideration of the relationship between New Labour and the media.

The growth of political marketing in the twentieth century

We are used to hearing that New Labour is 'all spin and no substance'. The Prime Minister's press secretary has been made into a star by newspapers stuffed full of correspondents who have known him for years. Given this hype, one could be forgiven for thinking that New Labour really have come up with something new, and that they treat the media in a way unlike any other previous British government. However, this is to give them far too much credit. New Labour certainly is media conscious, but it is hardly alone in this obsession. Anybody seeking a presence within the 'public sphere' must take media appearance seriously. Politicians are in good company here, since the media are obsessed with the media. Together they are part of what Nick Cohen has described as 'The Citadel' ... 'official London: Whitehall, Westminster, The City, Fleet Street, the BBC';[3] the 'Citadel' is a closed and self-supporting elite of people who know each other, observe each other and have fights with each other, while the rest of us peasants, who live in the provincial hinterland, are left to take up our required position as bored spectators.

But though connections between various personnel and their inter-locking backgrounds have some significance for an analysis of the nature of the relationship between political parties, the media, public relations and marketing, they are only part of the story. This close rela-tionship needs to be understood as a stage in the longer-term development of the organisation of politics, the media and marketing – in the UK and internationally.

There is a common conception that the marketisation and mediati-sation of politics began in this country with the decision of the Tory party to put the Saatchis on retainer, and that it was secured by the work in the Labour Party of Peter Mandelson as head of the Shadow Communications Agency under Kinnock. Chapter One, in a general and abstract way, considered the important changes in the relationship between political parties, media and marketing that became clear in the 1980s and 1990s. But that relationship, of course, has a much longer history.

A Press Office was first employed by the Conservative Party in 1906, and it eagerly targeted stories at newspapers. In 1929 the Conservatives employed an advertising agency to assist in the design of leaflets, and even at that early stage training was offered to candidates. With the help of cinema luminaries such as Alexander Korda (director of classic British costume dramas such as *The Private Life of Don Juan* and *Lady Hamilton*), Central Office made and showed films to thou-sands of voters, using mobile cinema vans.[4] While all this may not have had the scale and grandeur of the trains crossing the Soviet Union showing Eisenstein and Chaplin movies, in their own way the Tories were launching themselves into the modern world of mass propaganda.

Labour set up a publicity department in 1917. Prefiguring current developments in targeted political marketing and the focus group, Sidney Webb argued in 1922 for the development of 'stratified elec-tioneering':

> I should like to see a little variegated colour in electioneering ... Every elector has his own 'colour', if only we could discover it. He differs in character and circumstances, temperament and vocation, religion and recreation ... at present we tend to address them all in the same way, with the result of achieving a certain amount of 'misfit'.[5]

And in the 1937 local elections, under the guidance of Herbert Morrison, London Labour made use of public relations and advertising professionals.

After the war, and motivated by their landslide defeat in 1945, leading figures in the Conservative Party decided that they had to do something to change their party's image. In April 1946 Sir Joseph Ball, director of the Conservative Research Department, put out an internal party memorandum stressing the need to win the propaganda battle. Specialists in advertising and public relations were appointed to Central Office. Party Vice-Chairman John Hare wrote: 'We here [at central office] regard broadcasting as one of the most important instruments of propaganda and within our limited scope attempt to do everything possible to perfect our representation'.[6] Efforts to track down 'bias' in the BBC (and to implant their own) were duly initiated. The party began offering media training to members and put forward preferred lists of MPs for participation in television discussion programmes; and the 'Tactical Office Committee' issued 'Weekend Talking Points', described as being 'an official statement of policy which candidates and MPs could rely upon and accept as representing the exact party point of view'.[7] Speeches for broadcast had to be submitted to this committee in advance, and those about to appear on the media were told what subjects to touch on.

The spread of methods of statistical research and opinion polling also affected party campaigning, not least with the foundation of the Public Opinion Research Department in Central Office in 1948. And (given our focus on New Labour) we ought to recall here that that earlier 'revisionist' Labour leader, Hugh Gaitskell, was influenced by the famous *Must Labour Lose* pamphlet which, drawing on such data, came to the conclusion that the party needed to move to the centre and capture the middle-class vote. One of the authors of the report, Mark Abrams, was part of the 1964 Labour campaign team. As leader, Harold Wilson was careful to associate himself with aspects of the new popular culture and to make use of media opportunities.

This period also saw the growth of the view that democratic choice should indeed be understood as akin to consumer choice. Schumpeter (to whom we shall return on several occasions) interpreted democracy in terms of organised competition for political leadership. 'A party', he wrote in 1942, 'is a group whose members propose to act in concert in the competitive struggle for political power'. Given that it would never be possible for the public at large to spontaneously form a uniform opinion on all aspects of social and political life,

> party and machine politicians are simply the response to the fact that the electoral mass is incapable of action other than a stampede, and they constitute an attempt to regulate political competition exactly similar to the corresponding practices of a trade association. The psycho-technics

of party management and party advertising, slogans and marching tunes, are not accessories. They are the essence of politics'.[8]

In 1957 Anthony Downs developed and extended this sort of 'economic' theory of democracy, lending support to the view that, to be successful, parties should move to the centre, where they would find the bulk of the consumers.[9] Meanwhile, in the field of marketing itself, some began to advocate the widening of their own remit to include non-economic areas such as the marketing of ideas, values, politics and voluntary organisations.[10]

The growth and spread of such arguments (which, it should be admitted, have an aspect of the truth in their grasp, but also are capable of creating this truth) was both motor and mirror to the increasingly explicit use of techniques of marketing in political campaigning. Consequently, the UK in the 1980s saw a marked increase not only in political marketing but also in the use of advertising as a tool of government. By 1987 the British government was the largest advertiser in the UK. From 1979 to 1987 government expenditure on advertising increased from £31 million to £125 million. This was extremely important in the popularisation and legitimisation of the Tory policy of privatisation.

In terms of party competition, an important development was marked by the appointment of Gordon Reece as Conservative director of publicity in 1978. He led the process of differentiating the parties at an 'emotional' level. That is to say, it was officially recognised in British politics that electors might respond as much to the connotations associated with a particular party or candidate as to the policy itself. In 1978 the Saatchi-produced Conservative Party political broadcasts changed the ground rules by employing professional script writers and directors in a campaign aimed at shaping the connotations of the Conservative Party and Margaret Thatcher.[11] The appointment of Reece was, belatedly, matched by that of Phillip Gould and Patricia Hewitt to Labour's Shadow Communications Agency. Following this principle of connotation, they argued that Labour's 'brand' was all wrong since it was associated with austerity rather than affluence.

We have to see New Labour's relation to the media in this context. They did not initiate the marketing of democracy – Labour have often played quite a passive role in these developments. Nor did they invent the practice of ensuring MPs are 'on-message'. But this continuity does not mean that there have not been important changes, shifts or developments. Where earlier techniques were essentially unsubtle propaganda, with the political machines simply adapting to demands made on them by new forms of media, the last two decades have seen a shift, with the growth of political marketing proper. As Wring suggests, during this time 'opinion research as representative of the electorate begins to take on an important policy perspective in addition to its existing presentational role'.[12] Or, as Scammell argues of the Conservatives, marketing concepts may not have directly influenced policy, but they shaped 'the tone and tenor and indicated that certain policy options were electorally out of bounds'.[13]

Politics and the mass media

This increasing use of the techniques of marketing and advertising in politics is not a perversion of democracy; it is an outcome of the way in which democracy has been practised in capitalist commodity economies. This development is part of a logic internal to the practice of electoral, representative, democracy within an increasingly individuated and commodified society held together by communicative networks dominated by television, which allows the direct transmission of information, ideas and values from a central location, and to a body of persons that is simultaneously a 'mass' and a collection of individual units of consumption (or 'households'). What, for us today, could politics possibly be without communications strategies? And if, for most people, the primary source of information on politics is the mass media, then why on earth would politicians do anything other than try to act in ways that ensure they get their point across on television, or that prevent the media from making them look stupid or ridiculous? This is intrinsic to democracy as we now experience it.

But the media present politics in a peculiarly distorted fashion. The broadcast media are formally committed to neutrality and objectivity. Yet it is impossible to occupy such a position within democratic politics. In a democracy all positions are up for contest. Democracy entails the right and the capacity of people to challenge the truth-claims of politics, even to challenge the very terms in which politics is conceived. Presenting all this in an ostensibly neutral and objective fashion can thus only be a form of bias, which may simply serve to reinforce the predominant way of seeing things. But an even more serious problem is that this form of presentation turns politics into an object, a specific domain of activity that can be made to appear as if it is demarcated from yet equivalent to others, and so gazed upon (even though this very differentiation submits politics to the same logic as everything else). The subjection of practical politics to this gaze in turn necessitates the closer attention of parties to the way in which they appear under it. This furthers the tendency of publics as well as pundits to see it as a realm in which we are not directly involved and that is to be evaluated like a game: the strategies and styles are of as much interest as the content of a political programme. This is not to suggest that there was a time when politics was pure and not concerned with presentation. But it is to point out that most people today make sense of what politics is through modern mass media; and that these media understand politics in partial and limiting ways. Political movements have, in response, limited themselves and built on that agenda.

The relationship between New Labour and the media, then, is a structural feature of the contemporary organisation of politics. From the moment television emerged out of the light, producers were eager to establish for their 'new' medium a key place in all the central activities of the society. And also right from the start, any tensions between the media and politicians were balanced by a mutual interest. As Ralph Negrine points out: 'The mass media have become an integral part of a complex network of institutions and they contribute and give meaning to the relationships between institutions and groups in the political system'.[14] That is to say, the relationship between the media and politics cannot be understood simply as the outcome of the interaction of elite personnel. Politicians and media pundits often conceive of the relationship as mutually hostile, while critics such as Chomsky claim it is mutually supportive, serving to reinforce a dominant interest or ideology (and neither of these views is wholly without foundation). But both these viewpoints downplay the deep-rooted structural and organisational relationship between the conduct of politics and the operations of the media.[15] No longer do two separate 'institutions' deal with each other – they are part of the same complex. As we saw in Chapter One, politics, science, art, commerce and entertainment must all, if they wish to have any public presence at all (and what, nowadays, can be said to 'exist' if it is not passed before the ever more mythical 'public'), have to struggle through the terrain of the media.

Some, such as Baudrillard, talk of the collapse or implosion of 'the social' as the outcome of this proliferation of commodified images. There can no longer be any public stage, in the sense developed by Hannah Arendt, no place of 'being-in-common', that is not also the media stage. Politics, Manuel Castells points out, cannot take place other than in the media. It is not that the media determine what politics is in the sense of a simple causality, or that politics has somehow been 'captured' by television. Rather, 'the logic and organisation of electronic media frame and structure politics'.[16] Politics can take place, in some ways, as it always has. Politicians must go out and shake hands with the people, they must continue to stage political events; but these have taken on the character of what Boorstin called 'pseudo-events', whose real purpose is simply to be captured and broadcast on television.[17] This is why one cannot help but sense something disingenuous when the media crow about the stage management of political events, as they did for example about New Labour's election campaign launch at a primary school in 2001. The launch was staged like this because of the demands and expectations of television. Again Castells puts this well, arguing that while the media is not all there is to politics, 'all politics must go through the media to affect decision making ... politics is fundamentally framed in its substance, organisation, process and leadership, by the inherent logic of the media system, particularly by the new electronic media'.[18]

Tied into this capacity for opinion polling, direct marketing and the rapid-response techniques of opinion management, the political space begins to be closed down. There is still conflict, still a plurality of positions, but they are tied into, and framed by, media processes. But, to make the point again, this is not simply the outcome of ill will or stupidity. It is a structural effect. The media are a market. They have to compete for audience share; and this, now, is only marginally less true for the publicly owned media networks, which have to prove their worth through market success. News media have to compete with each other, and they all compete with other forms of entertainment. News thus tends to foreground whatever can be portrayed as exciting, which is usually taken to mean conflict.[19] But, at the same time, news journalists must play by the rules of fairness, neutrality and objectivity, since to break them runs the risk of losing the credibility that is precisely part of their market value. The news media must simply report on and not engage with the issues they report. This exacerbates their baleful effect. Politics cannot be considered on the basis of detached neutrality without ceasing to be politics, the arena where a divergent public exercises its differences in common. In striving for objectivity, news media put the event to the fore rather than what underlies and explains that event.[20] Castells suggests that politics turns into horse racing: commentators adjudicate on the status of the runners and riders and their likely form. I prefer the metaphor of a football match. Political events (policy announcements, reactions to them, etc) are commented on in terms of how they will affect the standing of the parties in the game. Instant opinion polling can keep us informed as to the score and the impact of any change in the selection of players or in their style of play. We, the former public of citizens, adopt the role of spectators at the match, having forgotten that in this competition the result is not based on the number of goals scored but on the decisions we have to make and have made.

This process exaggerates the importance of individual personalities and increases disaffection from politics; in turn this can lead to support for third parties and forms of political action independent of the mainstream system (though pressure group politics also engages in the production of spectacle). This is, it hardly needs to be said, not a phenomenon unique to the UK.

The embedded relationship between media, markets and politics has effects deeper than the simple perpetuation of a symbiotic link between two central spheres of social power. It facilitates (perhaps forces) the growth of a form of governance to which media and communication is fundamental. A notable aspect of New Labour's first term in office was that it appeared to continue to campaign, suggesting the intensification of the phenomenon of the 'permanent campaign'. It continued to invest in advertising (as a government) and to work hard at maintaining a tight rein on what stories the press would be able to run. In the first three months of 2001 the Labour government spent £62.9 million on advertising.[21] The Strategic Communications Unit, which consults other media officers in Whitehall and runs the Downing Street website,[22] costs a little under £850,000 per year. This is in addition to the usual costs of the Downing Street Press Office and the official Whitehall media systems. The release of these figures caused pundits to line up to opine and worry about them (ably assisted by opposition politicians). It was routinely pointed out that government spending on advertising was higher than Unilever's – though it did not seem to occur to commentators that it might be appropriate for information about government to be spread more widely and shouted more loudly than information about soap powders and detergents: the latter is seen as legitimate because it is simply marketing, whereas the former is illegitimate propaganda. But the dividing line between propaganda and mere attempts to persuade is notoriously difficult to place. O'Shaughnessy, for example, attempts a rough distinction between propaganda and marketing by pointing out that propaganda is essentially didactic, aiming to impose a view on the receivers of the message. Marketing, by contrast, necessarily places the emphasis on what the recipient (the customer) wants and so proceeds via market research.[23] But O'Shaughnessy admits the difficulty of establishing a secure distinction. He is wise to do so for it is no longer possible and isn't relevant. Governments in the democratic states do not engage in propaganda precisely because they can use marketing. And this fact, in itself, has a 'propaganda effect'. The ideological content of political marketing is not contained in the message (which is just a sales pitch like any other, and which, in any case, nobody really believes), but in the very fact that politics has to go the market in the first place, that it has to submit to that logic and cannot develop its own. Propaganda is unnecessary if the mechanisms of ideological reproduction and legitimisation can occur through the dominance of the market itself. The central question, from the point of view of assessing the condition of democracy, isn't whether or not media manipulation extends into the shaping of policy choice. Clearly politicians in and out of government desire and need media coverage, and are prepared to put a great deal of time, money and effort into media management. It is also clear that New Labour has refined the centralisation of communication in the hands of the Prime Minister's office[24] and that policy may be influenced directly by presentational concerns, for example when the government promises not to enact policies unfavourable to the interests of powerful media figures such as Rupert Murdoch. The more significant issue is that encapsulated by Peter Mandelson's comment: 'If a government policy cannot be presented in a simple and attractive way, it is more likely than not to contain fundamental flaws and prove to be the wrong policy'.[25] Media management and presentational policy is not simply about maintaining a government and continuing to ensure that it is successful in the opinion polls. It is, itself, a way in which government takes place and the ideology of market relations is secured. A policy can only be a good policy if it can be sold, because nothing has any worth if it cannot obtain value at market. Similarly, Mandelson has also declared that 'the era of pure representative democracy is slowly coming to an end'.[26] Government prefers to employ citizens' juries and focus groups, to spread its message 'directly' to the public through mail-shots, advertisements, road-shows and chat-show appearances, rather than enduring tedious debates in the legislature which, in any case, are of no interest to anyone outside of a narrow circle of initiates. Thus, Mandelson's comments can be understood as rational within the context of the need to respond to a media system that is not only resistant to carrying substantive information about policy, or presenting arguments unaccompanied by substantive comment of its own, but is also itself part of a market and compelled to compete. Consequently, the media system forces those who want to be part of it to compete for attention. Mandelson and New Labour have ceded the ground to this media system, and accepted that a policy which cannot properly be explained to a population is not much good as a policy in a democratic society; populations ought to be able to be clear on such things not only so that they can consent to them, but also so that they can be a part of their implementation. And if the explanation of a policy has to go through a competitive media system, with its own rules, routines and procedures, then media management and presentation becomes, necessarily, part of a shift in the overall mode of governance. Policy is not policy if it cannot be disseminated to good effect. This gesture, regardless of the content, is central to governance in the capitalist-media-liberal-democracies. As Armand and Michelle Mattelart put it:

Communication now occupies a central place in strategies whose object is to restructure our societies. Via electronic technologies, it is one of the master instruments in the conversion of the major industrialised countries. It accompanies the redeployment of powers (and counter-powers) in the home, the school, the factory, the office, the hospital, the neighbourhood, the region and the nation. And beyond this, it has become a key element in the internationalisation of economies and cultures. It has thus become a stake in the relations between peoples, between nations, and between blocs.[27]

The problem of distance

Another effect of the increased spread and capacity of forms of communication, along with other technologies, is the intensification of distance. We like to think, in McLuhan's phrase, that they introduce a global village. But, as Scott Lash argues, the reverse is in fact the case.[28] In a primitive form of social organisation many things may be at a great distance from us, but they don't really matter. The world we actually encounter, the world of objects, persons, relations between things, is close at hand. This may be an enclosed, limited and limiting, form of life; but the gap between what is 'here' and what is 'out there' is so large that life can be experienced as closely embedded in the nearby. The extensions characteristic of modernity, incorporating large scale transport and communication systems and the stretching of our social bonds, do, at one level, bring things nearer; but this simultaneously means that things near enough to have an impact on us are actually far away. We experience what has been termed 'time-space distanciation' in Giddens's terminology, or a 'flattening' or 'lifting-out' of forms of life in Lash's.[29] We engage in a permanent and intense relationship with forms of technology (internet, WAP phones, satellite, cable and digital television) that routinely keep us tied into things that are at a distance. This makes them feel nearer but also means that we can become more isolated from the things around us. As Heidegger observes:

> All distances in time and space are shrinking ... Man puts the longest distances behind him in the shortest time. He puts the greatest distances behind himself and this puts everything before himself at the shortest range. Yet the frantic abolition of all distances brings no nearness; for nearness does not consist in shortness of distance. What is least remote from us in point of distance, by virtue of its picture on film or its sound on the radio, can remain far from us. What is incalculably far from us in point of distance can be near to us. Short distance is not in itself nearness. Nor is great distance remoteness.[30]

For Heidegger, in bringing the world closer to us we are trying to make it submit to us; thus, unable to treat things as things, to let them be what they are, we find them coming nearer but always staying at a distance from us.

One of the tasks New Labour seems implicitly to have set itself is that of reducing this distance. In election campaigns it encourages us to be interactive, to receive messages on our phones to access RUUP4IT (as the techno-forged youth campaign was called in 2001). It urges us to access health care through new technology and NHS Direct, to make the most of 'open' government on the internet. It tries to bring politics back in touch with the people, but (much to its confusion and annoyance) this succeeds only in making it feel more distant. Its approach to these new means of communication is part of the problem: it does not take on these technologies, or attempt (or argue for) their redirection. It succumbs to and becomes incorporated into them.

New Labour's pitch to the electorate, its attempt to reduce distance, to make us feel close to, even at one with, the party, is also evident in the way in which it sells to us the figure of the leader (see below). This too is part of New Labour's 'transcendental illusion' – a desire for a method of pure and transparent communication linking it directly to 'the people', an unmediated contact achieved through all the means of mediation available.

We can also see in the sales pitch a related aspect. The speeded up and networked world introduces a new orientation to the future. We no longer look to the past for support. This we reject as outmoded. Our economic growth depends not on past investment but on projected calculations of future returns. Ideology is ceasing to function by defining the past. It defines the past away and aims instead to claim the future. The future is where the problems are and whoever can advance the solution to things that are going to happen can claim to be the natural party of government. This 'problematisation' of the future also forms a key part of New Labour's pitch to us (as well as its policy programmes of 'modernisation'). The collapse of distance between leader and led; the governing of the future: it is to this 'pitch' we now turn.

'Behold, the man!'
The central image of New Labour's electoral marketing is Tony Blair himself. The leader takes the lead in the representation of the party, and at all times in ways that seek to reduce the distance between him and the people he wants to represent.

Let's go back a few years (in political terms a lifetime) to 1994. In September of that year the Labour Party unveiled their first party political broadcast since Blair took over the leadership. The broadcast opened with a shot of the Houses of Parliament. One does not need a degree in film theory to understand the message behind the sun rising in the background, giving the grand, slightly gothic architecture the glow of the new dawn. Accompanying this unsubtle imagery is a voice-over taken from Blair's speech accepting the leadership of the party. He accepts it 'with humility' (just as he would tell the schoolgirls of St Saviours and St Olaves school that he would face the 2001 election with a sense of humility and hope).[31]

The main thrust of the broadcast is a portrayal of the party leader as, well, leader-like. Having learned the hard lesson of the Kinnock years the party knows that it must, perhaps above all, have credibility; and that means, in large part, looking like you could govern if asked to. What you will do with governing is, in this respect, a secondary question to be addressed once the hurdle of appearing competent and reliable has been successfully leapt. The broadcast thus built on earlier attempts to portray a party leader in an all-round way and to convince the public that this was someone who could and should lead them.

This approach had led to a degree of ridicule after film director Hugh Hudson produced *Kinnock: The Movie* in 1987, which tried to personalise Kinnock at the same time as aggrandising him. But its musical accompaniment (Beethoven) and attempt to tell Kinnock's life story (with old still photographs and comments from elderly relatives) made it appear just too manufactured and false. The same fate befell John Major's attempt to portray himself as an 'ordinary' bloke, returning to his origins in London and acting surprised to find that 'It's still there!' as he drove up to his old home. In both cases the genre of encomium did not sit well with the British tendency not to trust politicians who put themselves above us, and at the same time to dislike those who pretend to be the same as us. The implied 'rags-to-riches' or 'my-struggle' narrative felt false and staged.

The portrayal of Blair in broadcasts aiming for the same effect is rather different. There is no narrative aspect to them, and the elements of personal background and personal style that are put on display are woven into the policy and ideological commitments he puts across. We are invited to believe in these not because they are rational and well argued but because they emerge from Blair's experiences; and it is in him we must believe. But, most importantly, the production style of the broadcasts is not at odds with the sort of thing people expect from television.

The 1994 broadcast was filmed by the widely admired 'fly-on-the-wall' documentary film-maker Molly Dineen. It showed Blair in a style that has become indicative of the overall portrayal of the leader. There he is in the back of a car, the camera, hand-held and shaky, giving a sense of documentary realism, which is important to the aura of authenticity but also familiar to television viewers more used to consuming docu-soap. The whole broadcast intercuts various vox-pops (touching all the key demographics – middle-aged women, young black men, thirty-something white guys in suits) talking of how they trust him, like him, think he is genuine. They are 'real' people not other politicians; they are like us and we are like them. We can feel that we are (socially, ethically, politically) close to them, and, perhaps, because of this identification, close also to Blair.

Throughout, Blair never talks directly to camera. He rarely does in such broadcasts. He is caught talking 'naturally' rather than delivering a more stilted script to camera, and always in action (as if the camera crew was just following him around). He is described as a figure 'from a new generation' and thus as one who has an understanding of the problems facing business and people today. He 'has vision' and he 'looks you in the eye'. We see him in action a little, touring factories, meeting and greeting, dynamically chairing the shadow cabinet. It is his voice that we hear over footage of schools, police, hospitals, etc. And when we see other members of the shadow cabinet, such as John Prescott, it is Blair they talk about: 'He has vision, he has courage and above all he offers hope'. The broadcast ends with Blair speaking of himself, but the words are taken from a speech and used as a voice-over, making their grandiosity seem more appropriate: 'I am ready to serve, we are ready to serve ... we can change the course of our history ...'.

The same theme emerged in New Labour's 1997 'bulldog' election broadcast. Here a British bulldog is seen falling asleep while the voice-over explains that, despite all our talents, we have been too long under the same master and 'in a rapidly changing world we seem, somehow, to have lost our sense of purpose'. The film cuts to footage of Blair getting out of a jag, pressing through a crowd, meeting with Nelson Mandela and Bill Clinton, while we hear that, 'Now, someone has emerged who is determined to give it back to us. He is the most talked about politician of his generation ... in three short years his energy and leadership have transformed his party'. Blair takes up the screen space, once again talking to the side of the camera, discussing crime, Europe and tax, and saying that 'we' (Britain) can make the country better, but 'I will not promise anything I can't deliver'. Indeed we are not urged to vote Labour but to 'Give Tony Blair your mandate on May 1st and let him give Britain back its sense of purpose'. The image of the bulldog, typically associated with a Conservative form of nationalism, is thus linked to the new man and the new style. Blair himself will place his hand on the dog and command him to rise up and walk once more.

This is an essential aspect of New Labour's attempted populism.

Blair speaks directly to the people in his own name, cutting out the party and the state. It is his strength, and was important in the early years of the Government when faced with allegations such as that surrounding the £1 million donation to the party by Formula One mogul Bernie Ecclestone. It was most strikingly employed in the days after the death of Diana. But, it is also an essential part of politics. The party, in order to co-ordinate and build up support around itself, needs a way of embodying something of its vision; a leader such as Blair is able to carry out this role, manifesting a 'myth', in the sense of an image, a symbolic cluster, to which people can assent intuitively as well as rationally. As Gramsci put it in his comments on Machiavelli, the prince must 'represent plastically and "anthropomorphically" the symbol of the collective will'.[32] But in Blair's case there is something else going on. He is not a revolutionary leader or a Fascist dictator. He must be the kind of charismatic collective leader that expresses forces that are already present, a kind of ready-made will that he won't define. This is why Blair tries to come off as 'one of us'. He seeks to generate an identification of equivalence rather than of some greater ideal to which we aspire. We do not want someone we can look up to, someone whom we feel to be better than us in any all round sense. We want someone who is close to us (diminishing the distance that is a symptom of the illegitimacy of politics), but who also seems to possess a pair of capable hands to get on with the task.

This way of attempting to represent the leader was clear in an election broadcast of April 1997. Once again we see Blair talking as if in a docu-soap, to the side and not at us. But, extraordinarily, we get to hear the voice of the interviewer off camera. This is a striking break with the conventions of election broadcasts, which, until recently, have often consisted of a figure speaking directly to us, the audience (otherwise known as the electorate). But, in accordance with television conventions, this off-camera voice helps create a sense of directness and honesty, because we hear someone asking questions 'for us', acting as a present interlocutor.

In this broadcast there is another clever trick. As we see Blair in the media scrum, signing his name to a poster of himself, the camera films from behind the photographers, reporters and cameramen. We see the leader caught in the middle of them – doing what is asked of him (performing a photo-opportunity) while his voice-over talks about the trouble of being in politics, the fear of losing your sense of who you are. As the camera pans across the poster, with his face printed large across it, Blair reveals his wish that people, 'could go behind the image and see what sort of person you are'. (Blair regularly speaks of himself in the abstract, using 'you' as both general and specific. It is a phraseology that is self-deprecating, but which also raises him to the level of generality. It invites us to sympathise, to agree that, yes, you would feel like that.)

This broadcast, then, explicitly announces itself as getting behind the image, behind the media, to show us the real Blair. And this is 'the real' Blair inasmuch as it is the real image that he wants to put across. We should take it seriously. In everyday life we encounter each other's images and we judge that image, knowing full well that what people want to put across tells us something important about them. The media constantly confront us with real people forced to stand in as representatives of the ideal-typical (airport workers, police officers, hotel managers, ship stewards, etc). We know that we aren't seeing everything, but we also know how to judge their authenticity, to read what they do and say and, crucially, to evaluate them and their lifestyle in relation to our own. Blair's broadcasts work, essentially, like this, and their portrait is revealing in its generality and in its detail.

Blair talks casually in his kitchen, touching on his background in a way similar to the Kinnock and Major broadcasts, but he does it in an unscripted way, in response to questions that we hear and without any staged illustrative walkabout. Furthermore, he ties those experiences into policy positions, so bringing platform and person into line with each other. A statement of his commitment to the health service emerges out of talking about his father's stroke and mother's death. His commitment to education comes over in an exchange with one of his children about homework. But the whole is encapsulated in his stress that things can be done, we can do things better. He talks of 'a different type of politics rooted in values and convictions but not quite left or right'. He tries to explain that the Labour Party's approach to class-based politics got 'rooted in saying that's where you are, that's where you stay', when it should have become the 'party of aspiration'; and he implores us, over and over, to think about how things could be better. Along the way we see Tony playing football and tennis, but above all we see him in his kitchen. This image of the man casually chatting in his kitchen, drinking tea from a mug (embossed with the label of a cable company no less), is central. There is no pretence that this is a man who has 'made good'. He came from a well-off Tory family but he is a Labour man.

The same style and message were employed for the 2001 campaign. The broadcast *Leadership* clocked in at a little over four and a half minutes. Once again Blair criticised the media obsession with personality. This was mocked at the time because it seemed to be in contradiction with an advert solely concerned with him. But the broadcast is not all about him. Rather, it uses him to represent the party's new manner and ideology. It catches Blair in the favoured mode, relaxed, talking to someone off camera. His jacket off, he casually arrives into the shot to sit in front of some sort of brightly coloured patchwork banner. The caption states that we are in his constituency in Durham and the conversation delivered to camera frames the other images and constitutes the voice-over.

This too is 'common-sense' Tony. He denies the charge that, because he doesn't fit into a conventional political category, he doesn't have any principles. He says he is pleased he doesn't fit. He has 'no time' for 'the sort of 1960s libertarianism that says a criminal just did it because of a bad upbringing or poor social circumstances'. He re-states his personal purpose and the importance of the work of the government: 'I'm still basically someone who believes in the power of politics to change things'. To reinforce the sense that this is 'back-stage' Blair, we cut to a shot of him waiting in darkened wings about to go on and deliver a speech.

We see him casually laughing with locals, joking with the interviewer about his new baby, and all this is woven into the message that the conditions are set for renewal of public services. Tony is an ordinary member of the middle class, and vernacular speech plays its usual role – Tory plans to extend private health care insurance would mean we would have to pay 'forty, fifty quid out a week'. He personalises his policies, pointing out that he would not have become Prime Minister were it not for the doors opened by education, but moving quickly on to say that the country as a whole needs to be 'passionate about education', and that 'it would be crazy not to'. It is a 'passion morally and a common sense necessity' for the economy, and with it we are 'world beaters'. For this Tony it is all quite simple. People 'basically want the same thing, a decent job, pay the bills, low mortgages' … 'It's not rocket science as to what people want or need'. This is the leader as 'trust-me-Tony'. The pitch is neither policy nor person but the two combined. He wants us to believe that he wants to do it. He really, really wants to make everything better, and he wants us to want to help him. Everything is clear, and it only takes personal commitment to carry it through.

The extent to which the party sells itself through the image of the leader is also clear from the 2001 manifesto, titled *Ambitions for Britain* and sporting a large picture of Blair on the front cover. He is caught *au naturelle*, from the side, his hand gesturing to emphasise some point, but in such a way that it looks as if he is casually giving the thumbs up to us. It is a classic Blair pose. He is in action, preacher-like, but photographed as if from back-stage, thoughtful and expressive in front of an indistinct, out-of-focus audience.

Inside, next to his introductory statement, he appears again in a naturally posed image, sitting at a table somewhere, we presume in Downing Street. The jacket is off and the shirtsleeves rolled up, as he pens something on headed notepaper, a mug (not a cup and certainly no saucer) to one side. As Roland Barthes demonstrated, the photographic image, while embedded in a wider system of both production and signification, also has its own mode of communication.[33] At one level, of course, the image communicates only itself, the thing or scene it depicts or denotes. But it transmits other levels or layers of meaning, suggesting various connotations. Barthes offers as an example a photograph of President Kennedy. The pose, he argues ...

> prepares the reading of the signifieds of connotation: youthfulness, spirituality, purity. The photograph clearly only signifies because of the existence of a store of stereotyped attitudes which form ready-made elements of signification (eyes raised heavenwards, hands clasped) ... The message is not 'the pose', but 'Kennedy praying'.[34]

A photograph of a prominent politician can 'signify' many things, but for it to do so it must connect with attitudes and images that already exist in our experience, and that give new meaning to the photographic image and the politician it depicts. As such its meanings are dependent on the culture that produces it (and has a stock of stereotypes or iconic images through which a new image is interpreted); but they are also the way in which these systems of meaning are reaffirmed.

The manifesto image of Blair clearly attempts to connote a simultaneously relaxed and authoritative figure. The implication may be that what he is writing is that which we can read next to the image – his personal manifesto message signed by his own hand. There is a slight smile playing around his lips but it does not detract from the seriousness of apparent purpose. Rolled up shirtsleeves suggest a man getting down to work or, rather, a man aware that 'the work goes on' (as the 2001 election campaign slogan had it). And then there is that mug. Perhaps a whole thesis should be written on the significance of the mug in the presentation of Tony Blair. A mug took a starring role in the 1994 and 1997 election broadcasts focusing on the leader, and the motif reappeared in the 2001 version. In 1997 he was in his kitchen, still, at that time, a man with his own house and living at his own expense in 'middle-class' England. In 2001 the mug had a walk-on part as a cup of tea was delivered to him while he sat on a stool being filmed for his broadcast.

Certainly it is a cliché to associate tea with the British (or, more specifically, the English), but it has a truth to it. As a species we are good

at endowing otherwise mundane objects with great symbolic significance, making them into encapsulations of a whole way of life. What
wine is to the French and baseball to the Americans, tea is to the British.
It can signify sociability (we welcome strangers into our homes not with
the sacrifice of a bull and the offer of the entrails but with hot water
poured on leaves) as well as comfort and calm. It is a joke we make
about ourselves that the first thing to be done in a crisis is put the kettle
on. But, as much as it may be a symbol of a shared national pastime, tea
can also symbolise our social division. To drink it sweetened and in a
mug was once the exclusive preserve of the lower classes. Served in fine
china (with the milk poured into the cups first), it was the mark of the
aspirational petit-bourgeois. But now, as our cultural markers of class
dissolve (in the face of ever hardening financial ones), the mug of tea
(taken in Downing Street no less) is an emblem of traditional values in
a modern setting. That mug, accepted by Blair, held first around the rim
(too hot to grip) then turned so it can be held by the handle (no saucer
here) is a little marker of who and what we and Blair are (so long as it is
never revealed that it really contained a blend of Earl Grey and jasmine).

There are 35 different photographs in the 2001 New Labour election
manifesto (six of them are used twice). Seven of them feature Blair.
There are only three other politicians pictured. They are David Trimble
(of the Ulster Unionist Party), Seamus Mallon (of the Social
Democratic and Labour Party) and Nelson Mandela. Not a single
Labour MP other than Tony gets in. This is Blair's party and he
welcomes us to his world.

Behold, the future!

But the image of the leader is not, on its own, enough. It needs to be
supplemented by a more specific set of policies, not because these are
more fundamental to the political process, but because the policies are
part of the image, and the image is part of the policies. Government
does not take place solely through the implementation of administra-
tive tools. It also takes place through the creation of conditions and
perceived conditions that function so as to legitimate government itself.
It may once have been the case that government possessed a legitimacy
transcending its actual actions – because God or the natural order of
things sanctioned it perhaps. But, increasingly, government is only
legitimated by what it does, so that what it must do is permanently
legitimate itself. Just like consumer products on the shelves of super-
stores, we will only 'buy' into a political programme if it provides a
'product' we find useful or enjoyable. And part of the use-value or
enjoyment-value of a product is precisely that image.

And when it comes to policies and more substantial rhetoric we find, again, a surprising consistency. In 1994 Blair spoke of 'a new confidence for a land of opportunity in a new and changing world'; in 2001 he wanted:

> not just to win your vote [but] to win your heart and your mind for the change that our country needs to face the challenges of the future. And it is a change not just for its own sake but for this purpose in which I passionately believe, to create a society in which everyone, not just those at the top, everyone gets the chance to succeed and make the most of their god-given abilities.[35]

It is on the future that Blair's New Labour stakes its claim.

The main elements of New Labour's pitch on policies can be seen clearly in its promotional material for the 2001 general election. In the 2001 Business Manifesto the party spelled out 'The challenges ahead'. Globalisation and technological change were described as 'exciting new opportunities', and the role of government established as that of enabling business through creating the right conditions for strong growth and investment. Government would be an investor and a partner and a regulator to ensure full competition. The manifesto acknowledged that government could not stop or reverse the changes that led to redundancy, but stated that it could support those communities to move forward.[36] The business manifesto (priced at £10) was a glossy document, well laid out and full of impressive looking charts and boxes showing leading business figures endorsing the product. It was a prospectus for potential buyers of the New Labour portfolio.

The general manifesto concentrated more on everyday images of families. Promising 'prosperity for all', it depicted a 'typical' 'middle-England' family (sitting on an ugly rug in front of a reconditioned feature fireplace, dad helping his daughter with her homework, mum sitting the younger son on her lap so he can reach the computer, while the collie relaxes next to them all).[37]

Despite media griping, the manifesto was quite long and detailed and even outlined something of a philosophy. Blair's opening statement spoke of a 'chance to build the future properly' and to renew Britain. It listed the familiar themes of sound finance and a strong and dynamic economy, up to welfare reform and a strong world role for Britain, and suggested the election would decide ...

> whether more people will be able to realise their aspirations for them-selves and their children – to be able to rely on a stable economy where hard work is rewarded by rising living standards, to receive world-class education and health care, to enjoy a dignified old age, to feel safe and

secure in a strong community and to be proud to be British. Or whether we will be held back by the traditional British malaise of restricting life's great opportunities and blessings to a minority.[38]

This encapsulates the official ideology of New Labour. Blair begins with the interests of people who want to realise their aspirations, but is referring to people with children – families – not to individuals. To realise these aspirations, people need a good economy and a context where work properly pays, and where those who work hard move on up. Implicitly then, people's aspirations are essentially for themselves, and centred on work and earning. But this means that collective provision, or at least state-based provision, matters, since it can provide education, health and pensions. These aspirations are themselves housed in the wider circle of the community and then the country as a whole. Blair then goes on to counterpose this ideology to the 'traditional' way in which people are held back, 'by the weakness of elitism and snobbery, vested interests and social division, complacency bred by harking back to the past'. This is the 'glass ceiling' of British prosperity.[39] Though much of what this statement is saying could, in fact, be regarded as quite traditional, it presents itself as challenging tradition and looking to the future, thus rendering New Labour's philosophy of communitarianism as pseudo-modern, in its address to communities and families.

The front page offers five very clear pledges, and their choice is significant. The first is to keep mortgages low and to maintain economic stability. Second is a pledge on schools, followed by one on health, then crime and a 'families' pledge encompassing pensioners as well. The ordering of these pledges matches that in Blair's opening statement, and also the list of 'ambitions for Britain' at the end of his introduction – from economy through public services, welfare, strong communities and global position. The Blairite community is one of hierarchically nested relationships and obligations.

There is a hidden unity to all this rhetoric. The manifesto pledges on page six that 'a single aim drives our policy programme: to liberate people's potential'; this is a phrase deployed in many of Blair's speeches. And on page five he says that New Labour's ambitions 'will never be achieved by government alone' ... 'We know it is people who ultimately change the country'. This echoes his frequent statement in his speeches that, 'the future is people'. He signs off with, 'I deeply believe that, for Britain, the best is still to come. So I ask you to continue on this journey with us. Together we can achieve so much more'. This tone, again, is reminiscent of other speeches made by Blair, and of the party election broadcast *Heroes* that went out on 1 June 2001.

Heroes was clearly designed to put across concrete pledges – raising the number of teachers, nurses, doctors, police officers. But the message of the format was exceptionally clear. It looked at people whose names don't get in the headlines: 'they don't give political speeches but they're the real heroes – the quiet heroes who are building the future of Britain'. It then told us about 'a student nurse facing everyday pressures'. She needs a low mortgage and 'works hard to make ends meet'. We were also shown John Ewing, a retired police officer who won the Queen's police medal and 'made the streets in Derbyshire safer', and 'Patti Lane, a hero to all the six and seven year olds she teaches in Wednesbury'. Then a former soldier in WW2, who cleared a road in Sicily while under fire. He worked on the railways and on the iron works, and at 83 'is still working for Britain as a community volunteer in Stapleford'. Each little story was followed by pledges relating to the particular area featured (nursing, mortgages, policing, schools, pensioners), and relayed the details of what had been done already. These were people who work hard for their families: 'They are the strength and soul of Britain. The real heroes who are changing this country. Now together let's finish what we've all started'.

In his own broadcasts Blair spoke a lot about stability, investment, and of his 'commitment to people'. In his speech announcing the election of 2001 he said: the biggest strength of Britain is 'its people'. Consistently, support for the individual (e.g. at school) is linked to the benefit of the country. With *Heroes* we saw this filled out and placed in the neo-communitarian context of those nested responsibilities. The people depicted were clearly located in very particular places, the towns and communities to which they contribute. These are the ideal Blairite citizens, who deserve the support of the state because they in turn fulfil their duties to their community. Obviously this is a marketing strategy to flag up key marginals and to personalise policies, encouraging us to identify with these heroes. But it also demonstrates a reconfigured relationship between the individual (and it is definitely about individuals not classes or other groups) and the state. It is individual people on whom the future rests, and in whose potential we must invest if that future is to be shining bright.

In their first broadcast of the 2001 election Labour clearly showed their commitment to the future. *The Work Goes On* went out in May, a two-and-a-half-minute image and text based montage accompanied by the sound of 'The Lighthouse Family' singing their commercially successful song 'Lifted'. The broadcast was mostly noted at the time for a guest appearance by ex-Spice Girl Geri Halliwell. But it was one of the few 'positive' campaigns Labour ran in that election, aimed at listing and illustrating all the successful things achieved by the first term. Answering the question 'Has Britain changed since 1997?', it focused on changes in and for work, families, holidays, children, the NHS, pensioners, schools, crime, police, handguns, landmines, world debt, devolution, Northern Ireland, the economy and mortgages, ending with a shot of a union-jack-emblazoned kite being – yes – lifted.

It was a good advert. The tune is mellow and jaunty, bland enough to be inoffensive but upbeat enough to be catchy. The refrain of the song illuminated the theme of the broadcast and the message sent out to the country. But it showed no actual politicians. Here, as throughout the campaign, only Blair really mattered. The broadcast had the feel of a travelogue, from the opening shot flying across the coast line to the final shot of kids launching the kite. In the middle were various upbeat and happy images of families at play, people joyfully at work and other images that matched those used in the manifesto. These, as usual, showed the necessary mix of young and old, all different races and colours.

But the tag line of 'The work goes on' was perhaps the most significant aspect. Tied into the other broadcasts such as *Heroes*, and the manifesto images, and the consistent refrain of investing in the future potential of 'people', it illuminated the core ideological claim and practice of the marketing campaign and the actual government. Blair, it is now clear, was applying for a job. He was, almost literally, interviewed for it. He stated his credentials (all the things he'd done from transforming his party to, subsequently, running the country for a bit), and tried to communicate what he would do for the country by touching on the issue of how we the citizens would be managed. Blair believes in our potential to be a profitable enterprise once again. But he doesn't think this can happen through the old out-dated form of bossy housekeeping and mean management. He wants to encourage us all to be part of the team devoted to the delivery of total quality. He wants us to feel that all can play a part in building the future. He wants us to share his vision, to see that he is a bit like us; and the challenge isn't to drone on about all that stuff from the old days (the empire, the unions, class consciousness), but to see the dividends to come in the future. That is his promise. That is his pitch.

Conclusion

In order to provide a political project with solid ground to stand on, it is always necessary to clear a space first. Parties, movements and ideologies do this by establishing a crisis to which they have the necessary answers, so that they are the only reasonable response. Thatcherism was part of a New-Right reformulation, which posited the crisis of the Keynesian welfare state, blamed failure on socialism, and hence advocated that socialism be 'smashed' and the state rolled back from the economy.

Blairism established itself firstly within the Labour Party, as a response to manifest electoral crisis. It blamed that failure on bad party management, inefficiency, in-fighting and unworkable, un-sellable, policies. But it also pointed to the inadequate and out-dated branding of the party. The emotional connotations of the party were all wrong. The customer base, the electorate, had changed, and the party's image, structure and product would have to change if there was to be any hope of securing a market position. New Labour saw a shift in the market; it identified a new consumer need and a market opportunity. Through research, it developed a product and a strategy for placing it, found a chief salesman who could embody the company's values, and oriented itself so as to claim the future.

But there is always a context. New Labour's relationship with the media and its image and style is a continuation of developments that have been underway for some time. As I have argued, it is a response to prevailing conditions, but it is also a symptom of them, an outcome of developments in the relationship of the media – particularly electronic media – to the overall social formation; developments that make plain the extent to which government is just a nodal point in much larger networks and flows of power and resistance.

Having secured a place in the party, New Labour had to establish the basis on which it would stand within the more generalised context of the country as a whole. The national crisis to which it pointed, therefore, was much more complex. It began with an assertion about the absolute failure of traditional social democracy, arguing that it limited entrepreneurial spirit, stultified creativity and held back the potential of the people. But this was picking up where Thatcherism had left off, so Blairism had to put something new into the mix. What it did – what it has done – is to add to the Thatcherite critique of social democracy a kind of social democratic critique of Thatcherism. The latter could be seen as correct in seeking to clear out the deadwood of British industry and to break the illegitimate power of union or state where it hampered the development of a freely entrepreneurial culture. But Thatcherism had a fatal flaw – the rapacious forces it unleashed undermined the very things needed to secure the conditions for the sought-after entrepreneurial spirit. Just as some management theorists argue that firms need to maintain the consent and the willing participation of employees, so that they will be adaptable and hard working, so New Labour sees that there is such a thing as society, through which the conditions of compliance, through identification with the new economy, have to be forged. The economy can only function if there is a culture of 'trust' and 'social responsibility' to underpin it. The future, then, not the past, became the battleground. No longer was the party securing or defending the hard-won gains of past working-class struggles. Instead

it was shaping everyone up for a future in which the needs of corporations, national economies and social justice could be seen as unified. At
the head of the project was Tony Blair. If Thatcher stood for a nation
of shopkeepers, and petit-bourgeois 'Victorian' values, then Blair set
out to embody a nation of managers – playing football at the weekends,
worrying about the kids during the week. His task was to entrench the
new-managerialist belief that UKGov.plc needs to ensure that the
shareholders and workers believe in it, and are committed to its values.
The answer was (and still is) modernisation.

Notes

1. Tony Blair (1993) 'A Battle We Must Win', *Fabian Review*, Vol. 105, 5,
   Sept./Oct., pp. 1-3.
2. Mo Mowlam cited in Eric Shaw (1996) *The Labour Party Since 1945*,
   Oxford, Blackwell, p. 198.
3. Nick Cohen (2001) 'Democracy is Dead. Now What?', *New Statesman*, 11
   June, pp12-13.
4. See the useful history provided by Dominic Wring (1996) 'Political
   marketing and party development in Britain: a "secret" history', *European
   Journal of Marketing*, Vol. 30, 10/11, pp100-111.
5. Sidney Webb (1922) quoted in Wring (1996), p104.
6. Cited in M.D. Kandiah (1995) 'Television Enters British Politics: the
   Conservative Party's Central Office and Political broadcasting, 1945-55,
   Historical Journal of Film, Radio and television, 15, 2, pp265-284.
7. Memorandum from Mark Chapman-Walker, 5 March 1951, cited in
   Kandiah (1995), p271.
8. Joseph Schumpeter (1975) [1942] *Capitalism, Socialism and Democracy*,
   New York, Harper Colophon, p283.
9. Anthony Downs (1957) *An Economic Theory of Democracy*, New York,
   Harper and Row.
10. See Dominic Wring (1997) 'Reconciling Marketing with Political Science',
    Journal of Marketing Management, Vol. 131, 7, pp651-663.
11. Margaret Scammell (1995) *Designer Politics: How Elections are Won*,
    Basingstoke, Macmillan, pp68-9. For more detail on the marketing of
    Thatcher see also Margaret Scammell (1996) 'The Odd Couple: Marketing
    and Maggie', *European Journal of Marketing*, 30, 10/11, 100-113.
12. Dominic Wring (1996) p107.
13. Scammell (1995).
14. Ralph Negrine (1989) *Politics and the Mass Media in Britain*, London,
    Routledge.
15. Certainly Chomsky does argue that the media, industry and politics are
    structurally interlinked. The point I am making here is that this linkage is
    not only a matter of personal connections or of deliberate support for each

other. Rather, the shape of the culture and the organisation of social institutions changes because of the way in which media come to draw out the appearance of all things, and to be gatekeeper of that which is public. See Noam Chomsky and Edward Herman (1994), *Manufacturing Consent: The Political Economy of the Mass Media*, London, Vintage.

16. Manuel Castells (1997) *The Power of Identity*, Oxford, Blackwell, p312.
17. Daniel J. Boorstin (1962) *The Image*, London, Weidenfeld and Nicolson.
18. Manuel Castells (1997) p317.
19. On news values see J. Galtung and M. Ruge (1973) 'Structuring and Selecting News', in S. Cohen and J. Young (eds.) *The Manufacture of News*, London, Constable, pp62-72; John Hartley (1982) *Understanding News*, London, Methuen.
20. On the contradiction between news objectivity and the needs of democratic debate see Alan Finlayson (2001) 'The Problem of the Political Interview', *Political Quarterly*, Vol. 72, No.3, pp335-344.
21. *The Independent*, 26.4.01.
22. *The Daily Telegraph*, 14.4.00
23. Nicholas O'Shaughnessy (1996) 'Social Propaganda and social marketing: a critical difference?', *European Journal of Marketing*, 30, 10/11, pp62-75.
24. See Bob Franklin (2001) 'The Hand of History: New Labour, News management and Governance', in Steve Ludlam and Martin J. Smith (eds.) *New Labour in Government*, Basingstoke, Macmillan, pp130-144.
25. Quoted in Franklin (2001), p131.
26. Quoted in Franklin (2001) p143.
27. Armand Mattelart and Michelle Mattelart (1992) *Rethinking media theory: signposts and new directions*, Minneapolis, University of Minnesota Press, pxii.
28. Scott Lash (2001) 'Technological Forms of Life' *Theory, Culture and Society*, 19, 1, pp105-120.
29. Lash (2001) p108.
30. Martin Heidegger (1971) 'The Thing', in *Poetry, Language and Thought*, London, Harper and Row, p165.
31. See *The Guardian*, 9.5.01.
32. See Antonio Gramsci (1971) *Selections from the Prison Notebooks*, London, Lawrence and Wishart.
33. Roland Barthes (1977) *Image, Music, Text*, London, Paladin, p15.
34. Barthes (1977) p22.
35. See *The Guardian*, 9.5.01.
36. Labour Party (2001) *The best place to do business: Labour's ambitions for Britain's Economy*, p3.
37. Ibid. p9.
38. Labour Party (2001) *Ambitions for Britain: Labour's manifesto 2001*, p3.
39. Ibid. p3.

CHAPTER THREE

The Meaning of Modernisation

Introduction

If there is a single word that might capture the essence of New Labour's social and political project then it is 'modernisation'. The jargon and rhetoric of modernisation abound within the discourse of the Labour Party and government. In a study of 53 speeches of Tony Blair, Norman Fairclough found that the word 'modern' occurred 89 times, 'modernise' or 'modernisation' a further 87. It is, as he also observes, often used without reference to any specific practice or domain.[1] But 'modernisation' also crops up across policy fields, in statements, white papers, briefings and other documents released from Whitehall, where it appears to be a generalised process, applicable across the policy, governmental and social fields. As a result it has been adopted by the policy and academic communities and become embedded across a range of areas of discussion.

A number of competing interpretations of New Labour have considered the meaning of modernisation. It has been taken to be: the name of the process whereby the Labour Party adopted a Thatcherite agenda; a simple continuation, perhaps culmination, of the party reforms first attempted by Gaitskell; an empty term hiding the single sin of having nothing to say. But, as Kenny and Smith note, interpretations such as these underestimate the novelty of the political approach of New Labour and the complexity of forces, structural and ideological, to which it is a response. The ideological position of Blair represents more than just a capitulation to Thatcherism or the victory of a 'labourist' accommodation with capital. Rather, they argue, it entails the attempt to 'change the party's instincts and values in accordance with [a] new political economy'.[2] In this sense 'modernisation' represents the response of New Labour to a range of social conditions and conjunctural processes. Beginning with the transformation of the party, in order to make it fit for changed circumstances, this has been carried into a 'project' for the country. But there is a more immediate answer to the question of what 'modernisation' is. It is a word.

Words matter. Indeed, they are matter. Words are a substance, acting on things and being acted on by other substances and processes. They are one of the central materials of political action and mobilisation. We are perhaps too accustomed to accepting the idea that there is an easy opposition between rhetoric and reality. Our journalistic culture of political interpretation likes to contrast the 'fine sounding', 'high-flown' and 'empty' rhetoric of political debate and discourse to the reality of failed policy implementation and change. But rhetoric is part of the doing of politics alongside the restructuring of institutions and the injection or withdrawal of cash subsidies. Speech, as J.L. Austin so famously demonstrated, is an act and words can have a certain force.[3] Politics is concerned not only with deploying the force of words in order to achieve some desired effect but in giving force to words so that their usage can come to have such effects. The word 'modernisation' is just such a word. It is not a pure performative, in the sense of a word or phrase the saying of which is also the doing of it. But it is performative in a looser sense – a statement that acquires meaning and force only in the moment of its usage. Declaring that something is an act of modernisation is one way in which it becomes so (and also a way in which the word attains a more stable reference). Modernisation is a word and concept that attempts to 'organise' and 'structure' thinking and action. It can be understood and explained by focusing on it from three angles: its rhetorical function; its concrete reference and its deployment as a strategy of governance.

The discourse of modernisation is rhetorical in that it functions to persuade and motivate. It is an 'up' word, that makes things sound exciting, progressive and positive. But it is also ideological in that this rhetorical usage helps generate an appearance of structured and unified thinking beyond which is either nonsense or (by implication) out-dated thinking. It helps to render 'natural' and un-contestable that which is not necessarily so. Because the same word is used to describe constitutional reform, changes to the police force, health service and educational system, it seems that some sort of coherent approach is underpinning policy. Along with this unifying effect there is (as a necessary corollary) a simultaneous exclusion. That which is not modern is not of New Labour's New Britain, and that which is not part of it cannot lay claim to being modernised. At this level, the idea of modernisation links into certain ways of thinking about community, particularly national community, that add to its overall 'naturalisation'.

But modernisation does also have a concrete reference. Contrary to the implications of the above claims, and also to the numerous attempts simply to dismiss New Labour as all spin, modernisation refers to some very specific processes. Modernised things are technically advanced, they make use of the latest information and communication technologies, they are networked, lean, flexible, efficient and knowledge-friendly. Modernisation derives this meaning from the uses to which it is put, but those things also gain a meaning because they are linked together under the word and that meaning. Dividing up the functioning of the term into rhetorical/ideological and concrete is not intended to suggest that the latter is the 'real' meaning while the former is the gloss. On the contrary, the two aspects function together and support each other, allowing modernisation to refer to all sorts of things that have to be done in order to improve government and public services. This ties in to the third aspect of modernisation which I shall call its function as a 'strategy of problematisation' which shapes governance.

Modernisation serves as a mechanism for 'diagnosing' errors in the organisation and management of public services and for establishing their cure. Modern government works, in large part and especially in the areas of public service provision, by establishing 'problems' and specifying what exactly their nature might be in order then to be able to put forward the solution (in the form of government action or with-drawal for example). It is important to distinguish this level of the process from the more straightforward one of simply identifying 'things that should be done'. For example one might say that there is too great a level of poverty in the country. But is poverty the problem or is there another phenomenon or problem for which poverty is a symptom or index? For while poverty may be understood as an ethical problem this does not automatically make it a governmental problem. Government cannot act upon poverty. It can only act upon people and processes. So, the state or government has to establish what the problem is, what mechanical failure leads to poverty. One can imagine (without much difficulty) a political movement that sees poverty as the result of fecklessness and idiocy. The problem is thus not poverty but the poor. The solution that naturally follows is to treat the fecklessness by removing it (simply getting rid of the poor – not an unknown strategy in political history) or by 're-moralising' society (so that the poor are motivated to pull their socks up). This is a quite different kind of problematisation to that which identifies poverty as the outcome of structural features (such as the need of capital to have a 'reserve army' of cheap labour to draw on in times of rapid economic expansion). For the latter, different cures naturally follow (though here too they have, in political history, included getting rid of some people and re-moral-ising society). Thus, we might say that government functions through particular procedures of problem identification and generation.

Modernisation is a key strategy of problematisation used by New Labour. Indeed, we can go so far as to say that New Labour practises not only the modernisation of governance but a kind of governance through modernisation.

In this chapter we will examine some uses of the term 'modernisation' in Blair's own rhetoric and in government policy and advisory documents. This will help us explore its rhetorical function. We will then consider what the concrete referent might be before looking at how it works as a 'strategy of problematisation'. But we will begin with a brief consideration of some possible origins for the whole idea of 'modernisation'. Words do not come from nowhere and they never mean just whatever we want them to mean. They are shaped by their prior usage just as we try to reshape them by employing them in different contexts.

The origins of 'modernisation'

Dictionaries, rather unhelpfully, define the word modernisation in thoroughly tautological terms. It means the act of modernising or the state of being modernised; to adapt to modern tastes. This, naturally, leaves the content of the modern undefined. In this sense the word is certainly thoroughly modern. It denotes a state of always trying to catch-up with ourselves. However, to sociologists modernisation is probably a familiar and reasonably unproblematic term. For, in one sense, macro-sociology is about nothing other than modernisation. That is to say, it deals with the transition from what was 'traditional' to that which is 'modern', and analyses society in terms of these processes of change. Beyond that, of course, the meaning, causes and implications of modernisation are a site of doctrinal dispute. The modern may often be conceived as a disruptive force, something that transforms or uproots the way things have been. Indeed modernity is often understood within sociological theory as a condition defined by such uprooting. To be modern is to be aware that one lives in the now, at the present end of an historical process of some sort, unable to live according to the rules of the past, forced to form new ones all the time. In this sense, to modernise means to adapt, to adjust to new, changed, or changing conditions.

This means that, for the term 'modernisation' to have any meaning, a number of conceptual preconditions must be satisfied. The very idea entails a certain sense of history as some kind of forward (if not necessarily progressive) movement. It also implies some notion of tradition against which the modern is defined, and requires an object or body to be modernised or to be the agent of that modernisation. Typically, in political as well as sociological thinking, that body has been the nation.

For Marxist and liberal historians alike, the nation (and being a nation-state) has been understood as a hallmark of modernity.[4] The nation has defined the abstract form of community that predominates in the industrialised world to such an extent that, as post-colonial theorists from India to Ireland have argued, it comes to appear as if, to be modern, one must first pass through the necessary stage of acquiring nationhood.[5] The 'imagining' of national community derives from and entails notions of modernisation and combines within it a very specific sense of time, history and space. As Benedict Anderson argues, to imagine the nation is to imagine a large collective of people all occupying the same time and space. The nation is 'conceived as a solid community moving steadily down (or up) history'.[6] To imagine the nation means also to imagine a particular, and modern, notion of history as a sequence of causally related events moving in some direction. And the reverse is also true. To imagine time, or history, in that way means also to imagine the vehicle that moves in and through that history.

As we will see, 'modernisation', for New Labour, implies just such a notion of history in terms of some sort of progressive development driven by some sort of external force. As the nation is the body subject to the forces of modernisation, it is this which must be reconceived and re-branded, and it is in it that we must find the already written path to the pre-ordained future. Thus Blair frequently presents an argument in which the impulse or capacity for modernisation is found to be embedded in Britishness, while the need for it is allied to the desire to make Britain a world-class, world power.

But in addition to this general sociological reference, there is a more specific meaning of modernisation for some parts of the British left. The 'problematic' of modernisation has marked theories and analyses of the British state, society and economy for a long time. One left variant of this analysis crystallised in the celebrated Anderson-Nairn theses. Advancing their argument in a series of articles in the pages of *New Left Review* at the start of the 1960s, Perry Anderson and Tom Nairn developed an overarching theory of British society out of an analysis of its historical development.[7] They were motivated by the desire to explain what they saw as the crises of the British state, economy, culture and society. In particular their target was what we might now call the forces of conservatism that dominate (or have dominated) Britain. To simplify more than a little, they argued that the English Civil Wars were an incomplete, possibly 'premature', bourgeois revolution. By not having a 'proper' revolution Britain failed to eradicate the feudal legacy, leading to a compromise arrangement where new structures of capital co-existed with an archaic 'superstructure' encompassing aristocratic traditionalism. Britain was thus unable to undertake the necessary processes of 'rationalisation' and to develop a fully modern state form. The persistence of an *ancien regime* led to a continuing over-emphasis in the British economy on mercantilist forms of accumulation (commercial and financial capital) rather than modern forms of industry. Thus disabled, the state was unable to renovate itself and respond to changes in the nature of the economy. Consequently, Britain has a tendency to stagnate and decline. The state is inflexible, and weighed down by irrational traditions and arcane practices. It is incompletely modernised and new political projects can be analysed in terms of how they match up to the demands of modernising Britain.

It is impossible directly to measure the influence of such a thesis. Certainly Anderson and Nairn's arguments were provocative, even exhilarating new conceptualisations. They certainly provoked heated discussion within the New Left.[8] Furthermore, Anderson took up and redeveloped the argument again in the late 1980s while Nairn turned his attention to specific aspects of the charge such as England's lingering attachment to its monarchy.[9] These arguments were both a cause and an effect of a more general mood that Britain had been or is held back by too much emphasis on traditionalism, too great an attachment to the past rather than commitment to working for the future. Campaign groups devoted to constitutional reform; the numerous critiques of the habits of deference to authority, elitism and secrecy in Whitehall; charges of too much emphasis on the City of London rather than the mills of Sheffield are all members of the same family of ideas as the Anderson and Nairn thesis. It is an inescapable part of the intellectual landscape of most of the British left. It informs the contemporary analyses of Will Hutton, for example, and was a key point for analyses of Thatcherism developed by important writers such as Andrew Gamble and Stuart Hall.[10] In particular, modernisation formed an underlying theme to the perspectives developed in the 1980s in the pages of *Marxism Today* (see Chapter 3). Theories of British decline were predicated on variants of the Anderson-Nairn thesis and from them emerged the view that Britain required something called modernisation and that Thatcherism was to be understood as a failed attempt at 'regressive-modernisation'. Thus in 1987, for example, Eric Hobsbawm, in *Marxism Today*, called for Labour to establish a coalition of interests dedicated to bringing about modernisation of the British economy: 'Labour will return to office only as a party which offers such a New Deal: modernisation – and in a human and responsible manner. Whatever the long-term prospects for Britain, what the country needs now for any kind of future is such a transformation'.[11]

This entailed accepting some of the Thatcherite reforms, and an acknowledgement that Labour should be ready to 'disrupt old habits and practices'. Hobsbawm also called for a combination of market and state planning that would enable a socially responsible modernisation incorporating a commitment to social justice. Modernisation, at this level, means taking on the older and entrenched elements of state practice, reforming the structures and habits of government in ways that breakdown old privilege. It means challenging prejudices that hinder technological advance and rapid reactions to changing economic demands. It means refusing to rely on 'old' ways and rationalising the conduct of the state.

Such ideas can be related to other strands of the tradition of the British left and labour movement, such as the Fabian tradition which bequeathed to us a conviction that the way out of stagnation (social as well as economic) is better experts, able to exercise their judgement free from the interference of outmoded tradition. Such a notion of meritocracy allied to technical and scientific advance was central to Wilson's appeal to the party and the electorate in the 1960s. The talk then was also of a 'New Britain' that would overturn the old, landed establishment embodied by the Tory Party. In a stirring campaign speech in 1964 Wilson spoke (as Blair would a generation later) of the speed of technological advance, contrasting it to Britain's lack of will in making the most of the future:

> We are living in a jet-age but we are governed by an Edwardian establishment mentality. Over the British people lies the chill frost of Tory leadership. They freeze initiative and petrify imagination. They cling to privilege and power for the few, shutting the gates on the many …The Tories have proved that they are incapable of mobilising Britain to take full advantage of the scientific breakthrough. Their approach and methods are fifty years out of date.

The response was to galvanise the nation and let talent lead. Labour, Wilson said, 'wants to streamline our institutions, modernise methods of government, bring the entire nation into a working partnership with the state'.[12] The 1964 manifesto declared:

> At the root of Tory failure lies an outdated philosophy – their nostalgic belief that it is possible in the second half of the 20th century to hark back to a 19th century free enterprise economy and a 19th century unplanned society. In an age when the economy is no longer self-regulating and when the role of government must inevitably increase, they have tried and failed to turn back the clock.[13]

Here too there was talk of a modernised economy built around the new science and technology of the future, and an attempt to respond to generational and cultural change by re-shaping socialism for the affluent society.

These are only parts of the tradition of modernisation, though they are important parts of the history of the British left. They have shaped the meanings of modernisation in the past and in the present. But it would be a mistake to think that this word can mean the same now as it has in the past. Blair and New Labour's use of the term contributes to a reshaping of its implications at the same time as that use is shaped by the term's history. From its particular meanings for social historians, constitutional reformers and advocates of the white-heat of technological revolution, the word subsequently came to mean the transformation of the party under Kinnock. Here modernisers stood for reform and change, reassessment over retrenchment and opposition to the hard left cohorts with whom they struggled for power in the party during the 1980s. Where, in Wilson's mouth, modernisation meant rational management of the economy and planning for social advantage, it now came to mean something like the abandonment of even a limited Keynesianism. In the party, modernisation meant a kind of professionalism – the updating of organisational structures, the deployment of contemporary campaign techniques. Modernisation became a managerialist word, referring to the updating of procedures, structures, product placement and marketing.

Through all these changes the word keeps something of itself just as much as its meaning maintains mobility. It is a positive sounding word, it feels progressive. It is also a big word, that encompasses, potentially, the sort of grand theory and diagnosis found in the Anderson-Nairn theses. Because of its links back to the arguments of the 1960s it can feel like a Labour word, a Labour concept quite different to traditional Tory rhetoric about the need to preserve the past. As a term with a specific history in the British Labour Party it helps to anchor Blairite political discourses within the traditions of that party. It is thus a promising basis on which to shape what might sound or feel like a major new development in progressive political thinking. But rather than a simple historical development we find a kind of genealogy. The word-concept does not progressively develop according to any logic internal either to it or to a wider historical process. It undergoes a series of 'rebirths', related to but separate from each other, exposed to and entwined with other logics, different needs, desires, strategies and demands. This allows us to see the creativity behind each new employment of the concept, but also the ways in which it carries with it traces of prior usage. In developing a rhetoric of modernisation, the

Blairite New Labour Party is doing something new but it is not completely in control. Is modernisation uttered in the language of the labour movement and Labour Party, the language of sociology and Marxist history, the language of management theory, or a new language invented by Tony Blair and his advisers? It is uttered in all of these languages, enabling the modernising project to appeal to a variety of political, economic and intellectual constituencies. This history is a partial restraint on what the word can mean and shapes the practices carried out in its name. For example, 'modernisation' has implications of a deterministic kind (of the necessary and inevitable path of development the state must follow). The concept is intrinsically teleological. As a 'big' word, it helps New Labour feel like it is thinking big. It has set itself a 'historic' task of completely reforming the British state and society. There is a vision here and it guides policy formation and implementation as well as political practice: the country is weighed down by out-dated habits and institutions that are no longer fit to fulfil their stipulated tasks because the world has changed. While this change is understood by Blair as one that, of itself, brings about 'progressive' change and even 'emancipation', it also legitimates a vanguardist or missionary zeal on the part of those who are in tune with the forces of history and who must carry the national community forward to fulfilment. This, in turn, legitimates the centralisation of power in the hands of those who understand.

The rhetoric of modernisation

The speeches of Tony Blair are a good place to start exploring the 'logic' behind this contemporary rhetoric of modernisation. Blair's speeches before and after becoming leader of the Labour Party abound with references to the 'modern' party, his 'modern' vision and the all round newness of this 'modern' world. The first speech he gave to the party conference after his election as Prime Minister was quite clear in terms of this general vision. He wanted Britain to be 'nothing less than the model twenty-first century nation', the construction of which would depend on 'drawing deep into the richness of the British character ... old British values but a new British confidence'.[14] To this Blair added a populist twist by speaking as if the nation had been freed from a form of (Conservative) colonial subjugation. Addressing the conference after that first election victory he referred to the people as 'liberated' and spoke of government 'returned' to the people. This people was to be the bearer of the project, for there is 'a quiet revolution now taking place. Led by the real modernisers – the British people'.[15]

To legitimise the political project of modernisation. Blair locates the impetus for it, not in a cadre of political elites, but in the British people themselves. Conservative arguments that reform necessarily foists unwarranted change on the nation are trumped in advance by the construction of a story where change, renewal and modernisation are intrinsic to the tradition of the nation. Hence:

> From the Magna Carta to the first Parliament to the industrial revolution to an empire that governed most of the world; most of the great inventions of modern times with Britain stamped on them: the telephone; the television; the computer; penicillin; the hovercraft; radar ... change is in the blood and bones of the British – we are by our nature and tradition innovators, adventurers, pioneers.[16]

This claim was followed by a highly apposite quotation from Milton whom Blair described as 'our great poet of renewal and recovery'. It is a description of England taken from *Areopagitica*: 'a nation not slow or dull but of quick, ingenious and piercing spirit, acute to invent, subtle and sinewy of discourse, not beneath the reach of any point that human capacity can soar to'. The lines of Milton that follow those quoted by Blair could perhaps be seen as encapsulating the intended vision of the latter: 'methinks I see in my mind a noble and puissant nation rousing herself like a strong man after sleep and shaking her invincible locks'.[17]

The reference to the Miltonian intervention is particularly interesting in this context. With hindsight we can now see Milton's words as an opening sally in what would become a defining radical struggle of English history – and, as we have noted, the period most debated by historians interested in the 'modernisation' of Britain. That Blair should, however unconsciously, identify his project with that of one of the most epochal moments in British history is surely instructive. The upheavals and conflicts of seventeenth century England fostered a strengthened sense of particularity and identity and engendered crucial developments in the deployment of national consciousness in the name of the establishment of a new bourgeois class. As Matt Jordan has pointed out, Milton himself was writing at the time of an 'information revolution' in the form of the new (and powerful) printing press.[18] *Areopagitica*, in its content and its very publication, was an attack on attempts by the crown to censor and control printing. It tried to call into being a body of citizens prepared to partake of a democratic revolution and to become readers in the new public sphere of criticism and dissent, wherein they would be able to imagine a transformed nation free from monarchical authority.

Blair too wants us to be able to envision a transformed nation, or rather to become cognisant of the fact that it is already in the process of such change, animated by an information revolution. He also wants that change to be understood as inherently liberating and progressive. Thus, his rhetoric seeks to arrange itself on the side of 'the people' and hence (by implication) opposed to the anti-popular interests of the anti-modernisers. In his earlier, 1994, conference speech Blair had argued that 'the new establishment is not a meritocracy but a power elite of money-shifters, middlemen and speculators, people whose self interest will always come before the national or public interest'.[19] In contrast Blairism would transform the nation, or assist it to transform itself. However, Blair does not simply seek to occupy the terrain of Conservative patriotic populism. He aims to reshape that terrain, finding it to be fit for the 'challenge' of modernisation. Thus the country must draw on its deep character, exploiting the fact that it is one with:

> Proud democratic traditions ... of tolerance, innovation and creativity ... an innate sense of fair play ... a great history and culture. And when great challenges face us, as they have twice this century, we rise to them. But if we have a fault, it is that unless roused we tend to let things be. We say 'things could be worse' rather than 'things should be better'. And the Tories encourage this fault, they thrive on our complacency, I say it is time we were roused.[20]

This was three years before Blair did successfully rouse the people with, as a campaign song, the reminder that 'Things Can Only Get Better'. After that song had played its part in electoral success he told the conference that the country would be roused for a project of 'national renewal' ready to face the new world and embrace change. This is a battle of national historical significance, for the soul of the future, aiming to return to the nation its true inheritance, modernised and 'free to excel once more'.[21]

This talk is full of dynamic words like rousing, renewing and achieving, contained within a story about British history, national character and the requirements for their sustenance and continuation. Blair is trying to construct an appeal for transformation on the basis of the way things are so that modernisation can seem to follow naturally:

> We know what makes a successful creative economy. Educate the people. Manage the country's finances well. Encourage business and enterprise. But each bit requires us to modernise and take the hard choices to do it ... We have been a mercantile power, an industrial power. Now we must be the new power of the information age.[22]

It follows naturally from who 'we' are but also from the state of the present. After all, we 'face the challenge of a world with its finger on the fast forward button; where every part of the picture of our life is changing'.[23] Modernisation, then, seems to be a kind of code-word for 'what is to be done'. There will be 'hard choices' (like taking over failing schools, sacking teachers and so on) but these are forced on us by the imperative of modernisation which in turn derives from the inexorable progress of our island story. There is no alternative: 'The hard choice: Stay as we are and decline. Or modernise and win'. The NHS, 'the greatest act of modernisation any Labour Government ever did', requires adaptation in the form of: 'modernisation and hard choices'.[24] Perhaps the 'clearest' statement of what modernisation means is this:

> I say to the country in all honesty. You can have the education revolution, the health revolution, the welfare revolution. But it means hard choices. It means us all getting involved. And it means modernisation.[25]

Modernisation thus means everything we have to do, and we have to do what we do in order to be modernised, but this is OK because it is what we do anyway. The hard choices it entails are encapsulated in a kind of 'enlightened patriotism' that is the shell from which modernisation emerges. The principles of New Labour are the principles of Britain and there must be a 'supreme national effort ... held together by our values, and by the strength of our character, our nature as "a giving people"'.[26] We will be a beacon to the world if the people 'unite behind our mission to modernise the country'.[27]

In this way the notion of modernisation fulfils the crucial ideological function of naturalising Blairism and then placing limitations upon the scope of contemporary political thinking. As Michael Rustin has argued:

> It is a notable and defining fact about 'New Labour' that for the first time the power of capital and the markets which empower it is regarded as merely a fact of life, a reality to be accommodated to, and not a problem, a force to be questioned and resisted. The abstractions of 'globalisation', 'individualisation', even 'informationalism', can be used to reify the real agents and interests which dominate the contemporary world.[28]

The extent of such reification is related to the meanings given to the concept of modernisation. It is what this concept both reflects and produces since it tends to locate processes such as 'globalisation' in the exigencies of a social and historical development that is understood to be an unalterable given, and which is also rooted in the very nature of 'the people'. Thus, the widespread application of the term modernisation enables it to encompass everything that is held to be good and also necessary. It refers to everything for which Blair stands, and this is nothing less than a projected attempt at national renewal and transformation centred on new technology, global markets and the skills revolution. Whatever it is that the British education and heath system require can be called modernisation. In this rhetoric the nature of the times and the nature of the nation coincide; the essence of the people can be reconciled with the conditions of their existence and Blairism will abolish all alienation and antagonism. Modernisation is in accordance with the historic and innate sense of the British people, the logical extension of all that Britain has ever done. The nation is simultaneously in need of modernisation and already, of itself, engaging in the process, requiring only to be roused from its slumbers and revolutionised so it can face up to hard choices that it must accept or die. The hard choices foisted on us by the inexorable march of human progress will be lived up to by Blair's Christian world-historical movement.

This stress on nation is very much a part of Blairite rhetoric though it has not been much discussed by analysts. Perhaps this is because it does not quite fit with the usual ways in which nationhood has been deployed by British political leaders. For the Right it is clearly false, because Blair seems to stamp on so much of what they consider to be British (old values, old ways, fox hunting). And on the left it has not been much remarked on, perhaps because it is not couched in overtly racist terms; it can appear as if the Conservative opposition have a monopoly on patriotic language, in their own peculiarly xenophobic version, allied as it is for them with anti-Europeanism and hostility to asylum-seekers. In an interview during the 2001 election campaign Blair declared, 'I am British and I am proud of it but I have never regarded being pro-British as being anti-European or anti-anything else. It is an absurd position'. He went on to say that: 'In this day and age when the whole world is moving closer together the patriotic national interest is to be engaged in the alliances of which we are a member … the isolationist view of the world is just contrary to the way the world works'. Again, he tied this patriotism into the project of modernisation:

> Britain has always been a country heavily engaged in the future of the outside world. We've not been an isolationist country. In all the great moments of our history we've been engaged with the outside world. [The current Conservative approach] is just an attempt to dress up what is I think a very backward looking type of xenophobia as patriotism'.[29]

This kind of Blairite nationalism, often in the form of a communitarianism, is extremely important to New Labour.[30]

Meanwhile, the blanket use of 'modernisation' furthers the impression of inevitability, giving it a gloss of universality that adds another dimension to its naturalisation. Forces are at work bringing about the need for modernisation. They are inevitable and clearly definable – technological transformation, the 'obvious' failure of the social-democratic welfare state and globalisation. Since such forces are irreversible, the political challenge becomes construed as that of living up to them (as opposed to assessing them and deciding how politics should respond). Specific reforms to core state services can be justified on the basis of their *a priori* (and unquestionable) necessity: a response to what is. Changes to welfare policy, for example, are predicated on the belief that, in Alastair Darling's words:

> The structure of the economy has changed, industrial patterns and working conditions are very different and the labour market has needed to adapt accordingly. People's lives and their expectations have been transformed ... there have been profound economic and social changes since 1948. But the welfare state has failed to keep pace. Reform is therefore essential.[31]

We need skills, talents, education 'and every single part of our schools system must be modernised to achieve it'.[32]

While the word modernisation acts as a fully positive term describing all that must be done, a justification of its necessity and a point of mobilisation for the national community as a whole, it also requires the specification of that to which the New Labour 'project' is opposed – the enemies of modernisation. This is made necessary since the positing of an antagonist against which modernisation can be distinguished establishes for it a greater stability of reference and level of naturalisation. Hence the concept is also defined by its opposition to the anti-modernisation that had to be excised from the Labour Party, but is incarnated in the failed Tory Party. This turns into a crude dualism between old and new within the Labour Party. That which is not 'on-side' or 'on-message' is by definition anti-modernisation and out-dated. Blairism, by contrast, harnesses all the forces of progress. In his 1999 conference speech Blair declared New Labour 'confident at having modernised itself' and described it as 'now the new progressive force in British politics which can modernise the nation, sweep away those forces of conservatism to set the people free'.[33] He pledged the party to be in the business of creating a newly confident and strong Britain: to do for the country what had been done for the party and to bring about a political realignment favouring the 'progressive forces'. This sentiment has been expressed by Blair on several occasions. In one early pamphlet he set out his intention of putting right the historic split between the Labour Party and Liberal progressivism at the beginning of the twentieth century.[34] But Blair's progressivism has a distinct meaning, deriving from modernisation. In the 1999 conference speech he described his vision of:

> A New Britain where the extraordinary talent of the British people is liberated from the forces of conservatism that so long have held them back, to create a model 21st century nation, based not on privilege, class or background, but on the equal worth of all.[35]

This, for Blair, is the defining division of twenty-first century British politics: not capital and labour but progressivism and conservatism. The latter ...

> hold our nation back. Not just in the Conservative Party but within us, within our nation. The forces that do not understand that creating a new Britain of true equality is no more a betrayal of Britain's history than New Labour is of Labour's values.[36]

This allowed the injection of some 'classic' Blair populism. Responsibility for the failure of individuals is here not simply theirs alone. There is a 'them' that is at fault – elites and establishments that have run professions and kept out women and ethnic minorities:

> The old order, those forces of conservatism, for all their language about promoting the individual, and freedom and liberty, they held people back. They kept people down. They stunted people's potential. Year after year. Decade after decade.[37]

Having cited the winning of votes for women as a force of progress opposed by those of 'conservatism', Blair adds the NHS to the tally. Conservatism, on the other hand, was responsible for the murder of Martin Luther King and the imprisonment of Nelson Mandela. Through a neat segue Blair makes all the opponents of modernisation into opponents of progress and justice:

> These forces of conservatism chain us not only to an outdated view of our people's potential but of our nation's potential. What threatens the nation-state today is not change, but the refusal to change in a world opening up, becoming ever more interdependent.[38]

Here we see the final move in the naturalisation of this discourse and its internal closure. The narrative is, on inspection, quite clear. The world out there is changing. We have to adapt. Fortunately we are able to adapt because adaptability is something the British are great at and they are full of talent and potential. But some people don't want us to adapt to change. They want to protect their vested interests and not be threatened by transformation. Changing will not only allow more people to prosper, it is the very condition of that prosperity. The elites that don't want this to happen don't want others to prosper. But even they ought to realise that modernisation is the only game in town since, if the country does not sort itself out, everyone, including the old elites, will lose out: 'The old air of superiority based on past glory must give way to the ambition to succeed, based on the merit of what Britain stands for today'.[39]

The policies and acts of the government can easily be tied into this story. Devolution is modernising; opposing it is conservatism and nationalist separatism ('just the forces of conservatism by another name'). The forces of conservatism are not only Tories. They exist in the Labour Party too, such as those who opposed the reform of Clause IV. Thus: 'The Third Way is not a new way between progressive and conservative politics. It is progressive politics distinguishing itself from conservatism of left or right. New Labour must be the new radicals who take on both of them, not just on election day but every day'.[40]

Opening up the economy is opposed by the forces of conservatism, which also exist in education and in the medical profession. Lining up with modernisation and progress are concepts such as liberty, opportunity, aspiration, etc. Alongside conservatism, in contrast, are opposition to change (whatever the change), ideology, eternal doctrines:

> Arrayed against us: the forces of conservatism, the cynics, the elites, the establishment. Those who will live with decline. Those who yearn for yesteryear. Those who just can't be bothered. Those who prefer to criticise rather than do. On our side, the forces of modernity and justice. Those who believe in a Britain for all the people. Those who fight social injustice, because they know it harms our nation. Those who believe in a society of equality, of opportunity and responsibility. Those who have the courage to change. Those who have confidence in the future.[41]

'Modernisation' is a key word of New Labour and Blairite rhetoric, anchoring a rhetorical and conceptual structure. It ensures and justifies the inclusion of all that is pre-defined as part of the project, while securing this unity through consigning everything opposing it to a history that has been surpassed. The project is justified by reference to the nation which is ready and willing for modernisation but which also needs to be modernised and so cleared of reactionary forces. This is not just an ideology. It is a kind of social and political theory, even a philosophy, but with a solipsistic conceptual structure that is almost theological or cultic in its capacity to encompass everything or anything the movement might choose to do, while rejecting criticism as a kind of nonsensical heresy. This solipsism is fundamental to the rhetoric and theory of Blairism.

In his pamphlet on the Third Way, Blair considers (very briefly) the ways in which post-war political history has been shaped by wider social changes, on which political movements capitalised and to which they were a response. Now, he argues, we face social changes that have swept away neo-liberal dogma just as, in the 1970s, they swept away statist social democracy. He refers specifically to global markets and global culture, technological change and the information revolution, the changing role of women and changing political structures.[42] All these social and technological changes are understood as modernisation. In his speeches and other such interventions Blair places a singular emphasis on new technology and information super-highways. Addressing the TUC in September of 1999 Blair claimed that the transition to the knowledge economy was 'the fundamental issue' of our time and the importance of such 'change' is asserted throughout contemporary government publications and speeches.

In this respect, Blair's conference speeches as party leader are remarkable for their consistency of vision and employment of the same phrases and examples. At conference in 1994 he declared it 'time to break out of the past and break through with a clear and radical modern vision for Britain: Today's politics is about the search for security in a changing world'.[43] In 1995 he spoke of 'a new age to be led by a new generation', the popular culture generation of colour TV, Coronation Street and The Beatles.[44] The problem was that 'we live in a new age but in an old country', hanging on to an antiquated class system, yet needing to prepare to win the 'knowledge race'. This all related to promises about bringing the information superhighway to every school, library and eventually home. The 'patriotic party' would modernise public services and the constitution.

By 1996 we were hearing about 100 days for 1000 years, the 'Age of achievement', education, education, education and lots more technology. The age of achievement would stand against the age of decline, drawing on an intrinsic 'national ethos and spirit' such that the party would be 'part of the broad movement of human progress'. This, Blair said, links the Labour Party with the Old Testament prophets, Wilberforce and the

Union movement. Carried away with his own kind of Miltonian rhetoric, Blair spoke of the nation's intrinsic 'common sense', historic institutions, 1000 years of history and declared that his party was 'not just turning a page in history but writing a new book. Building the greatness of our nation through the greatness of its people ... let us call our nation to destiny'.[45] Thus, plugged into the world wide web, paradise is regained. The machines of state and the country itself will finally adapt to the new conditions that have been emerging since the popular culture generation learnt to play guitar in a college rock band.

In 1999 Blair was still talking about the model twenty-first century nation,[46] and declaring that there was 'all around us the challenge of change'. The spectre of technological revolution was haunting the world: 'Global finance and Communications and Media. Electronic commerce. The Internet. The science of genetics. Every year a new revolution scattering in its wake, security, and ways of living for millions of people'. These were the 'forces of change driving the future' that are now 'universal'. A knowledge-based economy and a strong civic society were needed to help us find a confident place in the world: 'Do that and a nation masters the future. Fail and it is the future's victim'.[47]

But there is a vacuum that is always threatening to open up within this rhetoric. The conceptual structure is strong in that it is so self-supporting; and all its parts – the claims about inevitability, the relationship to the essence of the national community, the drawing of borders of inclusion and exclusion – are mutually reinforcing. But they only work if one is already 'inside' this discourse, already finds it agreeable. Everything can be explained by it so long as the initial leap of faith has been taken. But what is missing is the motivation to make that leap of faith, to make modernisation seem attractive. The question of why we should want to modernise has to be answered.

Normally one might expect that the answer to this question would be that such change will bring about a positive benefit. But Blair's rhetoric has displayed a hesitancy about this, preferring to stress that we simply have to change and there is no choice about it. However, as time has gone on, Blair has become clearer about the positive advantages of the 'fast-forward' future. So in 1999, having already described modernisation, with implicit reference to Marx, as a spectre, Blair turned also to Rousseau: 'People are born with talent and everywhere it is in chains', he said. 'Talent is twenty-first century wealth'. Thus, 'Every person liberated to fulfil their potential adds to our wealth. Every person denied opportunity takes our wealth away. People are the contemporary resource that matters'.[48] Thus modernisation is given a positive aspect as well as a necessary one:

The cause we have fought for, these 100 years, is no longer simply our cause of social justice. It is the nation's only hope of salvation. For how do you develop the talent of all, unless in a society that treats us all equally, where the closed doors of snobbery and prejudice, ignorance and poverty, fear and injustice no longer bar our way to fulfilment. Not equal incomes. Not uniform lifestyles or taste or culture. But true equality: equal worth, an equal chance of fulfilment, equal access to knowledge and opportunity.[49]

Here the rhetoric of modernisation allows Blair to maintain his claim about a historic new opportunity in British politics, no longer seeing economic stability and social justice as antithetical. Just as the report of the Commission for Social Justice had argued in 1994, Blair declared that:

... lighting our path is this belief: that today a strong economy and a strong society are two sides of the same coin. To succeed as an economy we develop the talents of all. To be a fair society, we give opportunity to all. The political consequences are historic; self-interest and the common good are at long last in alliance ... What began as a moral crusade is now also the path to prosperity. What started as a belief in the equal worth of all is also a programme for wealth creation. Realism and idealism at last in harmony. [50]

This was the end of class war and the beginning of the struggle for equality: 'And it is us, the new radicals, the Labour Party modernised, that must undertake this historic mission. To liberate Britain from the old class divisions, old structures, old prejudices, old ways of working and of doing things, that will not do in this world of change'. This was a speech in which the phrase 'fulfilling our potential' was repeated over and over and, as in previous speeches, the neo-Miltonian rhetoric of liberation made a reappearance in the final flourish: 'Let us step up the pace. Be confident. Be radical. To every nation a purpose. To every Party a cause. And now, at last, Party and nation joined in the same cause for the same purpose: to set our people free'.[51]

We are now at a higher political stage, where emancipation and capitalist expansion, thanks to computers, are the same thing: 'Modernisation is not an end in itself. It is for a purpose. Modernisation is not the enemy of justice but its ally.'[52] With the riddles of social conflict solved by History there is little more to be said – except what modernisation actually entails.

The referent of modernisation
In politics the theological register will only carry your tune so far. An

electorate seeks salvation in this world and no other. We need delivery. By 2000 Blair was able to begin making claims that his vision had been put into practice and we could see what modernisation means in the 'real' world:

> Because 90% of new jobs will need skills with computers, there will be 6000 centres round Britain, giving access to the internet and help with technology. Everyone will get an 80% discount on computer courses, the unemployed will get it for free. There will be 1000 more technology centres for small businesses or the self-employed. Because we want to stay ahead in the new technologies we are investing £2¼ billion over five years in British science, the largest investment since the 1960s. Because we know small businesses are a big part of the future, we are setting up venture capital funds in every region, tax breaks for investment, cuts in small business tax and the new Small Business Service to act as their advocate and protector in government.[53]

It is clear that Blair sees himself and his government as operating at a unique and opportune moment. It is a fundamental aspect of 'third way' thinking that you can have it both ways; that 'sound' economic management need not be in contradiction to social justice and progress. It is the mission of New Labour to convince us of this. But what makes this possible is the nature of the 'new' economy and its dependence on skills and talents. In this sense a meritocracy is an absolute necessity, such that to be in favour of a strong economy one must also be opposed to all forms of exclusion and prejudice (these being the result of 'pre-modern' prejudices and not linked to the economy). Furthermore, the new economy necessitates that a community, or a nation, pull together and realise that its national accounts depend on 'people'. Because the real resource is now skills, and skills need people to live in, history has squared the circle and rendered disputes between capital and labour, private and public, redundant.

In the first 'Annual Report' published by the New Labour government in 1998 modernisation was part of the 'story' they had 'to tell about Britain'. We were reminded that the country is 'filled with creative, innovative, compassionate people' and that we led the world in an industrial revolution. But we had relied on past glories and needed to 'adapt to the new world and the global economy'.[54] 'The Truth', Blair wrote, 'is that in many areas Britain is not yet equipped to tackle the challenges of the next century – our institutions, our constitution, our attitudes. That is why I have challenged every part of the country to modernise ... Without modernisation, adaptability, creativity, we will fail to keep the pace, and fail to fulfil our lives'.[55]

The 'concrete' referent of modernisation is, in this sense at least, clear. It is a shift to regarding people as the fundamental resource of economic growth and social harmony. To modernise is to create a situation in which people are able to deploy themselves, or be deployed, in a way that maximises their output. This is intimately connected with the knowledge revolution in two ways. Firstly, information technology is understood as requiring skills in order to be useful, so investing in skills is a logical development. Old-fashioned work exploited people's bodies. Modern work will need the liberation of their minds. Secondly, new technologies facilitate the linking or networking of people, and form a circuit along which knowledge flows. Old industries consisted of enclosed and circumscribed units. Modern ones link them together, look for holism and ensure that information and know-how circulates through them like blood – a blood that will dissolve away all wickedly old-fashioned barriers. The practical aspects of modernising then boil down to introducing more computers and more people who can usefully sit at them.

At this point we have to look outside of Blairism to get a clearer picture. An interest in the knowledge economy, its anti-hierarchical nature and the ways in which we should adapt to it is not unique to New Labour. In the field of 'human resources' and management theory there has long been talk of how to keep up with rapid transformations and 'permanent revolution'. It is here that ideas about the knowledge economy and the value of intellectual labour have been most developed.

In 1989 sometime-management-cum-new-age guru Charles Handy described what he called 'discontinuous change'. As he pointed out, things do change all the time, but what we face now is a situation in which change is not incremental but rather consists of breaks, jumps and the emergence of new paradigms.[56] Other management theorists have chosen to characterise this environment by using a metaphor from biological science (one that, interestingly, was already a literary metaphor). They speak of the 'red queen effect'. Biologists use this term to describe the intense and permanent pressures of evolution, the fact that organisms facing a complex and highly competitive environment have to evolve, not in order to improve but just to survive. The phrase derives from Lewis Carroll. In *Alice Through the Looking Glass* the unfortunate Alice discovers that in the kingdom of the red queen you have to run as fast as you can just to stay in the same place. For Huseman and Goodman, the corporation 'competes in the *Realm of the Red Queen* ... While some companies may appear to master change today, perpetual technological innovation and rapidly increasing competition frequently negate any advantages that seem to be secure'. They add: 'To maintain a competitive position today, corporations must learn faster than others in their business environment. If companies do not build into their core strategy the ability to acquire and leverage knowledge, they will find that their competitors will simply pass them by in the *Realm of the Red Queen*'.[57]

They analyse this development 'historically', tracing the changing practices of the US corporation from mass production and scientific management in the first half of the twentieth century through to the stability, yet conformity, of what Whyte called the 'organisation man'.[58] Such companies were stable but limited, because their management and workers were conformist, cowed into conventional and routine behaviour by the structure of their workplaces. These were the organisations unable to cope with increased global competition, the growth of domestic small business competition and, latterly, information technologies. They were too stable to be able to respond to the changed conditions: 'By the mid 1960s the classic corporation was feeling the dual pressures of competition and technological change. Managers were desperate to meet the new challenge of competition, but the old hierarchy and management styles of the classic corporation were ill-suited for a quick turnaround, the classic corporation was designed to maintain the status quo'.[59] As a result the firm had to be 're-engineered', and in the 1970s and 1980s this led to a period of corporate mergers matched by the 'downsizing' of the workforce. In the jungle of corporate competition the firm needed to be more flexible and adaptable to survive the 'red queen effect'.

One of the earlier, and leading, gurus of all this was Rosabeth Moss Kanter, whose 1984 book *The Change Masters* was a bestseller. Here too the story was of intense change and the necessity of good new managers to lead their firms through the upheaval – or rather to recognise that upheaval was now to be the norm. She wrote:

> Those organisations which recognise the immensity and scope of the forces [of transformation] and carry out the required organisational changes will probably survive; many indeed will prosper enormously. Those organisations which either fail to understand the need for change or are inept in their ability to deal with it will fade and fall behind if they survive at all.

In other words, to quote Blair's later words with respect to the public services – 'modernise or die'.

Kanter argued that the corporate culture was suffocating the entrepreneurial spirit and undermining employee involvement at grass-roots level. The 'innovating company must provide the freedom to act which arouses the desire to act'.[60] This meant departures from tradition led by the new entrepreneurs. Such change was not only a threat but an

opportunity. It would radically transform the firm socially and culturally as well as productively, forcing it to break down barriers of
insularity and chauvinism. Social justice and economic growth, she
might have said, would go hand in hand, and the entrepreneur was
anything but a force of conservatism. There is an untold story here
(and sadly this is not the place to tell it). Kanter's first book was about
the managing of collective communes. Her discourse, like a lot of
management theory, is an odd blend of functional sociology and west-
coast hippie spirit, in which the corporation becomes treated as a
community. It is to be understood holistically or joined up.

The more recent growth area in such management theory has been
in the importance of knowledge, reflected in the increased readiness of
firms to train their staff, work at more long-term learning, pay for them
to take MBAs and so on (as does the British Civil Service). There has
also been the growth of the corporate university dedicated to the
permanent re-skilling of the work force. Here the mechanisms by
which a properly trained workforce is produced pass from the state
(once defined by Ernest Gellner as the body possessing the monopoly
over legitimate education) to the firm. But such education is also the
mechanism by which the corporation tries to retain the loyalty and
consent of its workforce. Integration and legitimation become one and
the same process. For the second term New Labour has pledged to
introduce lifelong learning into the NHS through the introduction of a
corporate university managed between the private and public sectors.

But, as Huseman and Goodman point out, this corporate learning
has then to be communicated through the firm. So we must construct
the knowledge organisation in which continuous learning and ongoing
improvement are embedded features. This can even be measured
through 'intellectual capital accounting'. But this too becomes part of
the project of making the firm communal. As Stewart describes it,
management has to operate through leading rather than controlling,
shifting from shareholder value to values.[61] The people who work in
the firm operate in 'communities of practice' which are 'the shop-floor
of human capital'.[62]

This is quite a trend. In order to function at its best the company has
to be a complete life world for the employee, who commits to the firm
not because they pay well and guarantee a job for life, but (like some
bastardised republican political community) because they share the
world view of the company. This will make them work better, it will
embed them loosely in the corporate culture (so that they are still free to
be entrepreneurial within those confines); but it will also help in the
overall marketing of a product which, it seems, is increasingly dependent
on the identification of the consumer with those corporate values, since

they are seen as a guarantor of quality. As one recent text argues, the image created by marketers must be shared by employees since they are the ones who deliver it. It is no use advertising a certain level of service if you can't be sure it will be delivered. To ensure this, it is not enough to control the behaviour of employees – this would only offer 'superficial compliance'. Their behaviour needs to be rooted in the organisational identity: 'Employees must feel the message they are sending with their behaviour, not just go through the motions … emotional and symbolic expressiveness is becoming part of the experience of doing business'. This can bring stakeholders together. Workers have to see their role in terms of how it effects the value of the firm – their place in the great chain.[63] For Arie de Geus, former head of Dutch Shell, the company is an organism, a living being, with a will, an intelligence, a memory and ecology. The company will have 'members, both people and institutions, who subscribe to a set of common values and who believe that the goals of the company allow them and help them to achieve their own individual goals'.[64] They will be helped to fulfil their potential.

The practical meaning of modernisation is very much entwined with this sort of post-downsizing management theory. Blairism looks to 'cutting-edge' management and business theory for its guidelines on what is modern. Underlying this is an absolutely fundamental aspect of New Labour politics. On inspection, it seems that most of the problems to which it directly addresses itself are not problems found in society, in the overall organisation of our productive, cultural or ethical practices. Rather they are problems of government itself. New Labour's project is more about redefining what government does and how it does it than it is about changing society. Ultimately, the objects upon which modernisation will be imposed are state institutions: Westminster, Whitehall and the public services need to be updated and properly inserted into the new flows of information. Where Wilson's form of modernisation entailed the full introduction of the state into the economy and engaged with society, Blairite modernisation effects the public only in as much as they (when at school, in hospital or on welfare) are the 'customers' of public services. Blairism seeks to 'modernise' the state by bringing it in line with business best practice (rather than find ways of changing business so that it acts in accordance with the interests or wishes of the people). This is symptomatic of the times. Business is once again believed to always, or in the last instance, act in the best interests of the people, because it is people who are the customers and competition will engender the right results. Having closed off the option of intervening in the private affairs of business, Blairism seeks instead to make the public services more like modern businesses. Modernisation thus comes to mean the harmonisation of state bureaucracies with contemporary neo-communitarian theories of private sector management. It is what the state does to itself – a kind of institutional onanism.

We can see this all over the modernising government programme led by the Cabinet Office and described as the 'agenda for modernising public services'.[65] The Cabinet Office declares that:

> Modernising government is a long-term project, which will transform the face of public services. Putting citizens first by ensuring public services are accessible to all. Overcoming barriers by shifting the focus of public services to the user's viewpoint. By joining government up to deliver better policies and seamless, quality services, thanks to public servants working better together. By using information age approaches to do this – and valuing public service at its true worth.[66]

This list of activities (or claims about activity) is highly indicative of what goes under the name of modernising government.

A Cabinet Office paper from June/July of 2000 lists some examples of achievements in the modernising of government. These include recommendations to remove the need of people to go through their MP when making a complaint to the public sector ombudsman, and plans to ensure that the ombudsmen work in 'flexible' and 'joined-up' ways. Particularly important are targets for electronic delivery of government (which means putting things on the web). The target is to have all government services online by March of 2005.[67]

In his introduction to the report 'Citizens First', produced under the auspices of the modernising government programme, Tony Blair claimed that the defence of public services requires us to move beyond the 'false choice' between big or small government. He wants to empower front-line workers.[68] In his introduction to the same report Ian McCartney admits that the term modernising government 'has a dry ring to it': 'But when you see what it means in human terms it comes to life'. He highlights a focus on the user, targets, efficient delivery, e-government, innovation and partnership.[69] This, then, all fits into the same story. The drive to modernise comes from the need for all organisations to improve continuously, demands from citizens to be treated as customers, the need to embrace diversity, new opportunities because of new technology, globalisation and the attendant need to show comparisons of performance and the need to show that public services matter.

This glossy and heavily photo-filled report lists detailed examples of modernising initiatives. In Poole, Dorset, for example, you can find up to the minute information on B&B vacancies via the council website.

Small businesses are being put in contact with the government via a website and e-mail forum, while VAT returns can be submitted on-line. There is a special welcome for a 'new brand', *Trade Partners* (complete with bee logo because it is a 'hive of information and support'), which offers online help for exporters.[70] Suffolk constabulary uses a computer handset system to collect votes from people on their views about police services. For this they won a Charter Mark and Beacon Funding. There are a range of 'communications strategies' for councils and their tenants. In Gloucester a Nye Bevan modernisation award was made for a one-stop cataract assessment service. Also cited are websites on childcare, NHS Direct and NHS walk-in centres, partnership schemes to reduce burglary, opportunities for electronic conveyancing, video-link kiosks in East of Riding Yorkshire Council, new adverts for pensioners' benefits starring Thora Hird. Even the army gets in there: the Armed Forces Youth Initiative and the Defence Diversification Agency (which provides information on technological developments to private businesses) are also examples of modernisation.

The very format of the report is informative. It is a glossy production with lots of pictures and a magazine-style layout (i.e. cluttered). The text is not written in the tone of usual civil service reports but is journalistic with headlines, sub-headlines (including poor quality puns) and quotations taken from interviews with the people behind the various initiatives. The report even ends with a 'human interest' story, about the modernisation of quarantine rules that allowed Bill Whitehouse ('a telecommunications consultant from Solihull') to live at home with his dog.[71]

Meanwhile, the Modernising Government White Paper promises 'government for people – people as consumers, people as citizens', and says that the programme will make sure services 'reflect real lives and deliver what people really want'.[72] This means more joined-up thinking and a focus on the 'delivery' of responsive services. The chapter headings are themselves an indication of what modernisation means: Vision, Policy-Making, Responsive Public Services, Quality Public Services, Information Age Government. Modernisation here means 'not being hidebound by the old ways of government'.[73] The paper specifies the importation of private sector management methods when it explicitly (and unfavourably) compares public service efficiency to that of the private sector. It lays out the faults of public services with what amounts to a manual of the public choice methodology. Public services don't work because they are organised around provider interests, focus on inputs rather than outputs, and are risk averse. They require better management and incentive systems.[74]

The White Paper also calls for a change in the processes of policy formation, so that it is structured around shared goals and meets the needs of cross-cutting policies such as those relating to social exclusion, women, drugs, etc, that require co-ordination between different agencies and ministries.[75] It also heralds the Centre for Management and Policy Studies in the Cabinet Office, described on the website as a new initiative 'to train and develop the senior management of UK Plc'.[76]

This, then, is what modernisation really means. Our world must be made to conform with the technologies we have created and the business environment which they facilitate. Because this technology is presumed to be non-hierarchical all hierarchy is assumed to be removed by it. Because business employs these technologies then business must also be non-hierarchical. The only thing left that is hierarchical is government, which must be so because it is not modernised. Therefore, the government will ceaselessly modernise itself. It must make sure it is not only networked but is a network itself able to deliver flexible best practice to its customer base of citizens.

Modernisation as problematisation

Many things can, and have been, 'modernised'. Even gambling is being reformed: 'The main thrust of the modernisation of the duty structure is to change the way of calculating the amount of general betting duty'.[77] There is a capital modernisation fund ('a central part of the Government's drive to renew and modernise the UK's public sector capital stock'[78]). The payment system in the NHS has been modernised and the home office is modernising licensing laws.[79] The post office has to change since, according to Tony Blair, it is 'a network that has not kept pace with technological change and which is in need of modernisation'.[80] The Home Office is working on its own general modernisation and funds have been allocated enabling it to 'modernise its IT infrastructure and support business change through public private sector partnerships ...' There is also a modernisation fund to help those who have plans to improve safety in the home from accidents. Training Standards Officers, it seems, are as in need of modernisation as the rest of us.

This language has spread up and down all tiers of government. Members of the assemblies in Belfast and Cardiff have called for modernisation of everything from waterways to roadways. Local government has also got in on the act, and many councils have produced modernisation strategies (which often involve redesigned web-sites and, as in Cardiff, 'cabinet-style' executives that get paid private sector salaries). But the most large scale and directed 'modernisations' are in the primary public services of health, welfare and education. In the schools, according to a Green Paper, http://www.dfee.gov.uk/buildingonsuccess/transforming_education/ 'Our drive for world class performance demands that we modernise secondary education...'.[81] Meanwhile NHS reform is the same as NHS modernisation.[82] In the words of the Secretary of State, 'realising the ambitions of the NHS Plan needs a modernisation movement which includes all one million NHS staff'.[83] According to the modernisation review (which is designed to assist in the implementation of the NHS plan): 'It will not be possible to deliver this ambition by simply doing more of the same. Delivering ... will demand new skills, new ways of working, new patterns of service provision and new investment in the infrastructure'.[84] The Modernisation Agency will reward those who respond well to the 'challenge' and identify those who do not and set them 'back on track'. It will be a 'centre for excellence' and a 'leadership centre', which entails disseminating information on 'best practice', linking into international and private sector networks, and 'developing staff into today's and tomorrow's leaders across all levels of the health service – from frontline staff to those in the most senior positions'.[85]

Modernisation cannot take place if nobody knows about it. Even though, according to Tony Blair, it is already happening and in the 'blood and bones' of the British, it must still be thoroughly monitored, audited and proven to exist. Thus, at the top of the NHS plan is a Modernisation Board chaired by the Secretary of State (accompanied by 'stakeholders' – representatives from healthcare organisations, NHS staff and patient groups). In addition to scrutinising the success of implementation the board will 'smooth away obstacles to change' and 'ensure the right groups of people are working together'.[86] There will be 'Local Modernisation Reviews' to 'engage' more stakeholders from users to voluntary sector workers and NHS staff. These will examine procedures of assessment and prioritisation so all may be validated.[87]

The modernising process goes all the way down to front-line services. Accident and Emergency departments are undergoing a modernisation programme, a financial investment in the improvement of physical resources that includes, of course, the dissemination of best practice and the finding of new ways to do everything. There is a pathology modernisation programme that offers awards to those who are modernising. Such schemes, in practice, tend to lead primarily to a change in the way in which people apply for funds that they would have applied for anyway. But a glance at a list of such awards reveals something of the concrete referent of modernisation. They go to those wanting to install or update IT equipment, particularly where this will include using web and other IT based systems to make information and data accessible. Projects will strive for 'integration' and 'collaboration' as well as a fair bit of 'dissemination'.[88]

Modernisation works in such policy formation and implementation as a keyword around which initiatives can cluster and cohere. It provides a conceptual and bureaucratic space in which certain actions can take place linking them to otherwise radically different practices, creating, perhaps, a sense of momentum and drive. As such the word is almost innocent in that it makes a complex and multi-layered set of processes thinkable. But, as we have seen, it also has a punitive function. One can be measured against the benchmark of modernisation. One might not be networked enough, insufficiently wired. This means that, as well as an opportunity, modernisation necessitates constraint. While some individuals will be freed up by this process and enabled to redevelop aspects of their work without the hindrance of older bureaucratic practices, they will simultaneously have to submit to new ones. Accompanying the decentralisation of modernisation is the centralisation of control through the introduction of ever more rigorous targets and more complicated systems of performance measurement. Because it is not a thing but a process (and one with a movable referent) this modernisation cannot ever stop. There will always be more reform to undertake. In this way it becomes not only a mechanism for finding problems but of generating them and of instituting new systems of control.

New Labour modernisation entails worries about the past (it weighs us down with its slow thinking). It also entails worries about the present (we aren't keeping up with the new), but above all it worries about the future. The future is what we must prepare for, the transformations ahead, the contingencies that must, at all costs, be insured against. Central to this is the gathering and interpreting of anxiety-inducing statistics. Think tanks such as Demos and the Future Foundation thrive on the production of statistics-led reports on the changes, 'earthquakes' and 'time-bombs' ahead due to an ageing population, the generation gap, the transformation in the attitudes of women, and so on. Government must plan for these immediately and individuals must begin to save for their pensions now in order to avoid societal crisis in thirty years time. Employers and businesses must adapt to a supposedly woman-friendly public sphere. Everyone must worry about the fact that young people appear to not be exactly like their parents. The discovery of such social changes (that are almost always discovered to be 'profound' in their implications) is – along with speculations about what technology will determine – essential to making modernisation into a strategy of problem generation, and, even more crucially, one of governing the future. This is a very particular political rationality.

Miller and Rose define a political rationality as

the changing discursive fields within which the exercise of power is conceptualised, the moral justifications for particular ways of exercising power by diverse authorities, notions of the appropriate forms, objects and limits of politics and conceptions of the proper distributions of tasks among secular, spiritual, military and familial advisers.[89]

As we have already seen, New Labour's claims about the need to update the constitution, reform welfare, renew education and so forth are contained within assumptions about the pace of change and the revolutionary impact of new technology and the new economy. We have also seen how these processes are given an air of inevitability. Thus, in imagining this process, something strange happens. New Labour is making claims based on its convictions about the changing nature of the present and its superior knowledge of them. Since these are irreversible, the political and social challenge is to live up to them – we must 'modernise or die'. Labour's authority is thus presumed to be based, in part, on its superior knowledge, just as Demos claim that politics must be based on 'clear values and a clear understanding of what motivates people'. Where past ideologies have based themselves on assumptions about human nature: 'Today we have a better understanding of the foundations of human nature. We know more about how evolution shapes our drives, our instincts as well as our capacity to co-operate'.[90] Policy towards the objectified economy must be formed on the basis of objectifying human beings – faced with a world that is beyond our control we must strive to develop the best knowledge about it so we can fit into it. As Leadbeater argues, there is no way round the global knowledge economy: 'we have to go through it … we have to steel ourselves to press on, not really sure what lies ahead, but knowing that retreat is no alternative'.[91] We need to re-design institutions 'to enable them to withstand the gale around them'. Anything else would be the pointless activity of a Luddite King Canute. This is why modernisation can mean a lot to those who advocate it, as it seems like the only way to respond to a situation that is out of control. But it is, at least in part, the discourse of modernisation that generates these problems, just as it generates their solution. The solipsism is lived as much as it is spoken.

Conclusion
The rhetoric of modernisation can be seen to function as a way of drawing antagonistic lines of exclusion and inclusion. On one side is that which is modernised or attuned to modernisation, and this is always good (if sometimes requiring a 'hard choice'). The other side is always, by definition, out of touch and anti-modernisation. Any insti-

tution or practice that is perceived as not working perfectly is held to require 'modernisation'. From this there inevitably follows the call for a new way that claims merit from recognising this supposed historical exigency and conforming to it. In a peculiar sense this aspect of the Blair project follows a certain vulgar Marxist tendency, in that it regards itself as in line with a given logic external to its own political interventions.

Modernisation thus carries with it certain tendencies. One noticeable strand in this rhetoric is the emphasis on the nation and the way in which modernisation is embedded in Britishness itself. Such an appeal to the nation is not unique to Blair of course. Indeed it can be found in the rhetoric of most party leaders whatever their colours. It is part of what Michael Billig has called 'banal' nationalism – the everyday way in which a concept of nation is renewed.[92] There are obvious reasons why politicians in a given nation state should base their rhetoric on an appeal to some aspect or given feature of that national community. It is a way in which an ideological project can achieve legitimacy. Finding itself rooted in the given history, traditions and character of a national people, a political project can present itself as simply operating in conformity with that people. Thatcherism certainly utilised a discourse of nation in this way. But Blair needs this kind of rhetoric for another reason. The party needs a 'team', a 'community' of some sort to be the body that both experiences and undertakes modernisation. He needs it also, so that there is someone or something to appeal to in the name of modernisation. And, finally, he needs it because it provides Blairism with a social or collective dimension that differentiates it from anti-statist neo-liberalism. The national/communal aspect of the modernisation project introduces the dimension of civil society. It means that modernisation is not a project that will be, or can be, undertaken only by the Labour Party or even by the state itself. It is a project of which everyone is a part and having everyone be a part of it is one of the things that defines it.

This legitimates and sustains a belief that government should no longer be seen as the only key to making social improvements. It cannot act without the effort of the country as a whole, everyone playing their part in making Britain anew. But, on the other hand it gives back to government a role in enabling this sort of nationwide effort. Thus: 'The Third Way recognises the limits of government in the social sphere but also the need for government, within those limits, to forge new partnerships with the voluntary sector'.[93] Government works with the communities of which it is simply an expression (given that its modernisation is in tune with the ancient British character). This is why Blair could say, in a speech to the Christian Socialist

Movement: 'a large part of individual responsibility concerns the obligations we owe one to another. The self is best realised in community with others. Society is the way we realise our mutual obligations – a society in which we all belong, no one left out. And Parliament and government, properly conceived, are the voice and instrument of the *national* community' (emphasis in original).[94]

This is a cornerstone of Blairite political theory. With this move modernisation and the third way retain a communal aspect, and take over the 'one nation' mantle from the Tory party. It allows the introduction of a strong rhetoric about duty, rights and responsibilities which, at least for its sympathisers, establishes beyond all doubt that New Labour is not simply Thatcherism in disguise. It enables them to argue that (as Blair so often stresses) maintaining a 'strong' and 'dynamic' economy need not be at odds with the goals of equality and social justice. The economy can only thrive because all the people in the country work together and modernise so that economy and society are united as one.

But the actual activity of modernisation is focused on the ways in which government works and public services deliver. Unwilling to attempt an old-fashioned form of state intervention, New Labour restricts itself to intervening into itself, reforming government structures. This connects with the wider public only in as much as new 'partnerships' are formed between agencies and citizen-consumers and between the state and private corporations. Modernisation provides government with a stick with which to righteously beat itself. It renders government intrinsically backward, untouched by the dynamism going on out there in private sector land. So it is that government must humbly accept lessons from business in how to do everything and go into asymmetrical partnerships with it. The purpose of the PFI and PPP, to which the government seems so perversely wedded, is not simply to bring in private capital. It is also to bring in private sector methods and a private sector culture. It is central to a rearrangement of the relations between state and economy that is quite different to simple privatisation. It also changes the relations of society and individual to their state and their economic lives. Ultimately it delivers a new kind of politics.

Notes

1. Norman Fairclough (2000) *New Labour, New Language?*, London, Routledge, p19.
2. Mike Kenny and Martin Smith (1997) '(Mis)Understanding Blair', *Political Quarterly*, Vol. 68, No. 3, p229.
3. J.L. Austin (1975) *How to do things with Words*, Oxford, Clarendon.

4. See, for instance, Anthony D. Smith (1983) *Theories of Nationalism*, New York, Holmes and Meier; Anthony D. Smith (1998) *Nationalism and Modernism: A Critical Survey of Recent Theories of Nations and Nationalism*, London, Routledge; Ernest Gellner (1984) *Nations and Nationalism*, Oxford, Blackwell.

5. See Partha Chatterjee (1986) *Nationalist Thought and the Colonial World: A Derivative Discourse?*, London, Zed Books for the United Nations University.

6. Benedict Anderson (1993) *Imagined Communities*, 2nd edn, Verso, London, p26.

7. See Perry Anderson (1964) 'Origins of the Present Crisis', *New Left Review*, 23; Tom Nairn, 'The British Political Elite', *New Left Review*, 23; Tom Nairn, 'The English Working Class', *New Left Review*, 24.

8. See the attack on Anderson and Nairn by E.P. Thompson (1978[1965]) 'The Peculiarities of the English' in *The Poverty of Theory and Other Essays*, Manchester, Merlin Press, pp245-301.

9. See Perry Anderson (1987) 'The Figures of Descent', *New Left* Review, 161; Tom Nairn (1994) [1988] *The Enchanted Glass: Britain and its Monarchy*, London, Vintage.

10. See Will Hutton (1995) *The State We're In*, London, Jonathan Cape; Andrew Gamble (1988) *The Free Economy and the Strong State: The Politics of Thatcherism*, Basingstoke, Macmillan; Stuart Hall and Martin Jacques (eds.) (1990), *New Times: The Changing Face of Politics in the 1990s*, London, Lawrence and Wishart in association with Marxism Today.

11. Eric Hobsbawm (1987) 'Out of the Wilderness', *Marxism Today*, October, p17.

12. See Harold Wilson (1964) *The New Britain: Labour's Plan Outlined by Harold Wilson*. Harmondsworth, Penguin Books, pp9-10.

13. Labour Party (1964) *A New Britain: Labour Manifesto*, 1964.

14. Tony Blair (1994) *Speech to The Labour Party Annual Conference*, p1.

15. Tony Blair (1997) *Speech to The Labour Party Annual Conference*, p6.

16. Ibid. p7.

17. John Milton (1973) *Areopagitica and Of education* (edited by K.M. Lea), Oxford, Clarendon.

18. Matt Jordan (2000) 'Determined Dissent: John Milton and the Futures of Political Culture', in Tim Bewes and Jeremy Gilbert (eds.), *Cultural Capitalism: Politics after New Labour*, London, Lawrence and Wishart, pp101-116.

19. Tony Blair (1994), *Speech to Labour Party Conference*, p16.

20. Ibid. p23.

21. Tony Blair (1997) *Speech to Labour Party Conference*, p7.

22. Ibid. p8.

23. Ibid. p7.

24. Ibid. p11/13.
25. Ibid. p14.
26. Ibid. p19.
27. Ibid. p20.
28. Mike Rustin (1998) 'Editorial: The New Labour Project', *Soundings*, 8, p11.
29. *The Observer*, 13.5.01.
30. The question of the origin of this latent and bastardised Hegelianism in Blairism will not be answered here. However, we may speculate that it is carried into Blairism by the half-understood and half-remembered remnants of Marxist thinking that lie behind it as well as that of New Liberalism and British Idealism.
31. Speech by Alastair Darling (secretary of state for social security) to the IPPR, 23/9/98. See also the Welfare Green Paper, especially chapter 1 (1998) *New Ambitions for Our Country: A New Contract for Welfare Reform*, London, HMSO, Cm, 3805.
32. Ibid. p8.
33. Tony Blair (1999) *Speech to Labour Party Conference*, p1.
34. Tony Blair (1995) *Let Us Face the Future*, London, Fabian Society.
35. Tony Blair (1999) *Speech to Labour Party Conference*, p4.
36. Ibid. p4.
37. Ibid. p5.
38. Ibid. p6.
39. Ibid. p6.
40. Ibid. p7.
41. Ibid. p14.
42. Tony Blair (1998) *The Third Way*, London, Fabian Society, p6. The Third Way is considered more fully in Chapter 3.
43. Tony Blair (1994) *Speech to Labour Party Conference*, pp11-12.
44. Tony Blair (1995) *Speech to Labour Party Conference*, pp4-5.
45. Tony Blair (1996) *Speech to Labour Party Conference*, p14.
46. Tony Blair (1999) *Speech to Labour Party Conference*, p1.
47. Ibid. p3.
48. Ibid. p3.
49. Ibid. p4.
50. Ibid. p13.
51. Ibid. p15.
52. Tony Blair (1997) *Speech to Labour Party Annual Conference*.
53. Tony Blair (2000) *Speech to Labour Party Conference*, p6.
54. *The Government's Annual Report 97/8*, HMSO, Cm 3969, p9. It is worth noting the connection between this and the party election broadcasts discussed in Chapter One. Despite appearances there is great consistency in New Labour's 'vision'.

55. Ibid. pp9-10.
56. Charles Handy (1989) *Age of Unreason*, Arrow Books.
57. Richard C. Huseman and Jon P. Goodman (1998) *The Realm of the Red Queen: The Impact of Change on Corporate Structure, Corporate Education, and the Emergence of Knowledge Organizations*, The Corporate Knowledge Center@EC2, Annenberg Center for Communication, http://www.ec2.edu/ckc.
58. See William H. Whyte (1957) *The Organisation Man*, London, Cape.
59. Richard C. Huseman and Jon P. Goodman (1999) *Leading With Knowledge: The nature of competition in the 21st century*, Sage, p41.
60. Rosabeth Moss Kanter (1985) *The change masters: corporate entrepreneurs at work*, London, Unwin, p142.
61. Thomas A, Stewart (1998) *Intellectual Capital: The New Wealth of the Organisation*, London, Nicholas Brealey Publishing, p50.
62. Ibid. p90.
63. Majken Schultz, Mary Jo Hatch and Mogens Holten Larsen (2000) *The Expressive Organisation: Linking Identity, Reputation and the Corporate Brand*, Oxford, Oxford University Press.
64. Arie de Geus (1997), *The living company: growth, learning and longevity in business*, Nicholas Brealey, p236.
65. See http://www.cabinet-office.gov.uk/moderngov/index.htm
66. Ibid.
67. See http://www.cabinet-office.gov.uk/moderngov/download/act0006b.pdf
68. *Citizens First: Modernising Government Annual Report*, http://www.cabinet-office.gov.uk/moderngov/anreport/index.htm2000, p1.
69. Ibid. p2.
70. Ibid. p5.
71. Ibid. p24.
72. *The Modernising Government White Paper* (March 1999), HMSO, CM 4310
73. Ibid. p9.
74. Ibid. p11.
75. Ibid. p16.
76. See http://www.cmps.gov.uk/whatwedo/psd/back_to_classroom.htm; Guardian 6.5.00.
77. See Budget 2001 BN 91/01. I should point out that I have read that sentence many, many times and I have come to the conclusion that it doesn't contain any real meaning at all. It says that the thrust of change in the calculation of betting duty consists of a change in the calculation of betting duty. This is a great testament to our expensively educated civil servants.
78. http://www.hm-treasury.gov.uk/docs/2000/capmod_3109.htm
79. *Time for Reform: Proposals for the Modernisation of Our Licensing Laws* (White Paper) CM4696.

80. *Counter Revolution – Modernising the post office network, A performance and innovation Unit report*, June 2000.
81. *Schools: Building on success* (2001), HMSO, CM 5050, p11. For a critique of the discourse of modernisation as applied to the teaching profession see Martin Merson (2000) 'Teachers and the Myth of Modernisation', *British Journal of Educational Studies*, Vol. 48, No. 2, pp155-169.
82. For a useful and open-minded assessment of the modernisation of the NHS see Jennifer Dixon (2001) 'Health Care: Modernising the Leviathan', in *Political Quarterly*, Vol. 72, 1, pp30-38.
83. Speech by Alan Milburn MP, *Shifting the Balance of Power in the NHS*, 25.4.01.
84. See http://www.doh.gov.uk/nhsperformance/modreview/background.htm
85. All information and citation taken from DoH website on the modernisation agency: http://www.doh.gov.uk/about/nhsplan/who/modagency.html
86. See http://www.doh.gov.uk/about/nhsplan/who/modboard.html
87. See http://www.doh.gov.uk/nhsperformance/modreview/latest.htm
88. See, for example, the summary provided by the Modernisation of Pathology Steering Group, Pathology Modernisation Programme, http://www.doh.gov.uk/pathologymodernisation/awards2000.htm.
89. Nikolas Rose and Peter Miller (1992) 'Political Power Beyond the State: problematics of government', *British Journal of Sociology*, Vol. 43, No. 2, p175.
90. Ian Hargreaves and Ian Christie (eds.) (1988) *Tomorrow's Politics: The Third Way and Beyond*, London, Demos, p3.
91. Charles Leadbeater (1999) *Living on Thin Air: The New Economy*, London, Viking.
92. See Michael Billig (1995) *Banal Nationalism*, London, Sage.
93. Tony Blair (1998) *The Third Way*, London, Fabian Society.
94. Tony Blair (2001) *Speech to Christian Socialist Movement*, 29 March.

CHAPTER FOUR

Politics: The Third Way

Introduction

Democracy, as we know it, is in trouble. Our political system requires citizens to turn up, once every four or five years, to a draughty church hall or crumbling infant school, in order to put a cross onto a small piece of paper using a tiny, blunt 2B pencil. These small pieces of paper (thousands of them) are then put in a box and moved, by hand and by van, to some spacious civic building (usually a sports hall with very bad acoustics) and counted by hand in order to find out who got the most crosses next to their name. That person then has to stand next to people in embarrassing fancy dress while another person, bearing the peculiar title of 'Returning Officer', will seize the opportunity to be officious on live television despite the sound of drunken jeers and cheers echoing off the breeze-block walls. The one who got the most votes will then get to go to the House of Commons and attempt to find a seat on narrow green benches where s/he will be empowered publicly to address members of the government in the hope that they will be promoted to a junior ministerial position, or (even better) get mentioned in a broadsheet newspaper gossip column.

But being horridly low-tech and unfashionable is not the only problem experienced by our democracy. Voters are becoming scarce. The General Election of 2001 featured the lowest voter turnout since 1918. In the 1997 election, at that time the lowest turnout since the second world war, 71.6% of those eligible voted. Four years later fewer than six out of ten bothered to place their cross. Party membership is also in decline. In the 1950s Conservative Party membership was believed to be in the region of 2.25m. In the 1970s it was 1.5m. Recent figures suggest it currently runs at about 350,000. Surveys from 1992 showed that members were aging: 5% were under 35 and the average age was 62. They are also less active than they used to be. Three-quarters of Conservatives do no active work for their party in an average month. For the Liberal Democrats the number of 'do-nothings' is just above half. While membership of the Labour Party increased through the 1990s, declining only a little after 1997, slightly under two thirds are in this 'do-nothing' category,[1] and with recent reforms in the structure of the party it seems that the members are decreasing in significance, as the party has turned itself into a professional electoral machine controlled from the centre and led by campaign specialists.[2]

Whiteley and Seyd attribute all this to wider social change: the decline of class politics leads to a decline in long-term commitments to a single party believed to represents one's class interests; the collapse of the rural economy has undermined the support base of the Conservative Party while the rise in the numbers of women working has also depleted a resource vital for them (while changing the expectations women have of political participation). At the same time the atrophying of local government has lessened the attractions of local politics and so grassroots membership. This is not solely a British problem. The 50% fall in party membership in the UK since 1980 is more than matched by a decline of two-thirds in France and 51% in Italy. The decline is less in Germany, at 9%, but there it is masked by the effects of unification. This goes along with a decline in all sorts of areas of public engagement, from churches and charities to trades unions. It would seem that the problem is not simply that of attracting people to politics but to civic life in general.

New Labour says it wants to address this problem. Tony Blair has written of 'finding new ways to enable citizens to share in decision-making that affects them', and of the need to 'encourage public debate on the big decisions affecting people's lives'. He has spoken of a 'drive to "reinvent" national government' and declared it 'incumbent on us to improve its image and effectiveness', stating that 'open, vibrant, diverse democratic debate is a laboratory for ideas about how we should meet social needs ... we want to revitalise the ethic of public service'.[3] Blair's adviser Anthony Giddens has called for the 'democratising of democracy', arguing that 'the crisis of democracy comes from its not being democratic enough'; he calls for a renewal of civil society, an expansion of the role of the public sphere and a cosmopolitan outlook for the state.[4]

Added to this are a number of New Labour policies that have been widely welcomed as potential motors of a radical transformation in both the conduct of British politics and attitudes toward it. Constitutional reform has been seen as the beginning of an unstoppable movement towards new forms of pluralism, decentralisation and civic engagement that will break conservative hegemony and allow new forms of radical politics to emerge.[5] Directly elected mayors for London, and some other large cities, may increase awareness of the relevance of municipal action. Citizenship classes in schools surely suggest an interest in revitalising the democratic tendencies of our society, while devolution of Westminster power forms a key plank in what the Blairites sometimes call 're-connecting' with the people. Certainly there is potential here for the enhancing of British political life. But to make sense of these developments we need to find out more about the ways in which New Labour understands the changing nature of politics. We need to consider its conception of 'the political'. Does it have a political theory that might specify in some way how politics should be understood?

One of the most important things any ideology does is establish a particular notion of what politics is, and is for. This limits the scope of potential challenges, but also provides a kind of legitimacy to a political position, in as much as it can be believed to derive from certain social facts. It can claim to practice politics the only way it can be done. This is why political theories are also always social theories of some kind. They posit something (or some set of things) as given, as the basic features of social life. From this it follows that politics is there to do certain sorts of things. Actions or aspirations that fall outside of this definition can thus be considered non-political, beyond the scope of political action, or just not possible. Of course, people do develop perspectives, or find it necessary to make demands, that fall outside of any particular definition of politics. This is one of the central issues underlying all political arguments. People do not just contest *how* things can be done but *what* exactly should be done and *why*. Changing the scope or definition of what may legitimately be considered political (and thus changeable by collective action) is one of the most radical (or conservative) of acts. New Labour's claims about the new society and economy we now live in, about modernisation, necessitate a call for a new politics. Each claim helps legitimate the other.

Consider, for example, an ideology that succeeds in convincing people that the test of good government is the tendency of the rate of profit to increase. It would follow from this that the options competing for the label of good government are small. Not one of those options would even qualify for election in a context where the test of rightness is the pure and Spartan lives of the citizenry. Typically, traditional Conservatives (a dwindling band) argue that the central problem for society is the maintenance of order. Human beings are unruly, driven by their passions and so damaged by original sin or hubristic rationalism (which, for this ideology, are essentially the same charge) that they need to live in a social system that is, above all, stable and ordered. Because 'man' is not God and is prone to frailty and fallibility, yet thinks himself more capable than he really is, evils follow. The task of conservative politics is thus clear: ensuring that society is protected from any great schematic impositions and that the status quo is maintained.

Such an ideology could also, of course, be explained by factors taken to be external to the ideology itself – the class basis of the society and the elite group that benefits from quietism, for example. But we are interested in how the ideology might work 'spontaneously', how it might operate when it is part of the clutch of assumptions, the conceptual resources, of a political movement. Within such ideologies we can see two moments to their thinking of politics. There is the explicit political activity that a movement advocates, but there is also its political 'ontology', its convictions about the basis from which its ideas derive. People can contest political parties or movements on either of these levels, but they are quite distinct analytically. We might accept the general claims of New Labour and only disagree with the way in which they seek to implement policies. But we could disagree with their fundamental assumptions about what society and politics are for. It is therefore important to be clear about the level on which discussion is taking place.

There is one particularly crucial aspect of this: the relationship between politics and economics. It is one of the defining features in the emergence of capitalist states that they attempt to constitute the political and the economic as distinct realms. Where, in feudal systems, the arrangement of power amongst Lords relates directly to their control of the primary resource, land, it is a founding principle of capitalist states that the political and economic structures should be separate. This division has carried on into everyday thinking but especially into the academy. Much of the time the two fields of politics and economics are presumed to carry on with quite separate theoretical frameworks and analytical tools, as if they are analysing totally distinct forms of human behaviour. Where there has been a recent intellectual relationship between economics and politics, in rational and public choice theories for example, this has often taken the form of a colonisation of one by the other. The 'spheres' of economics and politics are both spheres of social power; they are intimately related and in the form of the state find their most clearly unified expression. The state (as we shall consider a little further in Chapter 5) is an instrument for the control of both economics and politics and the battles fought over the state can sometimes be understood as battles over what should be dominant and what should be marginalised. A central aspect of contemporary ideological struggle is conflict over the extent to which emerging and expanding economic forces can in fact be controlled by any state structure. A crucial question for New Labour is whether it conceives of politics as an activity that can act on economics, or as one that is only acted upon by economic force. This is central to any 'ontology' of the political. This chapter seeks to explicate the underlying political 'ontology' of New Labour, its theory of society and of what politics is for. Despite derision from many quarters, this is what the Third Way amounts to.

The idea of a Third Way emerged during the first year Blair was in power but was derived from wider currents, the most important of which was the 'triangulation' strategy of the Clinton democrats in the USA. For the Democrats this was more than an electoral strategy. It was a 'new progressivism' moving on from the 'top-down' government of the New Deal or Great Society.[6] Self-consciously directed towards 'transcending' the traditional division between social democracy and neo-liberalism, the aim of the Third Way was not solely to position Blair and New Labour as neither left or right but also to define them as 'progressive'. It was also the opening of a debate, an attempt to articulate and develop the basis on which New Labour makes its judgements: to name, create and make possible a 'big idea' for the government. Circulating before Tony Blair or Anthony Giddens had published their writings on it, the term served to open a space within which thoughts could be formulated and developed.

In May of 1998 Blair hosted a seminar at Downing Street on the idea. Subsequently, Anthony Giddens wrote a book on it and the Prime Minister a pamphlet. While a hostile press reaction to the presumed vacuity of the term has meant that since these early days ministers and attendant advisers are reluctant to talk explicitly about the Third Way, it is still the case that ideas shaped under its name inform government thinking. Understanding something about it can help us see how Labour 'makes sense' of what it is supposed to be for and of how it understands political life.

The Third Way has been used to describe a whole range of problems, solutions and policy areas. But what interests us here is the underlying themes that unite these areas, for they add up to a very particular theory of social change, from which a specific notion of politics derives. The very name 'Third Way' automatically implies that old ways are no longer relevant; that the models of social democracy and conservative neo-liberalism have failed; and that something new is in need of development. As we saw in our discussion of modernisation (Chapter Two), this sense of novelty is central to New Labour. It does not formulate political ideas on the basis of a substantial moral claim about the nature of society and the distribution of its resources. It does so on the basis of a 'sociological' claim about the novel condition of contemporary society; a belief that the world has been transformed, while our political ideas have not kept up the pace. As Blair puts it in his explanation of The Third Way: 'Just as economic and social change were critical to sweeping the Right to power, so they were critical to its undoing. The challenge for the Third Way is to engage fully with the implications of that change'. The Third Way response is to aim for a 'dynamic knowledge-based economy founded on individual empowerment and opportunity, where governments enable, not command, and the power of the market is harnessed to serve the public interest'. This means: the reinvigoration of civil society, partnership government and international co-operation.[7]

The socialist principle of universal welfare drew on ethical claims about social life and the importance of equality. Conservatism is based on normative arguments about social responsibility and the moral importance of order. Thatcherism was very obviously motivated, at least in part, by significant philosophical claims about the priority of liberty over equality and the moral right of individualism. But sociopolitical theoretical claims of this sort do not predominate in New Labour's 'Third Way'. Elements of reheated New Liberalism, communitarianism and Christianity are mixed in with the Third Way but they do not take priority. The moral claims of socialism have been reduced to claims about taking responsibility for ourselves and each other: social-*ism*. New Labour policy is rooted in convictions about certain social facts and their influence upon behaviour.

There are significant and complex theoretical, as well as empirical, roots to this aspect of The Third Way. To some extent they are global in their origin. However, I argue in this chapter that the Third Way as conceived by Blair (for all the global rhetoric) is actually quite parochial in its immediate origins. There are two main strands. The first derives from analyses associated with the magazine *Marxism Today* in the 1980s. The second comes from the kind of sociology exemplified by, though not restricted to, the work of Anthony Giddens. Both emphasise the claim that the condition of contemporary society necessitates a radical change in our thinking and thus our idea of what politics is and must do. We will examine these theories in a way designed to highlight how they lead to particular ways of thinking about politics. But first we will consider, in a little more detail, some aspects of the current 'crisis' of politics. This will give us a context within which we may understand the idea of the political held by New Labour and see it as a symptom of the times.

Politics?

Perhaps we are experiencing the fallout of the transition to what Colin Crouch has called 'post-democracy'.[8] We have passed the great era of democratic expansion when mass society produced mass parties able to, approximately, represent the interests of their mass memberships and struggle for control and influence of the institutions of state. Now, despite the rapid spread and deepening of democratic regimes across the world, as a by-product of the collapse of the Soviet Union and the shift in global power this precipitated, we in the 'old' democracies are bored by it all. Politicians are not well regarded by the populations that choose them. Declining faith in the competence of government is matched only by the conviction that it can't do anything anyway. As Claus Offe argues:

> Many of those political agents that were well known to political analysts of earlier times and were taken for granted by them seem to have been lost ... To be sure, states and governments, citizens and social movements, social classes and political parties, elites, administrative authorities, interest groups, coalitions, nations, blocs and associations are all well and alive; it is just that neither the spectators nor they themselves seem to have any clear notion about their distinctive domain of action. As their rules, roles and identities, missions and responsibilities are becoming uncertain, so is the very idea of political agency.[9]

Philosophically, democracy has always faced big problems of positive justification. There is no necessary connection between the reaching of a decision by the majority of the population and its truth content or efficacy. Rather, the advantage of popular consent has been that, if people feel involved in the taking of a decision, they might at least support it afterwards or refrain from taking up arms against it. No-one has ever convincingly argued that mass acclamation, of itself, makes a statement right or good. There was, however, the idea that democracy, in allowing wide ranging and unrestricted discussion, would enable an enlightened public to reach more rational decisions. Individual rights to free speech and association, protection from harm and the ensuring of a minimum of harassment make it possible for a people collectively to address themselves, develop their values and opinions and express them. But who, any more, believes that such a public sphere exists? It is almost banal to state the reasons why it does not and cannot. Where can 'the people' meet to thrash out their problems? The mass media perform such a function only in a simulated way. Journalists become stars for their capacity to harangue politicians, not for their ability to make them available for participation in open-ended and wide ranging social discussion. TV Talk shows and 'question-times' stage some sort of political discussion but participants are often so fearful of giving too much away that we end up with a stale form of one-way posturing. In any case, the sorts of issues discussed in these limited forums are not always the ones that a society needs to address. Wide-ranging moral and ethical issues are easily supplanted by the policy or personality issue-of-the-week. Deeper moral conversation is more likely to emerge around discussion of the latest developments in the soap operas. There is nothing necessarily wrong with that. The Ancient Greeks knew how to explore social and ethical issues through drama. But we are not sure how to regard such forms of entertainment and to take them too seriously is to invite ridicule. Ultimately, they play a limited part in our conscious societal self-reflection.[10]

So, there are few ways in which the people can discuss, in an open-ended and inclusive way, let alone in a manner that transforms the perspectives and understanding of the participants. But even if they could, it is no longer clear, and never really was, who 'the people' are. If democracy is rule by the people then it is necessary to define who that people is. Historically, the practical solution was the invention of nations. The people was the national people. Except they weren't. Initially it was only the national, propertied men who were counted and the whole notion was convincingly subjected to critique from those radicals who saw the nation as an ideological fiction and capitalist democracy as granting authority to such an abstraction only in order to hold things ever tighter in the grip of a very concrete elite. But democracy did 'reform' itself and slowly the rights of citizenship spread out to the unpropertied men and then women. But this increasing 'inclusiveness' of the notion of the people, while strengthening the legitimacy of representative democracy has, ultimately, weakened its efficacy. Once it is admitted that the people are not a pre-unified collective but a collection of disparate and mobile groups with differing and contradictory interests the whole abstraction begins to break down. Treating the social world as fractured only by mass classes allowed a holding pattern to emerge in which mass parties could represent (or fight over) those class interests. But it seems now as if such notions of collective unity, whether national or class, were always myths. Society is so clearly fractured along lines of class, region, occupation, ethnicity, gender and so on, that the constitution of them as a 'people' capable of speaking with, to and for each other either is no longer desirable, or requires greater resources of political imagination than we currently have.

Meanwhile, many of the problems to which we want solutions cannot, it seems, be resolved at a national level. To function, democracies have required not only meaningful discussion and a sense of the collective will, but a clear and authoritative body to whom that will could be expressed and so acted upon. But, as governments and numerous pundits never tire of telling us, national states no longer have the power to act on all of such collective decisions. The global firm can exercise power over national governments and effectively force them to concede to it in certain areas of fiscal and employment policy. Under the influence of neo-liberal ideology, the British government has withdrawn from many areas of what was once public provision and seems, as Crouch argues, to have lost confidence in itself as a provider of anything. Unsurprisingly, the public loses confidence too. Subject to the influences of a powerful global corporate elite, government finds it even harder to pretend that it represents collective interests, and the cycle of disaffection extends itself.[11]

But this process should not be understood as simply an inevitable development deriving from fixed tendencies in social organisation. It is made possible by such processes, but entrenched by political decisions, values and ideologies. Crucial here is the growth in influence of 'public choice theory' and other 'economic' theories of democracy which, while they originated earlier in the twentieth century, took off in the 1970s and 1980s. Apparently arcane 'academic' theses can have an influence that is almost impossible to measure, for they are disseminated through leading universities and institutes (such as Nuffield College in the UK) to politicians, civil servants and opinion formers. Such theories usually consider themselves to be neutral and objective methods of political study, and they are incapable of conceiving of their own capacity to create the very conditions they purport to merely describe. But, as Colin Hay trenchantly argues, with regard to Anthony Downs' theories of electoral competition: 'New Labour has learned to play the "politics of catch-up" by Downsian rules largely because it has come to accept (for a variety of reasons) many of the assumptions which inform such a theory of electoral competition'. With regard to the use of focus groups and opinion polling to reposition the party he roundly declares: 'A more distinctly Downsian strategy could scarcely be imagined'.[12]

The initial principle of public choice theory is quite straightforward: that economic theories of decision-making can be applied to non-market choices. The behaviours and rationalities assumed by utilitarian and individualist models of economic choice are put to use in making sense of those in the public sector. Despite working in public and non-commercial organisations, it is argued, state employed bureaucrats make decisions akin to those of market choice. Political choice (from voting in a legislature to electing an MP), budget demands from public servants, and policy decisions by ministers, can all be understood by, essentially, the same model as is used to explain purchases in a supermarket.[13] Bureaucratic actions can be understood as the private choices made by individuals. Thus economic theory colonises political science, putting itself forward as rational, scientific and non-normative – the philosopher's stone of positivist social science. Public choice theory prides itself on being an accurate depiction of what actually happens in processes of political decision-making rather than a method clouded by collectivist sentimentality. All politicians and bureaucrats act in self-interested ways. As Downs put it: '[a bureaucrat] acts at least partly in his own self- interest, and some officials are motivated solely by their own self-interest'.[14]

The result of this is the view that public based systems of provision will inevitably lead to excessive spending. Public Choice Theory applies the logic of microeconomics to politics and generally finds that 'whereas self-interest leads to benign results in the marketplace, it produces nothing but pathology in political decisions'.[15] Because they are not subject to the profit motive and the rigours of competition, there is no limit to what bureaucrats may demand. Similarly, politicians will seek to maximise self-interest by supporting expenditure on programmes that benefit them politically, rather than on programmes that are necessarily effective and fiscally efficient (this point is, naturally, a coded attack on Keynesianism). The conclusion is that the incentive system in public services is all wrong. Actors are encouraged to focus attention on the input side of their organisation (such as finance, staff levels, etc) rather than on the output side (what they actually achieve). The solution is to shift the balance of incentives. In Britain in the 1980s this led to the contracting out of services, the spread of internal markets and outright privatisation. It also led to measurement of outputs through forms of performance assessment and to league tables for schools, hospitals and so on.

This is very damaging for democratic politics because public choice theory treats problems as managerial rather than political. Errors can be rectified through the careful design of managerial systems and structures in ways that bring about the desired change in behaviour. It may well be that because there were minimal constraints in the past, doctors advocated the maximum range of treatments rather than the most efficient ones. It may also be the case that bureaucrats were in a position that encouraged them to act in ways that benefited their organisations more than the people they were supposed to serve. But creating structured incentives is a very particular response to this problem. What it achieves is a guarantee that public servants will act in ways designed to meet the criteria by which they are adjudicated. For example, in universities the introduction of forms of assessment based on published research has only served to cause academics to write and publishers to print more. This may have created a further incentive to employ and promote those who publish most (so, perhaps, rewarding the hard-working), and to remove those who were not publishing so much. But the downside is clear. Those with skills in areas not related to publishing (such as teaching) may not be rewarded. The increase in published research is matched by a decrease in attention to teaching. The introduction of performance measurement results, naturally, in a herd-like rush to fulfil those requirements. Innovation decreases and the volume of published material rises dramatically without any necessary increase in quality. Whatever damaging pursuit of self-interest was hampering the growth of quality in public services has not been eliminated; instead it has been redirected, because acting on self-interest has been re-legitimated not de-legitimated. Academics are encouraged to write not for each other or for a wider public but for their curriculum vitae. The public choice solution to problems across the whole range of public services is to change behaviour via alterations to the environment in which people work. It adjusts the stimuli which act on the organism – the worker or service; it is a system of control and rule rather than a plan for political change. It has nothing to say about what we actually want a public service to do and cannot offer any guidance on this question. Certainly a regime of assessment measures and targeting can change the culture and values of an organisation. But it cannot decide on what we should try to change those values to. That is a political decision related to values and judgements of a kind quite different to merely individual choice. In entering the public services as a mechanism designed to ensure only efficacy, public choice theory, or the New Public Management, masks the fact that encoded into it are a set of value judgements about the public services. These are removed from the clear purview of political discussion, and shifted onto narrow notions of efficiency. This leads to two factors that further contribute to de-politicisation.

Firstly, public choice enables government to blame policy failure on the ineptitude of managers who are now kept at arms-length. This was central to the Thatcherite restructuring of the state. If an independent trust hospital fails then government can blame the managers of the trust. If schools fail then responsibility lies with the staff. If prisoners riot then errors must have been made by prison staff and governors. Decision-making can come to appear to be non-political, merely an 'operational matter'. As Du Gay argues, the split between policy and delivery is 'the ideal organisational innovation for ministers': ... 'ministers still retain formal accountability to Parliament for the conduct of policy and yet are simultaneously able to decide what is and is not a policy issue, they are now in a position to have their cake and eat it'.[16] This process, started by the Tory governments under Thatcher and

Major, has been continued by New Labour. Indeed it may have particular advantages for them in that it separates them from total responsibility for public sector wages. Unions will have to negotiate with employers rather than with government, so freeing the latter from involvement in damaging industrial relations disputes. Of course, this is a strategy that poses problems for government, in that citizens may not be so nuanced in their approach to issues and may continue to regard hospital failure as a proper concern of government. But it is operating in a context in which public services have been undermined politically and organisationally, with the expectations of the public systematically lowered. It thus contributes to a declining sympathy for politics, which it is in the interest of politicians to foster, because it enables them to shift blame for policy failure onto executive agencies, quangos, private contractors and so on (see, for example, Railtrack).

The perverse truth, then, is that all this does actually make sense for those in government in our particular political system. Our form of representative democracy has developed in such a way that, feeling distant from the institutions of state and constituted as an electorate rather than a body of active citizens, people tend to judge the government in terms of their apparent competence as opposed to the actual values which they manifest and attempt to engender in state and society.

This is particularly the case in the field of economic management. Because the ideology and social system that underpins our government is that of capitalism, and it is axiomatic that the state should not really try to interfere in the free actions of economic agents, the government believes it cannot act on this fundamental area of social life. The state, in short, is structurally dependent upon capital. Thus, as Colin Hay makes plain, New Labour must 'convince capital of the fiscal probity and responsibility of their measures ... while sustaining a popular political project capable of providing a sufficient electoral base'.[17] Given that it has these constraints coming from one side, but is likely to be punished for them from the other, electoral, side, social democratic politics is almost always stuck between Scylla and Charybdis. It thus becomes quite rational for a government to downplay the power it has and to reduce the areas over which it claims political control. Keynesian social-democratic governments fell into crises of legitimation, because they could not deliver simultaneously the conditions desired by capital and those promised to labour. Rather than attack capital, such governments vacillated until they fell and were replaced by New Right governments which willingly attacked labour. New Labour has subsequently rejected a politicised engagement with the economy, arguing that it cannot really interfere with it because of the constraints imposed by the globalisation of finance. Instead it prefers to set up rules to which it will adhere in the hope that this will ensure stability of expectations and so confidence in the market, while devolving power to bodies such as the Monetary Policy Committee of the Bank of England. Through this mechanism New Labour can 'seek to evade direct responsibility for high interest rates and the high value of sterling, thus establishing its credibility with the markets whilst, at the same time, increasing the pressure on labour and capital to become more competitive'.[18] The advantage of all this (New Public Management plus a hands-off economic strategy) is that it appears to remove political calculation from the process of economic management. This is deemed an advantage to the markets but also an advantage to the state, in that it cannot be so easily accused of screwing things up since it was only following pre-set rules. Of course, at the same time, it is the government that sets the rules; and what is offered with one, decentralising hand, is taken away by the other which intensifies systems of regulation and rule-setting, allowing government to pretend that it is on the side of the citizen and is bashing those nasty professionals in their name. De-politicisation is thus a highly political strategy, with the effect of shifting regimes of accountability and influence away from the elected and thus away from the electors. This has even wider effects on 'political culture'

Which brings us to the second way in which public choice and attendant ideologies contribute to a general depoliticisation. It adds to, and extends, an individualisation of all public activity. Far from combating individualism, the ideology of new public management entrenches it, reinforcing the values of market individualism rather than bolstering those of public service. It facilitates (and one cannot help but suspect this was the purpose) the spread of values of individualism and the virtues of market mechanisms of allocation over all others. This happens at the level of the manager but also at that of the user of a public service. The introduction of managerialism into the public services is also a process 'through which new subject positions are created, through which "administrators", "public servants" and "practitioners" come to see themselves as "business managers", "purchasers", "contractors", "strategists", "leaders" and so on'.[19] Workers in public services are encouraged to see themselves as entrepreneurs and 'change agents', as individual actors rather than parts of collective enterprises. Indeed, this is understood as a positive form of liberation, moving away from hierarchical and protective forms of activity to empowering and open networks. To be sure, this may well have the effect of undermining certain monopolies of power, and of damaging forms of prejudicial and defensive inertia, but the cost is that of further breaking public services away from their public positioning, undermining their collective commitment and replacing it with a looser sense of public good based on satisfying customer need. Thus, the individualisation goes all the way through the services and starts to reconfigure the user and the user experience. Here, the New Public Management and public choice theory combine with more general management theory, which (as we touched upon in Chapter Two) advocates a focus on attracting and holding onto customers through the provision of an all round quality consumption experience. This may encourage service managers to see the people they serve as diverse and differentiated and as something other than a homogeneous mass requiring and deserving exactly the same things. As such the move towards a customer oriented rhetoric is not simply a product of the New Right obsession with efficiency; it also accords with New Left critiques of the bureaucratic nature of state services, and the defensive and restrictive power of organised professionals.[20] However, as Clarke and Newman argue:

> Consumerism can help authorities to advance from considering individual members of the public as passive clients or recipients of services … but it will rarely be enough to turn members of the public into partners actively involved in shaping public services … it does not go far enough to effect a radical shift in the distribution of power.[21]

Our immediate interest here is not in how this discourse of consumerism effects public services, but in its wider impact on understandings of the political. Here Clarke and Newman are incisive when they comment on the Thatcherite reforms of the state, and their development of market relations in public services: 'These changes aimed to dislocate collectivist notions of the public and the public interest, challenging the legitimacy of any claims (other than those of national government) to be able to speak for the people'.[22]

This, then, is the background against which New Labour's commitment to the 'democratising of democracy' must be placed. On the one hand there are genuine shifts in the ways in which people perceive themselves and their aspirations, as well as their expectations of what politics can do. People are more aware of their variations and distinct needs, and we do now live in societies made up of people with more diverse lifestyles and backgrounds. It is harder for the media to function as a meaningful public space (and they are not much inclined to do so), and nations and national states appear to be less significant determinants of social life. But these shifts are inseparable from the wider context of democratic practice in liberal capitalist societies, in which certain centres of power – those rooted in economic activity – are not to be challenged by government, and where the primary form of political power that can be exercised by the citizen is the vote or party membership. Political decisions lie behind the deregulation of media, and their insertion into market logics that militate against their playing a more considered public and democratically accountable role. The extension of public choice and of market mechanisms throughout the public services has been a matter of political will, and it has spread and secured an ideology that is hostile to collective action, and ensured that political problems are mostly seen as attributable to management failure. As Hobsbawm succinctly puts it:

> Market sovereignty ... is an alternative to any kind of politics, as it denies the need for *political* decisions, which are precisely decisions about common or group interests as distinct from the sum of choices, rational or otherwise, of individuals pursuing private preferences. Participation in the market replaces participation in politics. The consumer takes the place of the citizen.[23]

Politics thus comes to lose all appeal. It seems an unwieldy way of making decisions that are essentially to do with my personal preferences rather than with any attempt I may make to see things from a collective or public point of view. The management of personal life just as much as the management of industry or social services becomes a matter of calculating what is most efficient, what has minimum opportunity cost, what will be most immediately profitable.

The problems suffered by democratic politics today are the result of political decisions, choices and acts. What is the Third Way response?

The Third Way, Marxism Today and 'New Times'

In the latter half of the 1980s, in its role as 'theoretical and discussion journal' of the Communist Party of Great Britain, *Marxism Today* engaged in the promotion of a theoretical political agenda loosely brought together under the name of 'New Times'.[24] It advanced a particular analysis of our changing socio-economic environment as the way to understand the failures of the British Left and the ascendancy of the New Right. This magazine had a level of influence that is surprising given its relatively small circulation and affiliation to a dying political party. But it had a distinctive agenda for left renewal (and a distinctive politics within the CPGB) that brought together a number of political currents dissatisfied with the old left and sharing a similar view of the problems needing to be addressed. It was also very concerned to make links with those in the Labour Party who were thinking along similar lines. Thus many of those who wrote for it now have direct links with New Labour. Blair wrote for it. Geoff Mulgan, a key participant, has since become special adviser in Downing Street. Charles Leadbeater, who was also closely linked to the magazine, is now one of Blair's 'economic gurus' and collaborated with Peter Mandelson on the New Labour government's competition policy. Even Stuart Hall, the central intellectual associated with the 'New Times' ideas, and someone who has always been critical of New Labour, has admitted that: 'I feel a peculiar responsibility for the Blair phenomenon ... we're responsible for launching some of these new ideas which have then been appropriated cosmetically and installed in a different kind of project'.[25]

It is not possible to understand the analysis of *Marxism Today* without acknowledging that it was developed by people working within the Marxist tradition. The most important part of that tradition was the work of Antonio Gramsci, and the understanding of politics as the establishment of hegemony. This conception was put to work most notably by Stuart Hall in his famous analysis of Thatcherism, crucial to which was an attack on orthodox Marxist conceptions of politics as predicated on the inherent dynamics of class conflict. For Hall, Gramsci offered a way of theorising the political crisis of the Left and understanding how the Right had come to dominate. This entailed recognising that Conservatism had been reconstructed and that ruling class politics was not working in the way the traditional left generally understood it.[26] Thatcherism was not a simple continuation of class domination but a 'project', concerned to 'transform the state in order to restructure society: to decentre the whole post-war formation.' It was a hegemonic project, aiming to reverse 'common sense', and to alter the automatic consensual assumption that a welfare state and mixed economy, managed by a state that could represent a general social interest, were inviolable features of the British form of capitalism. Thatcherism had responded to the incomplete development of the British social formation by instituting a 'regressive modernisation', that constructed 'a politics and an image of what modernity would be like for our people'. The purpose of a historically effective ideology, for Hall, was 'that it articulates into a configuration, different subjects, different identities, different projects, different aspirations. It does not reflect, it constructs, a "unity" out of difference'.[27]

This construction of unity is the essence of Hall's understanding of how hegemonic politics inserts itself into people's experience and common sense, redefining their identity and sense of interests so as to form them into a new 'coalition'. This claim was a break with traditional Marxism, since it follows that, 'interests are not given but have to be politically and ideologically constructed'. In other words, class position does not determine political aspirations and needs. Politics extends beyond the narrow realm of the state and government, reaching into and shaping the cultural sphere where our everyday perceptions are formed. It is the process of binding together and redefining these perceptions, building wider social legitimacy for a project of transformation. Politics is not the algorithmic application of a theory of society, but the open-ended and strategic production of collective political identities. Hampered by erroneous and historically redundant assumptions, the Left, Hall argued, could not understand this sense of politics, or the need to unify diverse political forces far beyond the traditional base of the Labour Party. The 'economic-corporate, incremental, Keynesian game' was 'closed' and 'exhausted'. There had to be 'a renewal of the whole socialist project in the context of modern social and cultural life', a strategy for taking on new technical and cultural trends and leading them in the direction of the Left.

New Labour has inherited from *Marxism Today* this sense that it requires more than a set of policies; that it needs a guiding theme enabling its critique of the present, the shaping of an alternative, and the transformation of political culture. The Third Way has been one way in which it has sought to produce and shape just such a project. As Hall has acknowledged, the recognition in The Third Way of the importance of economic globalisation, new individualism and so forth, occupies common ground with the *MT* analysis.[28] The aim of Labour 'modernisers' is to make the party into the 'natural party of government', the hegemonic force that shapes the new century. The Third Way attempts to render the Labour Party and the current socio-political situation coincident.

But for Hall it is still not right. The analysis of new times may be similar, but the political responses are very different. One error has been to try and be all-inclusive, believing that all old oppositions should be transcended. The Third Way is, in Chantal Mouffe's phrase, 'a politics without adversary'.[29] New Labour fails to realise that there is still a conflict of 'social solidarity, interdependence and collective social provision against market inequality and instability ... [that] ... there might be structural interests preventing our achieving a more equitable distribution of wealth and life-chances'.[30] Globalisation is treated by New Labour as an inevitable force, and neo-liberal theories of the market remain dominant. The project is, in this sense, *insufficiently* modernising, remaining dependent on vacant populist claims and media gloss. It has taken the easy way out, failing to live up to its historic opportunity, serving only to adjust us to a post-Thatcherite settlement.

But it was, after all, *Marxism Today* that advocated co-operation between Liberal Democrats and The Labour Party; that argued for the salience of new technologies in the economy and culture. In 1991 the magazine ran a series of articles on 'modernisation' that today make familiar reading. Modernisation then entailed decentralisation of power and more active citizenship; a new constitution; more attention to science and technology; restructuring of defence expenditure; a new sense of open nationhood.[31] Then Shadow Employment Spokesperson, Tony Blair wrote of 'a new settlement between the individual and society which determines both their rights and obligations'; a notion of citizenship understood as embedded in community; 'a new approach – neither old style collectivism nor new style individualism'; and a policy debate no longer dominated 'by a battle between state and market'.[32] His 'new agenda' was 'fundamentally different from the issues that dominated debate in the past'. It entailed constitutional reform and devolution, and a 'non-ideological' recognition that 'the market is essential for individual choice'. Collective action was no longer about 'war for supremacy between management and labour', but a question of enhancing 'the power of individual employees, not just to protect their position from abuse, but also to grant them the capability to use or exploit capital'.[33] It was about the application of technology and the better education of workers, the liberation of 'untapped potential'. All these claims, which remain fundamental to Blairism, at that time seemed in tune with the general analysis of *Marxism Today*.

But Hall's approach was a fundamentally socialist one, and a critique of capitalism, if not always brought to the fore, formed the ethico-political core of his analysis. Blairism may still have a claim to being ethically socialist, but it is not committed to a critique of capitalism in this way. It shares considerable amounts of the 'sociology' of *Marxism Today*, but very little of the politics. To understand the implications of this, and the influence of that sociology, we need to consider some of the wider New Times arguments.

New Times, Post-Fordism and the Knowledge Economy

New Times was about appropriating and 'grasping the future',[34] assessing the present balance of social forces and the nature of social organisation to develop new strategies of political intervention. The 'New Times' were understood to derive from a shift from the uniform, mass production of 'Fordism' to a diverse and flexible 'post-fordism', shaped by computer and information technology. This led to an over-whelming concern with 'the knowledge economy' and the impact of IT on industrial organisation and consumer lifestyle. This was as impor-tant a part of the New Times analysis as it is of New Labour and the

Third Way. In *The Manifesto for New Times* (*MFNT*), it was argued that:

> At the heart of the new times will be production based on a shift to information technology and microelectronics. New technology allows more intensive automation and its extension from large to smaller companies, pulling together the shop-floor and the office, the design loft and the showroom. It allows production to be both more flexible, automated and integrated.[35]

This changes the nature of work, blurring the division of blue and white collar. Service industries become the main source of employment, with women's part-time employment increasingly important. The basis of traditional union organisation is undermined and there is 'enormous pressure for established institutions, from the family to the welfare state, to be refashioned in the new times'. Along with the internationalisation of finance and the globalisation of the firm, this was believed to have led to a transformation in competitive pressures, the undermining of policies for full-employment and the rise of 'an assertive individualistic consumerism'. The goal of 'progressive modernisation' was therefore 'to sustain people through providing them with the skills, confidence and security to engage in productive work'; to protect the environment; democratise the workplace; develop an 'ethic of progressive consumerism' and redefine public interest.[36]

Post-Fordist analysis was not only a rethink of the massification of industry, but a rethink of massification as such: 'Mass production, the mass consumer, the big city, big-brother state, the sprawling housing estate, and the nation-state are in decline: flexibility, diversity, differentiation, mobility, communication, decentralisation and internationalisation are in the ascendant ... our own identities, our sense of self, our own subjectivities are being transformed'.[37] Fordism was not merely an industrial arrangement. It was an overarching social formation, defining a relationship between state, individual and society. Under Post-Fordism, it was argued, social interests were fragmenting such that no state could effectively and legitimately represent them. This led to a critique of class-based socialism, and was related to debates within the CPGB. However, this aspect of *MFNT* differs from the arguments of Hall (who was never a member of the CPGB), in that its beliefs are derived not from theoretical reasoning but from a claim about industrial change and diversification. Economic restructuring, it was argued, disrupted class formations and undermined traditional forms of identity. New patterns of consumption were believed to be transforming individuality: 'Choice in consumption, lifestyle, sexuality, are more important as an assertion of identity. The dynamic area of most people's lives is where they can assert their difference from others'.[38] In both *MFNT* and the Third Way, Post-Fordism is the analytical key to understanding Thatcherism, the eclipse of Keynesianism, and of defining what is to be done. A Demos collection on The Third Way, produced shortly after the 1997 General Election, similarly spoke of ...

> the profound forces of globalisation, which have sharply altered the operating environment for government. Governments can no longer easily erect barriers to the exchange of money, regulate precisely what media their citizens consume, insulate their economies from global business cycles or pursue autonomous defence strategies. One of the core challenges is that of achieving the transition to an economy based on the intensive application and development of knowledge.[39]

There is no mystery about the ideas in play here. The distance from the *Manifesto for New Times* to *The Third Way: New Politics for a New Century* is not very great. It is an ideology based on 'sociological' analysis of economic and social changes, and subsequent decisions about the best way to manage them.

But to completely equate the 'New Times' analysis – which in any case was never a homogeneous set of ideas – and the Third Way would be a mistake. The latter has a very different conception of politics to the Gramscianism of Stuart Hall. Claims about Post-Fordism do not of themselves necessarily constitute a critique of Marxist or 'Labourist' theory. They are simply a particular analysis of productive conditions, and of the social arrangements within which they exist. By contrast, Hall's arguments were written (at least partly) as a critique of traditional Marxist philosophy and epistemology. This was even more clearly the case with Ernesto Laclau, whose related arguments were also important to *MT*.[40] While both Hall and Laclau did endorse significant chunks of 'Post-Fordist sociology', the core of their claim was that reductionist Marxist class politics were mistaken. It wasn't just that they had been rendered out of date. Social changes made it clear that they had never really been right. This is a significant distinction but not one that was always clearly brought out. The difference can be seen in looking at the politics derived from 'Post-Fordism', and comparing it to that of Laclau and Hall. The former is much closer to New Labour than the latter.

Leading enthusiast of the knowledge economy Charles Leadbeater, who contributed to the *Manifesto for New Times*, argued in *Marxism Today* for a socialism in which the index of progress was not the expansion of the public sector, but 'the progressive expansion of the sphere

of individual rights and responsibilities.' In a passage that could have
been written yesterday, but is actually some thirteen years old, he said:

> If the Left stands for one thing it should be this: people taking more
> responsibility for all aspects of their lives. Whatever issue the Left
> confronts, its question should be this: 'How can people take more
> responsibility for shaping this situation, determining its outcome?' It
> should not be, as it often is, 'What can the state, the council, the expert
> professionals, do to solve this problem for people'.[41]

This was not a rolling back of the state but the encouragement of its
withering since productive forces were making this necessary. It led to
advocacy of an individualism believed to be different to that of
Thatcherism: 'individual citizenship rather than individual
consumerism ... an expansive individualism which offers people rights
to influence decisions in production as well as consumption; political
and civil rights as well as the right to buy'. Collective social action had
to be made 'accountable to, and designed to fulfil, individual needs',
and the left had to 'renegotiate the contract between those who finance
collective services, those who provide them, and those who consume
them, to ensure they provide value for money, efficiency, flexibility and
choice'.

Post-Fordist flexibility, or what Blair calls the 'fast-forward future',
creates and requires a new individualism and autonomy that should be
enabled, not interfered with, by the state. This is an analysis driven by
assessments of technological transformation and changes in the market.
But the analysis of Hall or Laclau was predicated on a theory of politics. In common with other writers in *Marxism Today*, they rejected
the assumption that political identity could be reduced to position in a
class structure. But in place of this came neo-Gramscian notions of
politics as the process by which social meanings are contested, and
political alliances and identities formulated and reformulated. The challenge for the left was to analyse the social forces and develop new
strategies beyond a simple appeal to class allegiance, that could
generate a wide enough constituency for a hegemonic project of
socialist renewal. For Laclau the problems of the Left, 'had nothing to
do with the working class and its actual struggles but rather with the
very idea of a "fundamental social agent" of a historical transformation
and with the notion that there is *one* project of global emancipation ...
the whole conception of history as a unified process'.[42] The 'New
Times' are not understood as a 'break' within capitalism, nor are political identities thought to have been reconstituted in the form of new
individuals or even a plurality of autonomous, 'post-modern' libera-

tion movements (feminism, anti-racism, gay liberation, etc). Rather, the destabilisation inherent to capitalism is understood to have been radically extended, dislocating social identities and making it necessary to realise that politics expands across social relations; and the relationship between class and politics is understood to always have been one of political articulation and construction, never as something which could be 'read off'.

Socialism was thus reformulated by Laclau, with its ethical basis cohering in the radical expansion of democratic forms of life, based in discourses of rights and with equality as the fundamental principle of free society. Such democratic politics does not cohere within the central state or a single agent or process of reform but spreads to every social relation. And Hall celebrates Gramsci as *'par excellence* the theorist of the political', giving to us 'an expanded conception of "politics" – the rhythms, forms, antagonisms, and transformations specific and peculiar to it as a region'.[43] This is quite different to the 'technologism' of other interpretations of New Times. It is this understanding of politics that has made Hall critical of Blairism, which he believes capitulates to, and seeks to de-politicise, social and economic trends initiated by Thatcherite neo-liberalism. Blairism does not seek to constitute new political subjects but assumes they are 'already out there, fully formed, requiring only to be focus-grouped into position'.[44]

Two strands (at least) of analysis stood together in the *Marxism Today* stable. One was focused on the social changes deriving from new economic conditions; the other was concerned with how to use such an analysis in a re-theorisation of anti-capitalist social and political theory. It is the first of these that exercises most influence on the Third Way. For this version of 'modernisation', 'late' capitalism became the object of sociological and economic analysis, but the development of a political philosophy through which a socialist alternative could or should be advanced was eclipsed. The design of a new politics became dependent on a very particular analysis of the condition of capitalism, one that saw the benefits of autonomy and individuality deriving from trends inherent within it. It is a kind of technological futurism. There is an irony in this. The Hall and Laclau analyses were a much stronger and wholesale critique of Marxism than that of Leadbeater et al. But they were still socialist. The *MFNT* was more (crudely) Marxist in its commitment to deriving politics from economic change. It is these 'Marxists' that have now joined New Labour. However, in the latter the socialism has been jettisoned.

Without the ontological and ethical commitments of socialism, or any serious reformulation of them, their critique of capitalism as such turned into a critique of the particular capitalism of Thatcherite neo-liberalism. It ceased being a *political* claim and became a *managerial* one about how to run things better. The development of a hegemonic strategy that could seize the future by understanding the state of current social forces, and design a political strategy to mobilise them, turned into a desire to adapt to a pre-ordained future. The sociological analysis became a normative claim and rather than the servant of political will it became the master.

This was a possibility always contained within the neo-Marxist sociology that was being deployed; that strain which derived its ethical claims by turning 'sociological' insights about the direction of history and the productive forces into a normative claim about the future. This was exactly the Marxism that 'New Times' sought to critique and transcend. The ethical and political claims of socialism suffered further in Eastern Europe, and the voters rejected Labour in the 1992 election; socialism became effectively supplanted by beliefs about how to understand correctly the shape of present day capitalism and how best to organise a population to respond to it. This is what New Labour's Third Way is primarily about. The Gramscians sought to reformulate analysis of the agents that could form a coalition to bring about social change and the ethico-political basis which would legitimate it. What we might call 'the Demos tendency' developed a kind of vanguardist futurism. Here the purpose of politics is 'to resolve the big conflicts of interest and lend direction to complex societies'. It is conceived as 'a way to solve problems and as a means of providing security and a stable sense of belonging'.[45] This is a vision of a new politics for the direction of a world of change. It is certainly not a narrow or traditional conception, in as much as it does see politics as taking place across spheres of society. But it does not conceive the political as the place where the steering of society is decided upon. It is where it is enacted. In this sense, despite the rhetoric, the modern Demos is Platonic rather than Aristotelian. Hence the tendency to fall into a technocratic programme of futurism that seeks an ontology in objective forces of truth. Modernisation, as we have seen, happens because it must, not because we want it to or have demonstrated that it is ethically better.

But with the rejection of socialist, moral objections to capitalism, this kind of Third Way lacked an ethical and normative core. In an effort to deal with this problem and develop the Third Way there was (in the early days of the 1997 Labour government) promiscuity and flirtation with notions of citizenship, community, stakeholding and so forth, some of which have left an imprint. But ultimately The Third Way left political theory behind to seek a normative and ontological basis derived from a description of present society that could also provide an ethic.

Giddens and the sociology of the Third Way

Giddens' political analysis shares with 'New Times' the conviction that certain specifiable social conditions demand a new form of politics. But he criticises the Stuart Hall analysis for adhering to the 'unchanged doctrines of the traditional Left', to counter capitalism through the state. For Giddens, 'If social democrats are to have real purchase on the world their doctrines have to be rethought as radically as half a century ago when social democracy originally broke away from Marxism'.[46] The transformation underway is much greater in scale than anything socialists had imagined. Modernisation 'means reforming social institutions to meet the demands of a globalising information order. It is certainly not to be identified solely with economic development'.[47]

Old ideas of socialism and Keynesianism are obsolete, Giddens claims. Our concepts of knowledge and control need to be rethought to fit a society too complex, too fluid and diverse to be managed by a central state. Class politics is no longer viable since the manual working class has declined, and anyway 'class isn't usually experienced any longer as class'.[48] There must be a new politics that strengthens individual responsibility and relations of trust; a 'life politics' concerned with the emancipation of lifestyle, identity and choice. As with New Times this includes an extension or deepening of democracy, the development of a more decentralised, enabling politics (that Giddens calls 'generative'), and a realisation that the social forces that can bring about such change must be broader than those to which the Left has traditionally turned.

The Labour Party, Giddens has argued, must abandon the socialist critique of capitalism (in as much as it ever really believed it). But it cannot endorse Thatcherite neo-liberalism. This is criticised because it undermined social relationships, failing to understand the context of the new world. Its hostility to the social prevented it from seeing the necessary cultural and moral underpinnings to market society. But what could this new politics be? Communitarianism is insufficient because the kinds of communities it advocates cannot, and should not, be brought into being. They are archaic and would run counter to the changed conditions and 'new' individualism.[49] Similarly, Christian socialism cannot provide a new politics in a world of multi-faith pluralism. It too is inappropriate because not in tune with the times. Communitarianism and Christianity fail properly to analyse and understand the new social context. They are, in a sense, insufficiently sociological.

Instead, Giddens develops a politics led by an analysis of the nature of contemporary social relations. This theory also sets out ontological and ultimately normative claims, that offer to theorists of 'new times' and political modernisation an alternative ethical basis to that of socialist anti-capitalism. This is concerned with redeveloping or repairing social cohesion and solidarity. It is a 'philosophic conservatism'.[50] But these claims are not made in the manner of political theory. They are developed on the basis of a sociological method and interpretation, such that they are legitimised by being found to flow from the nature of contemporary social life itself. To understand how this works we need to look at Giddens' more general social theory.

Giddens has always been interested in the specification of sociology as an intellectual endeavour and discipline. One could argue that his preoccupation is not society so much as sociology itself. This is not necessarily a criticism since, for Giddens, a kind of sociological mindset is the one best placed to act well in modern society. Reflecting on sociology is a way of reflecting on society. The core of his thought is precisely concerned with grasping the fact that people are in some degree conscious of the procedures by which they act and are continually evaluating and re-evaluating social rules.

For Giddens, sociology ...

> concerns itself above all with modernity, – with the character and dynamics of modern or industrialised societies ... More than any other intellectual endeavour, sociological reflection is central to grasping the social forces remaking our lives today. Social life has become episodic, fragmentary and dogged with new uncertainties which it must be the business of creative sociological thought to help us understand.[51]

This makes it particularly interesting that Giddens has moved directly into political thinking, and that with New Labour political thought is subordinated to sociology. For, by implication, sociology is vastly superior for thinking about politics to political thought. Not simply because of a superior methodology, but because what it studies is the basis for any political questioning. By its very nature sociological thinking enters into our ideas about social life and so alters its character, thereby necessitating a further revision of sociological thinking.[52] Giddens' role as an adviser to Blair is a culmination, not merely of personal talent, but of a logic that inheres within the very project of sociology as Giddens has delineated it. Philosophers have only interpreted the world in various ways, and political theorists sometimes try to change it, but in re-interpreting the world sociologists actually contribute to changing it.

This is one reason why Giddens' book *The Third Way* has a tone quite different to works of normative or analytic political philosophy. It is not concerned with the careful discussion and dissection of normative principles but with laying out objectively the components of the social organism. Its mode of discourse is diagnostic and prescriptive, giving recommendations for good health in an ailing society. *The Third Way* is a kind of manual, specifying the appropriate mentality for government in the era of 'reflexive modernisation'. The legitimacy of the argument does not depend on the coherence of logical principles, in the way it would in a work of normative political philosophy, but on the fidelity of the diagnosis and the coincidence of sociological reasoning with the reasoning characteristic of the present – one that transcends old deterministic dualisms of political thought: left and right, state and market, individual and collective.

The transcendence of dualisms is a hallmark of Giddens' theories. The primary dualism he has sought to overcome in social theory is that of structure and agency. Sociological analysis tends to oscillate between two opposed conceptual and analytical approaches. One emphasises the determining effect of constraining structures of social organisation. The other emphasises the capacities of individuals or agents. Giddens is critical of both structuralist/functionalist and subjectivist/interpretative theories. One is an 'imperialism of the social object', the other an 'imperialism of the subject'.[53] The aim of 'structuration theory' is to 'put an end to each of these empire building endeavours' and to transcend the restrictive dualism. Giddens does this by making the social sciences into the study not of individual actors nor of a social totality but 'social practices ordered across time and space'. Social action (agency) is understood as productive of the conditions (structures) that, in turn, order it. Social activities are 'recursive', continually recreated by actors: 'In and through their activities agents reproduce the conditions that make these activities possible'.[54]

The features that make up a particular social group are thus understood as the result of routine practices and not the sum total of individual wills or theoretically 'external' social forces. The crucial feature of social practices is their reproducibility, which in turn means that actors have a certain practical consciousness of what it is they are doing, if not a complete mastery. Motivations for action may be unclear to individuals but they do monitor their activities and their context, maintaining 'a continuing "theoretical understanding" of the grounds of their activity ... actors will usually be able to explain most of what they do, if asked'.[55] Social action is thus marked by 'reflexivity', 'the monitored character of the ongoing flow of social life'.[56]

This is not simply a description or argument. It is an ontological claim. Social life is intrinsically historical. Time-space is the terrain of social action within which actors reconstitute that social action by reflecting upon it. This inherent reflexivity of human beings is the condition for both society and individuals. The routines it enables provide 'ontological security'. It is not only something that we *do* do but *should* do. Therefore individuals must have the tools, and live under conditions, which enable them to be such actors. For this theory power is understood as the capacity 'to be able to do otherwise' or 'make a difference'. Without it, an agent is not agent. Power is not a resource in itself: 'resources are the media through which power is exercised' and are intrinsic to forms of social life. As such, concentrations of power and attempts to dominate all social life from one centre are ontologically in error. This legitimates a politics designed to encourage the capacity of social agents to act and justifies a state that fosters them – one that is not conceived as directive but as 'generative'. But while this theory of social action and structure is ontological it incorporates in itself a reflection on the historical dimension. Since social action is reflexive it includes reflection on the history of social action. There cannot be any over-arching theory of social action and history, such as historical materialism, since this would presume determination outside of reflexive time-space. But a theory that is itself reflexive can be attuned to processes of social change as well as being part of that process. Thus sociology has primacy in the analysis of modernity and the practice of living in it.

To get a sense of how Giddens analyses modernity we can consider his arguments about its relationship to tradition. Traditions guarantee a kind of order and regularity to a social group, shaping the continual interpretation of its collective memory. But they are not merely functional. They have a normative and moral character,[57] offering a 'formulaic' truth of ritual, rather than the truth of philosophical reasoning; an affective ontological security formed through repetition that creates meaning and identity. But, 'Modernity destroys tradition'.[58] The pace and scope of change it engenders, and its new social institutions (the modern state, city or industry), undermine tradition. Our world becomes increasingly interdependent and our local actions have global consequences such that we are increasingly exposed to new forms of risk. This globalisation and 'radicalisation' of modernity have begun to uproot even deeply held traditional assumptions about personal areas such as the family or sexual intimacy.[59] The local contexts on which our 'practical consciousness' of social action has been based become subject to the influences of distant, often unaccountable, forces. They become 'disembedded', and we experience 'the lifting out of social relations from local contexts of interaction and their restructuring across indefinite spans of time-space'.

In this 'post traditional' context we can't rely on old routines, for 'we have no choice but to choose how to be and how to act [to cope with] the multiplicity of possibilities which almost every aspect of daily life ... offers'.[60] What 'New Times' saw as characteristic of post-fordism is thus seen by Giddens as the condition of 'high' modernity or 'reflexive modernisation'. This is an extension of modernity, the understanding of which is crucial to the formulation of a new politics. Early modernity adapted pre-existing traditions and invented new ones, but globalisation and the 'evacuation' of traditional contexts introduce abstract systems and new risks into intimate local contexts: 'In the present day, the destruction of the local community, in the developed societies, has reached its apogee'. We see the 'dissolution of the local community'. Local customs may persist but they can no longer exist in isolation from each other. As a result social conflict between value systems changes. Traditions which could once be taken for granted increasingly have to justify themselves. They can try to further embed themselves or disengage from others, but the possibilities of succeeding at this are increasingly limited, something which applies to religious or ethnic traditions but also to phenomena such as traditional conceptions of gender. Increasingly the choice for such traditions is between engaging in discursive justification or resorting to violence and domination.

At the heart of this is a claim that social relations cannot now be assumed or relied upon. They are not inherited but are always being made. We are open to more risk in social encounters and require new forms of trust to engender the possibility of dialogue rather than violence. Old forms of authority must be replaced by dialogic forms of democracy, and new forms of solidarity based on a 'new balance between individual and collective responsibilities'.[61] This also means recognising the opportunities and possibilities of risk in high modernity, the chances it creates for new forms of lifestyle. Indeed this is the ethical requirement since if we do not foster this kind of open-endedness the alternative is anxiety or the violence and limitations of fundamentalism. So Giddens calls for a 'social investment state' that develops an entrepreneurial culture and offers protection in a way that encourages risk and opens possibilities.[62]

Thus, a political ethic of open-ended democracy, advocacy of a re-design of the role of governance, the demand for greater orientation towards the encouragement of risk and the entrepreneurial life-style, is derived from a social analysis of present trends and forces – against which, it seems from Giddens at least, there is no point waging any resistance. To some extent this feels similar to the arguments of Hall et al. But the Hall analysis was intended to be of use in the design of a strategy that might harness the social forces made available by social change to a project of radical transformation. In Giddens though –

despite some of his claims to the contrary – the process appears to have a logic all of its own. Furthermore, and crucially, unlike most the 'New Times' authors, Giddens is not convinced that capitalism has structural tendencies towards exclusion or exploitation. Indeed, he does not understand contemporary society through the prism of an analysis of capitalism at all. His is a more general conception of modernity, and within that framework he presents a critique of both socialism and market fundamentalism. He does not consider conflict to be constitutive of society, as someone influenced by Marxism, such as Stuart Hall, might do. Thus the more technological and futurist side of New Times, that which predominates in a think-tank like Demos, can find in Giddens' theory the ethical and ontological basis it lacks. The theory of the sources and importance of social solidarity, 'ontological security', can be extended to cover economic as well as social processes, and provide to the New Times, post-Marxists what they lost when they abandoned socialist anti-capitalism. An index of what this means for New Labour's political theory is the reconfigured place of the concept of equality in their 'New' social democracy.

For Giddens, equality matters because inequality leads to disaffection and conflict, undermining social cohesion. Equality of opportunity is not enough, since 'a radically meritocratic society would create deep inequalities of outcome, which would threaten social cohesion'.[63] The ethic of equality is not derived from its being a principle as such but because the effects of its absence are an offence against the constitution of a cohesive society. Thus Giddens endorses the redefinition of equality and poverty in terms of inclusion and exclusion. We have seen this trend across New Labour for several years now, for example in the important report issued by the John Smith inspired Commission on Social Justice.[64] It is part of what Ruth Levitas deprecatingly terms 'the new Durkheimian hegemony', in a reference to the French sociologist whose concern for social solidarity in industrial society is of course a key inspiration for Giddens.[65] Equality is recast as inclusion, and inequality is seen as the enemy of social harmony. The concept of inclusion can be a concept applied across policy areas – education, pensions, culture, for example. But its ethical justification derives from a sociological analysis of the condition of society. Inclusion is understood as the only way to bring security to people in the new society and as part of the logic of the new economy which must draw on all the talents and creativity of people. It means bringing people into the knowledge economy and enabling them to be the kinds of well educated and technologically literate individuals both made possible by 'New Times' and made necessary – since without them there will be nobody to produce or consume the weightless economy. Thus reconceived, a commitment to equality as inclusion is both a moral justification of The Third Way, evidence of its belief in community, and proof that only it can manage capitalism in the twenty-first century.

This entails a specific approach to politics. We can no longer understand things in terms of the badness of the market, not even in terms of good and bad at all. We have to leave behind the outdated 'politics of redemption'.[66] If this is a left politics, it is fundamentally different from old left politics, in as much as it seeks to replace emancipatory politics with this 'life politics'.[67] The old battles are over. Fiscal and social questions, Giddens believes, are now separate, and the role of government now has much to do with supporting personal and sexual freedom. This is the 'radicalism' of Third Way politics, that 'accepts the logic of 1989 and after' and sees that left and right are of declining or changing significance. Government must be rebalanced in relation to the economy and civil society, to ensure investment in human capital and respect for diversity.

Some of these may be acceptable sorts of prescriptions. But there is a fundamental political problem. A diverse society in which there is the capacity for all to fulfil their potential is a welcome idea. But how do we get there? The fundamental claim of socialism was that we could only get there by restructuring society away from capitalistic forms of accumulation, since these were understood as fundamentally in contradiction with the open and free development of all. That was why much of socialist theory was devoted to analysing the forces of opposition that would reject such a social model, and that would have enough structurally embedded power to do so. The Third Way (of Blair, of Giddens and of the techno-futurists of *MT*) has no conflictual edge, and cannot devise what used to be called a 'theory of transition'. Instead it sees the transition as already achieved, as already incipient in the flows of social change. Thus the belief is that we will get there simply by moving from an old politics of equality to a new politics of lifestyle. What is ruled out is the possibility that this might just be the way in which we are tied back into the 'old' forms of power, that this democratisation might in fact be a capitulation to marketisation. The Third Way theory of politics does not think in terms of collectives or movements but of individuals (albeit ones sometimes ensconced in communities, though these are moral before they are political). But of course this does not mean that individuals no longer need to be managed, and for third-wayers the market is the mechanism to do it.

Marketisation or democratisation
An economy fundamentally understood as a kind of entity unto itself will direct us more than we direct it. And when that economy is over-

whelmingly focused on the sphere of consumption, indeed on the necessity of consumption, then the logic of consumerism and consumer choice will blend into other areas of social and political life with marked effects. It means that liberation offered with one hand can be accompanied by increased control from the other. Some have expressed confusion at the government's twin instincts of devolving and decentralising power at the same time as tightening control.[68] But these are moments of the same process. The industrial revolution made necessary demands for greater freedom from the absolutist state and the development of individual autonomy. It also necessitated forcing people to take the opportunities offered them by a free labour market. Teaching people to read freed them from a feudal clerisy, but it also required restrictions on how much subversive literature they could read. Opening up education to the free choice of parents requires simultaneous specification and standardisation of the goods on offer. Schools therefore have to draw on a universal curriculum and submit pupils to standardised tests, the results of which can be published in uniform tables. Universities can be opened up to non-traditional entrants but only if their staff submit to uniform measures of assessment, regardless of their actual circumstances, so that choice between them can be free and clear.

This is decentralisation through levelling down. Freedom and democracy are extended through the individualisation of actions, and concomitant limits placed upon the social institutions that get in the way. The other side of the process is the simplification of that which can be chosen and the concentration of power at the top. The public realm is hollowed out and choice reduced to private transactions between service provider and consumer (or politician and voter). In consumer society everything must be reducible to a common currency of exchange. A central authority must assume the responsibility for establishing such a basis for comparison. Where some things are not comparable to others or do not easily submit to simple measurement, they must be made to do so.

This process, of simultaneous centralisation and decentralisation, is reflected in numerous aspects of the New Labour project. It was developed early in the internal party reforms. Here the membership is free to exercise its consumer choice over the goods made available to them by central selection committees. The sense that the party could be about incorporating myriad groups, which could reconfigure the terms of political choice, is lost. The same phenomenon is also apparent in the tendency to engage in direct populist appeals from leader to people, and the fancy for citizens juries and focus groups. But these, to quote *Renewal* editor Paul Thompson, 'cannot be the sole or main bridge between government and an active society. When combined with the seeming tendency to heavily manage the selection and performance of Party representatives, new Labour is in danger of producing an ever sharper contradiction between centralised Party and decentralised public polity'.[69] People get consulted directly but only on specific and limited matters.

This can also be seen, very clearly, in one of the central areas where New Labour has made a great effort to open up and 'democratise' the government: e-democracy. For modernisers, information technology and the internet hold out the promise of reconnecting people to politics. But there seems to be a split purpose here. On the one hand e-government means modernising government services, improving the relations and the flow of information between them; on the other, it means using the internet as an access point or portal for users. Here the talk is of customers, and the use of new technology as a means of democratic empowerment allowing access to relevant information. This sometimes extends into wholesale exhortations on the virtues of 'digital democracy', and new methods of citizen participation, such as smart card voting systems, which have been tried out in local elections in Manchester.[70] Along with this there have been numerous attempts at new sorts of consultation: 'Citizens' juries, citizens' panels, visioning, community planning and other such terms have all become part of the everyday language of modern local government, and have crossed over into other parts of the public sector.'[71] Consultation is one of the key principles of the 'Best Value' framework, set up as part of new legislation on modernising local government. But, as Pratchett shows, these moves do not emerge from a simple commitment to democratisation, but from a confluence of agendas that also include the commitment to a customer orientation and the need to secure legitimacy. When citizens panels gather together a statistically representative group of residents to seek their views through surveys, a form of consultation takes place but not necessarily participation. Citizens juries that hear and evaluate policy options have no statutory power, although they may allow participants to develop knowledge and may break the closed loop of policy networks. But on the whole these sorts of initiative draw on focus groups and other marketing techniques. They derive from the shift to a customer-orientation in the public sector in the 1980s.

This conception of democracy is predicated on assumptions about the virtues of individualism and choice that are analogous to those of the market. It indicates an attachment to the principles of market freedom, and a hostility to intermediate collective political institutions. Committed to inclusivity, New Labour does not like institutions that get in the way of the direct relations between individual citizen and their political market choice – just as neo-liberals claim not to like anything that gets in the way of the individual consumer and their purchase. Thus there is a dislike of any arrangement or institution that perpetuates 'out-dated' forms of 'sectarian' identity and organisation, since they hinder the formation of a single coherent collective out of a society made up of differentiated individuals. There must be an imme- diate relationship between party and membership. The capacities of trade unions or LEAs to mediate the relationship of individual to service provider must be restricted because they distort market choice.

Such 'marketisation' is antithetical to democratisation. Marketisation implies that it is enough for the individual simply to make a political purchase from the range of choices already available, and encourages a form of politics oriented towards preference accom- modation rather than preference shaping. But true democratisation involves expanding the range of choices conceivable, making it possible to change the terms of choice and to alter the range of options available. This is why sectional institutions and collective organisations that provide spaces for ongoing debate are crucial to democratic societies. Without them we really would be faced by fickle mob rule and the tyranny of the majority. Democracy is not reducible to the aggregation of individual market choices. It is a transformative process that can alter ways of thinking about society and our place within it.

Conclusion

This chapter has looked at some of the specifically British intellectual elements woven into the Third Way. It has been argued that the key to it is a form of sociological analysis that has a tendency towards a tech- nological futurism. This shapes policy. For example, the drive of welfare reform to include people in the game of risk, the encourage- ment of entrepreneurialism and the obsession with the high-tech and design economy.[72] Thus, any demand for Labour to present a coherent political philosophy will not be met. The Third Way derives its argu- ments from a sociological assessment and not a philosophical one. All these claims are based on grasping the truth about how society works and how it is changing. This is a deep-rooted political mindset, for which political theory is, as Mulgan has it, redolent of 'the cloying atmosphere of the seminar room', interested only in abstract 'generali- sations' and not really political at all. Without the Third Way sociological mind-set, 'society is viewed from outside, without any sense of membership or responsibility'.[73]

The Third Way can simply be dismissed on the grounds that it is empty and bland. More sophisticated critiques might argue that it is intellectually or logically inconsistent.[74] A political denunciation can, of course, simply argue that it represents a complete capitulation to the New Right, a point that seems well founded when Tony Blair and Gerhard Schroeder argue that the new social democracy must set itself the task of creating 'a positive climate for entrepreneurial independence and initiative', and that 'small businesses must become easier to set up and better able to survive'.[75] But this does not, on its own, constitute a grounded criticism. However weak critics may find the Third Way, and the ideology of New Labour, they will get nowhere by refusing to take seriously what is being argued. The Third Way is not simply cynical spin, and the very fact that its advocates exist, and are attempting to present some kind of analysis, is surely evidence of this. Arguments that it is inconsistent are on surer ground, but they do not necessarily undermine the Third Way in total. It is quite possible for the arguments of the Third Way to be unclear and insufficiently sophisticated, without their being erroneous in their entirety. Meanwhile simple political denunciations are useless. The claim of the Third Way is that old style socialism and social democracy are redundant. Therefore, any criticisms that base themselves simply on the assertion that they are not and they are good and workable political models will fail to hit the mark.

Rather, the Third Way needs to be assessed on its own terms, but without capitulation to those terms in advance. For example, we can ask if the conviction that an adequate social scientific analysis of society is the place from which to formulate political ideas is acceptable. Although Giddens' sociology is not simply functionalist, it is interested in the way social systems function and in how they shape the experiences and responses of human beings understood as self-conscious actors. Combined with the kind of Marxist functionalism I suggested was implicit within strands of 'New Times', the Third Way forms a politics based on the fallacy of empirical sociology – that social trends are always clearly identifiable and neutral phenomena as long as you have enough statistics. The point then becomes to establish these social or economic trends so that they may create rational policy. The result is a tendency to accept economic developments (e.g. globalisation or de-industrialisation) as non-political, even natural, phenomena. This blunts analysis and conflicts with aspirations for social change. It also leaves political activity in a paradoxical condition. On the one hand the state cannot be understood as a body capable of directing the actions of individuals –and this is both impossible and undesirable; but, at the same time, the state has the responsibility of ensuring certain social conditions and enabling people to respond to the new environment. This is *not* simple neo-liberalism. Indeed, one of the key aspects of the Third Way is a recognition that deregulation of markets can undermine or corrode the social conditions that make the functioning of markets possible. But where social democrats might once have seen the role of the state in terms of taking over from markets, in order to avoid the fallout associated with them, Third Way thinkers reject this option because it would restrict the market and because it is out of tune with the new aspirations of post-fordist citizens. But they also reject any conservative nostalgia for a time past when women did not go out to work, and a certain orderliness could be based on deference and subordination. Instead they speak of encouraging the 'responsibilities' of citizens, and the combination of a strong economy with social solidarity, since these are, in fact, natural partners. As Tony Blair and Gerhard Schroeder put it, social democracy has 'found new acceptance because it stands not only for social justice but also for economic dynamism and the unleashing of creativity and innovation'.[76] Here the emphasis, yet again, is on updating policy instruments for a changed world and moving beyond the old ideas about state intervention, but this is clearly allied to a moral agenda. The 'universalist' approach, it is argued, undermined the individual's responsibility for themselves and their obligations to others. Blair and Schroeder endorse the idea of a market economy but balance this with the rejection of a market society. Politics therefore, they say, has to change. Politicians must use 'best practice' and 'search for practical solutions to their problems through honest well-constructed and pragmatic policies'.[77] They must be as flexible and adaptive as voters have to be. The justification for such policies, however, is the veracity of the analysis of the social trends which it leaves untouched. In this sense, the Third Way is conceptually dependent on a repression of the possibility that social change is something to which politics responds by directing rather than ameliorating. It is not able to conceive of politics as the activity by which a society collectively decides on the way in which it should live and the courses of action to achieve it. The way we live (the fundamental, even foundational, ethical-political question) is thus (and this is typical of contemporary liberalism) left out of politics. Instead the way we live is simply derived from the way things are. But, of course, a normative aspect does (as it must) creep back in, since it implies that the way we should live is in accordance with the social arrangements that have simply developed around us. Thus, the Third Way departs from a simple liberal refusal to allow government to be concerned with fundamental values. Instead it insists that there cannot be such universal values in a pluralized and pluralizing society. But it also argues that there have to be such values if society is to cohere and be capable of maintaining systems of social support as well as economic dynamism. So the Third Way leads one to argue for the transparency and downscaling of state institutions (their opening up) but also for personal responsibility.[78]

This is related to the ontological assumptions in Giddens' theory of the need for security, which lead to his arguments about the reformulation of solidarity. Combined with the parts of the *Marxism Today* analysis that emphasised the uprooting of social relations caused by Thatcherite neo-liberalism and called for a reconstitution of public interest, this leads to a pre-occupation with developing some overarching sense of unified identity. We see this in the elements of national populism that Labour has played around with, but also in an obsession with the reconstitution of some notion of community. There is an element of Giddens that is concerned with the classical sociological 'problem of social order'. In framing the question of how to account for order in society and its maintenance, it is a short step to regarding society as itself the phenomenon of social order, and sociology as the mechanism for grasping the principles of such order. A group of post-Marxists who believe they have grasped the direction of the productive forces might tend towards incorporating this in a way that leads to a conception of government as the business of shaping us all up for the new world, forcing us to be reflexive. This feeds back into the Third Way conception of politics.

Giddens, the *MT* writers and latterly third-way thinkers talk a lot about the reconstitution or reinvention of politics. As I tried to show above, part of the New Times analysis involved the development of a concept of politics as the ontological condition of society. Politics was understood as existing in all social relations, in a plurality of spaces and in competing forms of identity. But this perspective emphasised the constitutive nature of conflict. The technological futurists did not complete this move away from Marxism, and in the Third Way this expansion of politics becomes a normative claim deriving from the ontology of the present. In a sense politics becomes a particular form of managerial reflexivity.

The crucial difference this makes was noted by Perry Anderson, in response to Giddens' earlier arguments about dialogic democracy. Anderson argued that this conception tends to downplay (even deny) the presence of structurally induced interests, in favour of an open ended dialogue wherein people are expected to modify their interests (in the interest of dialogue) if not to actually leave them at the door. Concepts of politics as strategy, as a contest for power, or resources of power, are thereby lost and replaced by the search for a new popular consensus that can accord with the given drift of the global economy. The Third Way understands politics to be the technocratic application of a certain form of knowledge. It is therefore absolutely essential for it to conceive of the social world as a collection of individuals and families rather than power blocs or coalitions of interests, since the latter would invalidate their conception. Politics can then apply itself to managing the relations of and between these people, because they can't any longer do it for themselves. But for the same reasons government is not in a position to do much either. The end result of this kind of thinking is the Third Way conception of politics and society as symbiotic, each needing the other for any security or legitimacy of existence. Government and people alike must be reflexive actors.

The combination of elements at work here leads to a sense of historical mission, legitimated by an ontology derived from an interpretation of our historical context, which believes that not only does this context generate the right conditions for economic transformation, but it is also the source of legitimacy for it, or rather the place where legitimacy will be constructed. Such solipsism can be dangerous and is the hallmark of repressive ideologies that base themselves on a notion of destiny, or derive their claims from some external, given, cause. In the form of fascism or of communism this has legitimated all manner of social destruction.

The Third Way, needless to say, does not quite work in this way. It is not fascistic or totalitarian. Those ideologies were essentially millenarian or eschatological in their narrativisation. They cast themselves as the heroes of their own stories, the ones blessed with insight into the movement of class struggle or the true spirit of the people. They saw their task as that of leading the people into the promised land. The Third Way (true, in a way, to its stunted Marxist roots) sees the change as already upon us. Its role is not to lead us into the promised land but to follow us, mopping up the stragglers. This sense of the agency of government does not work by constituting a bloc which can then employ the resources of power upon a population, and against those who oppose it. Rather it reshapes from the ground up – a strategy about which third-wayers are quite explicit. Where 'old' ideologies, including fascism and communism but also social democracy and neo-liberalism, directed themselves at management of the overall productivity of the nation, this is no longer seen as a valid object of political strategy. Communism and fascism could see the social world as a vast productive enterprise to be ordered and directed by the state. But the Third Way sees the productive activity of society as already taken care of within its own terms. Government has to act to service that productive aspect and ensure the conditions that sustain it. It is no longer the base of the CEO of UK plc; it is the personnel management department. Thus the emphasis of political activity shifts from economic instruments and towards the cultivation of techniques oriented to smoothing out the social space. It turns to issues of crime, family morality, and 'the quality of life', and becomes 'etho-politics', where, as Nik Rose puts it, 'life itself, as it is lived in its everyday manifestations, is the object of adjudication'.[79] Thus, for example, 'Modernising the police is about much more than extra money and new technology, it is about modernising attitudes as well'[80]. Threats and penalties to be awarded to the welfare recipient are attempts to induce certain forms of behaviour, to change the outlook and culture of the people concerned.[80] It is neither accident or sentiment that has made the primary policy concerns of New Labour education and welfare, with both legitimated by reference to their central role in sustaining the economy (See Chapter Four).

Through this new 'technology' of 'governmentality', we are 'enabled' to become self-regulating, our progress and direction monitored through the setting of parameters of action assessed through the agencies of state governance. This individual-oriented strategy combines with the general re-structuring of state and government, such that 'joined-up government' demands an internal reflection by agencies upon their own efficiency, measured by their ability to generate and draw on the resources of contemporary social scientific research and knowledge. Government becomes an information hub. We access our welfare rights through kiosk technology and by paying attention to television advertisements; school-teachers are updated on the latest findings; 'best practice' is disseminated throughout the medical profession. This feeds back into the process of legitimation since it finds and forges a new role for government. No longer will it intervene directly to halt the disruptive actions of capitalist enterprises, nor will it find cash to inject into failing public services. But it will gather and circulate 'evidence based research'.[82] Government, too, must put itself up for continual reinvention, receiving validation through continually grounding itself in the effectiveness of its outcomes as assessed by us, the consumers of the governance state. The practice of Total Quality Management in the firm extends into government and out into the management of communities. Just as personnel managers have been encouraged to see their working environments as active communities, so the community becomes a kind of firm that will cohere only if the patterns and flows of control and participation are correctly administered. By happy coincidence, for the discourse of Blairism, the old divisions of society, economy and state are gone. The management of the economy, the protection and development of communities, the freedom and security of individuals, all become part of one overall process of setting things free to thrive in the ever changing world of global financial transfer.

Thus politics disappears. The social world is conceived as a smooth surface comprised of an infinite number of activities and operations. The agents of those operations are freed to undertake them, but only under the condition that they conform to the requirements of modernisation. Thus, crucially, politics (or governance) directs itself at the agents – us, the subjects of New Labour.

Notes

1. Paul Whiteley and Patrick Seyd (1999) 'Slow Collapse', *Guardian* 5.10.
2. See Patrick Seyd and Paul Whiteley (2001) 'New Labour and the Party: Members and Organisation', in Steve Ludlam and Martin J. Smith (eds), *New Labour in Government*, Basingstoke, Macmillan, pp89-90.
3. Tony Blair (1998), *The Third Way: New Politics for a New Century*, London, The Fabian Society, pp15-17.
4. Anthony Giddens (1998), *The Third Way: The Renewal of Social Democracy*, Cambridge, Polity, pp69-78.
5. See for example Andrew Gamble (1998), 'After the Watershed, the Conservative Eclipse', in Anne Coddington and Mark Perryman (eds.), *The Moderniser's Dilemma*, London, Lawrence and Wishart, pp15-31; Stewart Wood (1999) 'Constitutional Reform – living with the consequences', *Renewal*, 7 (3), pp1-10.
6. See Democratic Leadership Council-Progressive Policy Institute (1996), *The New Progressive Declaration*, Washington DC, DLC-PPI.
7. Tony Blair (1998) *The Third Way: New Politics for a New Century*, London, The Fabian Society, pp6-7.
8. Colin Crouch (2000) *Coping with Post-democracy*, London, Fabian Society.
9. Claus Offe (1996) *Modernity and the State, East–West*, London, Polity, pp vii-viii:
10. On the ways in which soap operas intersect with everyday talk about everyday issues see Christine Geraghty (1991) *Women and Soap Opera*, Cambridge, Polity; Mary Ellen Brown (1994) *Soap Opera and Women's Talk*, London, Sage. For a more positive assessment of talk shows see Sonia Livingstone and Peter Lunt (1994) *Talk on Television: Audience Participation and Public Debate*, London Routledge.
11. See Colin Crouch (2000), pp22-36.
12. See the excellent third chapter in Colin Hay (1999) *The Political Economy of New Labour*, Manchester, Manchester University Press, pp94, 96.
13. 'When I go to vote I am doing something similar but not identical to what I do when I go shopping. In both cases I "buy" what I "want" ... there are obvious differences between the cases ... but they are similar enough for the public choice analyst to have things worth saying about the citizen's decisions of whether and how to vote, and also about what politicians,

bureaucrats and pressure groups do' (Iain McLean (1989) *Public Choice: An Introduction*, Oxford, Blackwell, pp9-10).

14. Anthony Downs (1967) *Inside Bureaucracy*, Boston, Little, Brown and Company.
15. Paul Starr (1988) 'The Meaning of Privatization', *Yale Law and Policy Review*, 6, pp6-41.
16. Quoted in John Clarke and Janet Newman (1997) *The Managerial State*, London, Sage, p144.
17. Colin Hay (1997) 'Anticipating Accommodations, Accommodating anticipations: The Appeasement of Capital in the Modernisation of the British Labour Party', *Politics and Society*, Vol. 25, No. 2, pp235-6. See also the revised version that makes up chapter 5 in his (1999) book *The Political Economy of New Labour*, Manchester, Manchester University Press.
18. Peter Burnham (2001) 'New Labour and the Politics of depoliticisation', *British Journal of Politics and International Relations*, Vol. 3, No. 2, p139.
19. John Clarke and Janet Newman (1997) *The Managerial State*, London, Sage, p92.
20. This is well summarised in ibid, pp109-112.
21. J. Potter (1994), quoted in ibid, pp108-9.
22. Ibid, p123.
23. Eric Hobsbawm (2001) 'Democracy can be Bad for You' *New Statesman*, 5.3.
24. See Stuart Hall and Martin Jacques (eds) (1989) *New Times*, London, Lawrence and Wishart.
25. L. Terry (1997) 'Travelling the Hard Road to Renewal: A Continuing Conversation with Stuart Hall, *Arena Journal*, 8, p55.
26. See Stuart Hall (1988) *The Hard Road to Renewal: Thatcherism and the Crisis of the* Left, London, Verso.
27. Stuart Hall (1987) 'Gramsci and Us', *Marxism Today*, June, pp16-21.
28. Stuart Hall (1998) 'The Great Moving Nowhere Show', *Marxism Today*, 1998, pp9-14.
29. Chantal Mouffe (1998) 'The Radical Centre: A Politics Without Adversary', *Soundings*, No 9.
30. Hall (1998) p10.
31. *Marxism Today*, October1991.
32. Tony Blair (1991) *Marxism Today*, p32.
33. Ibid. p34.
34. *Marxism Today* (1998) October, p3.
35. *Manifesto For New Times* (1989) p7. This was a document produced by the CPGB itself, not the *Marxism Today* group; it was influenced by the 'New Times' analysis, but was also the product of compromise with other views within the party.
36. Ibid, p26.

37. *Marxism Today* (1988) October p3.
38. *Marxism Today* (1988) p15.
39. Ian Hargreaves and Ian Christie (eds) (1998) *Tomorrow's Politics*, pp1-10.
40. See e.g. Ernesto Laclau (1987) 'Class War and After', *Marxism Today*, April, pp30-33.
41. Charles Leadbeater (1988), 'Power to the Person', *Marxism Today*, October, p14.
42. Ernesto Laclau (1987) p31.
43. Hall (1987) p vii
44. Hall (1998) p9.
45. Geoff Mulgan (1997) 'Introduction' in Geoff Mulgan (ed) *Life After Politics: new thinking for a new century*, London, Fontana, pp x, xii.
46. Anthony Giddens (2000) *The Third Way and Its Critics*, Cambridge, Polity, p28.
47. Ibid. p32.
48. Anthony Giddens (1996) *In Defence of Sociology*, Cambridge, Polity, p247.
49. See Anthony Giddens (1996) 'The Labour Party and British Politics', in *In Defence of Sociology*, Cambridge, Polity, pp240-271.
50. Anthony Giddens (1994) *Beyond Left and Right*, Cambridge, Polity, pp10; 27-30.
51. Anthony Giddens (1996) *In Defence of Sociology*, Cambridge, Polity, pp3, 6.
52. Anthony Giddens (1984) *The Constitution of Society*, Cambridge, Polity, p xxxv; Anthony Giddens (1991) *The Consequences of Modernity*, Cambridge, Polity, p15.
53. Giddens (1984) p2.
54. Ibid. p2.
55. Giddens (1984), pp5-6.
56. Ibid. p3.
57. Giddens (1996) p18.
58. Ibid. p46.
59. See Giddens (1991); (1996).
60. Giddens (1996) p28.
61. Anthony Giddens (1998) *The Third Way*, Cambridge, Polity, p37.
62. Ibid. pp99-101.
63. Ibid. p101.
64. *Social Justice: Strategies for Renewal, The Report of the Commission on Social Justice*, London, Vintage, 1994.
65. Ruth Levitas (1996) 'The Concept of Social Exclusion and the New Durkheimian Hegemony', *Critical Social Policy*, pp5-20.
66. Giddens (2000) p38.
67. Ibid. p40.

68. David Marquand (1998) 'The Blair Paradox', in *Prospect*, 30, pp19-24.
69. Paul Thompson (1998) 'Editorial Commentary: Changing the People', *Renewal*, 6, 3, p6.
70. See Rachel Silcock (2001) 'What is E-Government' in *Parliamentary Affairs*, Vol. 54, pp88-101.
71. Lawrence Pratchett (1999) 'New Fashions in Public Participation: Towards Greater Democracy ?', *Parliamentary Affairs*, Vol. 52, 4, pp616-633.
72. See also Stephen Driver and Luke Martell (1998) *New Labour: The Politics of Post-Thatcherism*, Cambridge, Polity, pp41-46.
73. See Geoff Mulgan (1998) 'Whinge and a Prayer', *Marxism Today*, 1998, pp15-16.
74. See, for example, Alan Carling (1999), 'Labour's Third Way', *Imprints*, 3, 3.
75. Tony Blair and Gerhard Schroder (1999), *Europe: The Third Way – Die Neue Mitte*, London, Labour Party and SPD, p5.
76. Ibid, p1.
77. Ibid, p3.
78. See Anthony Giddens (2000), *The Third Way and its Critics*, Cambridge, Polity, p56.
79. Nikolas Rose (1999) 'Inventiveness in Politics', *Economy and Society*, Vol. 28 (3), pp477-8.
80. Jack Straw (1999) *Speech to Labour Party Conference*.
81. Frank Field (1997) 'Re-Inventing Welfare: A response to Lawrence Mead' in Alan Deacon (ed) *From Welfare to Work: Lessons from America*, London Institute for Economic Affairs, 1997, cited in Desmond King and Mark Whickam Jones (1999) 'From Clinton to Blair: The Democratic (Party) Origins of Welfare to Work', *Political Quarterly*, Vol. 70, No. 1, p71.
82. See John Lloyd (1999) 'A New Style of Governing', *New Statesman*, 4.10, pp12-13.

CHAPTER FIVE

The Subject, Citizenship and Welfare

This chapter examines political theories of 'the subject', using them to help our analysis of New Labour while showing that they have fed into the discourse or philosophy of New Labour itself. Because New Labour attempts to address the complex relationships between the individual, society and the state (wanting to steer a middle course between unbridled individualism and strict collectivism), it is drawn to ways of harmonising the potentially conflictual relationship between the individual and society, believing it can and should resolve the opposition between them. This is manifested in a particular conception of citizenship (shaped by the concept of social capital), and expressed in policies intended to increase 'social inclusion' through incorporation into the labour market. These suggest that New Labour operates with a particular, implicit, concept of 'the subject'; one that is presupposed by this emerging political discourse, and towards which policies aim.

To make sense of this we will first consider theories of the political subject, especially in relation to concepts of citizenship. Then we will examine the idea of 'social capital' opening the way into a longer look at the ways in which New Labour has responded to so-called 'crises' of the welfare state. This will prepare the ground for a fuller consideration of welfare and economic policies in Chapter Five.

Contemporary theories of the political subject

The changeability and instability of current forms of social life (to which the third way is meant to be a response) have made questions of subjectivity (our grasp of ourselves as selves) and identity (the particular sort of self we imagine we are) that much more salient. Because we are exposed to the lifestyles, habits, views, opinions, cultural practices and values of so many different social groups (we meet each other in our cities, see each other on television, read about each other in newspapers, consume each other's movies and music), the culture we might once have called our own begins to feel less secure and more contingent, its once apparent naturalness challenged by the mere existence of something other. Furthermore, as Giddens argues, the re-structuring and de-structuring of 'traditional' forms of life (which includes, it should be said, the end of once secure communities built up around industries such as mining or steel production), and their replacement with transient and fragile forms of work and social organisation (or nothing at all), exposes once stable frameworks of identity as 'mere' habits. This, in turn, occasions new forms of questioning about who and what we are, since even this can no longer be taken for granted.

Because of this increasing dislocation within social life, recent movements within political theory and political sociology have come to recognise the ways in which ideologies and movements depend upon particular notions of the agent and object of political strategy, and turn upon claims regarding identity. Similarly, they have come to study the ways in which systems of social regulation can function to 'produce' particular sorts of subject. We might go so far as to say that the concept of the subject is central to contemporary political analysis.

That said, while concepts of the subject can be found employed across theories of politics, sociology, literature, history and so on, there is no unanimity about its meaning. 'Subject' does not meant 'self' in a straightforward way. Nor is it a synonym for identity (although this can be a closely related concept). Rather, the concept of subject refers us to a series of particular configurations of what (or who) a self or an identity is. A self becomes a subject by grasping itself in certain ways. This is why there is an affinity between notions of the subject and concepts of human nature. The idea of 'human nature' as an object of study has been one of the central ways in which an understanding of the subject has been framed (and it is one that persists in the current vogue for 'evolutionary psychology', which, its proponents believe, gives to public policy a solid and scientific basis). But many critical theories emphasise their discontinuity with concepts of human nature, understanding the subject as a construct of some kind rather than an *a priori* essence. It follows that there can be a history of subjectivity, in that humans have not at all times and in all places exercised or shaped consciousness of themselves in the same way. Such a history is, in large part, not a history of the subject, but of the discourses, the cognitive frameworks – such as that of 'human nature' – through which subjectivity is grasped, experienced and acted upon. One does not have to be a pure Hegelian to accept the point that: 'the opposition between subjectivity and objectivity ... had not yet come up in Plato's age. The independence of the "I" within itself and its explicit existence was foreign to him; man had not yet gone back within himself, had not yet set himself forth as explicit ... the fact that man is in and for himself free, in his essence and as man, free born, was known neither by Plato, Aristotle, Cicero, nor the Roman legislators ...'.[1] That is to say, a concept of subjectivity, of selves grasping themselves as such, becomes possible when (long before Giddens) we find ourselves no longer cushioned by simple theologies, superstitions and traditions. Exposed to the 'vertigo' of the modern, we are 'free' to begin to grasp ourselves as we are, or as we might be; to become our own makers. This was how the modern 'liberal' subject was born. The emergence of notions of (implicitly) secular freedom allowed humans to think in, of and on themselves; to try and establish what is them and what is not, what is part of their free will and what is not. In the history of political thought, therefore, the concept of the subject is deeply involved with concepts of liberty and citizenship. To be a subject one must be free, but one is free only because one is a citizen, which is to say because one is subjected (in)to some form of state.

The political idea of a subject, then, begins not with Descartes's conception of an isolated mind grasping its own existence but with Kant, in whose theorisation the liberty of the free subject is won only when a free republic subjected to the universal law is established.[2] The subject is thus founded out of a kind of split – free but only in as much as it is able to achieve consciousness of this freedom via its membership of a polity which subjects the free subject to the categorical imperative. With Hegel the 'split' is understood in terms of an alienation which will be overcome historically through the identification of the individual with a political community or state. In this respect both Kant and Hegel owe a debt to Rousseau, who so strongly expressed the experience of this paradoxical condition. For him the individual, alienated by the falsity of modern life, becomes free only in the moment of accepting subjection to the General Will of the communal state. The Marxian twist on this was to extend the Hegelian historical schema and to locate the alienation of the subject in the exploitation of labour and thus within the context of the specific socio-economic system that was founded upon it.

In a sense, to simplify much more than a little, all of these positions turn on a fundamental problem. The individual, in order to be free and able to realise his/her full potential (perhaps their *telos*), must be part of a community, engaging and being with others. But this undermines the autonomy of the individual. Hence the penetrating force of Rousseau's question regarding how one can be free and a citizen at the same time. This problematic persists in contemporary Western thought and has recently been replayed in the 'debate' between liberals and communitarians.[3] Giddens, meanwhile, has given it a sociological twist. 'Reflexive modernisation', deriving from de-traditionalisation, condemns individuals to a life in which they have 'no choice but to choose' in their search for 'ontological security', and this new individualism requires new forms of state. For Giddens, as for some 'postmodernists' (though with further inflections), this generates a greater role for politics centred on identity, since the subject is now a self permanently trying to grasp itself and its world and this must be the basis on which political structures are founded. The freedom of the subject to define itself for itself is understood as greatly extended, but this also presents all sorts of new risks and anxieties.

But while there is agreement among many that the increased scope, scale and dislocation of social and cultural life causes or allows a proliferation of anxieties and claims about identity, there is less agreement about what this means for politics. For Giddens and others (as we have seen), it makes possible new forms of freedom. The state should facilitate and assist individuals by generating the capacities to help them cope and flourish in the new environment. For some strands of postmodern political thinking, with a self-proclaimed radical agenda, it makes possible a new emancipatory politics centred primarily on axes of identity considered marginalised or suppressed (be they related to ethnicity, gender, sexuality, etc). Here identity politics often comes to be equated with liberation (and there is a link here between this sort of 'postmodernism' and the sociology of Giddens). But the strand of thought deriving from Marx, passing through the Frankfurt School and redirected by forms of poststructuralism, interprets this new freedom very differently. Foucault, for example, understands freedom as the precondition of forms of liberal governance which act not on conduct but on the conduct of conduct. As we 'moderns' have become increasingly conscious of our self-hood, the operations of social power have shifted away from marshalling, punishing and dominating us and towards structuring that very self-consciousness, shaping the ways in which we shape ourselves. Liberal government then, is government by (not in spite of) freedom. The proliferation of forms of identity that is characteristic of modernity and of liberal societies is thus also a proliferation of locations for conflict and subjection.

The relationship between subject and citizen as conceived by, for example, Kant, runs along the axes of state-individual and operates through the law. But in an increasingly complex society there are many more sites of such subjectivity-subjection. As free labourers or workers, for example, we are subjected to the disciplining of the firm. This can take the form of time and motion studies and other such Taylorist methodologies, or of more contemporary systems of control – usually termed personnel management – that act on 'human resources' and operate through inducing self-assessment via the mechanism of permanent performance review, with the consequent anxiety of being declared the 'weakest link'. The family – distanced from 'traditional' societal networks – also becomes a site of intervention, not only by governments, social service agents and family experts, but by ourselves as we eagerly purchase manuals of practical parenting and constantly monitor our own family experiences to ensure they match up to a projected ideal. The function of community in generating secure boundaries to identity becomes displaced from the intensity of closed locality onto the abstraction of the nation, and then onto a much looser framework of 'culture' (be it that of ethnicity, gender, profession, etc), while the market generates forms of consumer-based identity to which we are subjected, and by which – often willingly – we are disciplined. In each case, we might say, a sense of self is turned into a subjectivity by being suborned into a framework within which the practice of self takes place. I come to see myself primarily as a parent, a family member, a worker (or a 'professional'), a man, a subject of sexual desire (maybe even an object of it), a British citizen and so on, or I see all of these as inter-related in special ways that make me what I am. Each is a category of being to which I aspire and on the basis of which I may be classified, evaluated and judged.

This Foucauldian approach has effectively forced us to ask not what political subjects are (the liberal question), but how it is that they get created. Rather than see power as something that exists independently of the rational subject (such that it can be legitimately or illegitimately exercised and one can be shielded from it through rights and so forth), Foucault contends that it is power that constitutes such subjects. 'Rights' and 'responsibilities' are not merely neutral concepts or properties that can be derived from or attached to the independent subject. Rather, they create new kinds of subject, 'subjected' by new formulations and practices of power. For Foucault, liberalism is a particular 'rationality of government', 'a system of thinking about the nature and practice of government ... capable of making some form of that activity thinkable and practicable both to its practitioners and to those upon whom it is practised'.[4] In a liberal political culture, where the subjects of government are formally free, the task of government does not require repressive measures so much as the instilling in subjects of particular sorts or modes of behaviour – or rather the creation of conditions whereby subjects define themselves by their adherence to these behaviours. Thus, following Foucault, Miller and Rose regard government as 'the historically constituted matrix within which are articulated all those dreams, schemes, strategies and manoeuvres of authorities that seek to shape the beliefs and conduct of others in desired directions by acting upon their will, their circumstances or their environment'.[5] For them, 'Power is not so much a matter of imposing constraints upon citizens as of "making up" citizens capable of bearing a kind of regulated freedom. Personal autonomy is not the antithesis of political power but a key term in its exercise, the more so because most individuals are not merely the subjects of power but play a part in its operations'.[6] As such governance entails policies and practices designed to encourage particular forms of subjectivity.

This theoretical position makes it possible to engage in a particular sort of analysis of contemporary British politics. New Labour certainly has a theory of what the modern citizen-subject must be, and the context within which it formulates this is already clear to us. New Labour philosophy is premised on beliefs about the changing nature of social organisation as driven by technological transformation and the globalisation of capital. Just as this shapes the idea of modernisation as a given and non-negotiable process, so too it is out of this nexus of ideas that the New Labour subject emerges. The world is changing and we need to ensure that citizens are able to gear up for it, so that the innate inventiveness of the British population is 'freed to excel once more'. New Labour is also convinced of other social changes, such as the impact of the changing role of women on families and family structures – fully apprised, via Giddens, of the ways in which identity can no longer be taken for granted by anyone. All of these are held to necessitate strategies for the management and creation of new kinds of citizen. Before turning to these strategies (as found in welfare policy) we will consider more closely the connection between the concept of citizenship and the experience of subjectivity.

Citizens, subjects and the welfare state

Being a subject, then, entails a grasp of self in ways intimately, if not exclusively, related to structures of power within, and in relation to, the state. But the subject also has relations with other subjects and is often defined by such relations. It is to questions about this relationship of the subject to other subjects that the concept of citizenship offers an answer, suggesting particular kinds of bond and obligation and tying social relations into the phenomena of the political community. Citizenship (and 'good' citizenship even more so) is an important terrain on which the struggle to manage the relationship between individual freedom and collective necessity is waged, in ways meant to ensure that the very freedom of the citizen is the condition for the good of the whole and vice versa. In political thought we could (and this is only one way) map differing responses to this problem along a continuum from radical forms of republicanism to extreme forms of liberal individualism.

Within a republican schema, the subject-citizen is absorbed into a collective subject as a condition of free citizenship, and the interests of the two are held to coincide. This powerful and influential way of thinking has played a part in shaping the ideologies of socialism and Marxism (for whom Rousseau is a particular sort of influence). But, as is well known, it can shade into totalitarian forms of thought, inasmuch as the absolute unity of the individual with the communal good may legitimate the exclusion or eradication of those deemed insufficiently compatible with the needs of the commonwealth. The community can be conceived as a kind of 'super-subject', the needs of which outweigh all others. This can tip into a kind of nationalism, where the interests of the nation are taken to be the precondition of the interests of all and the primary concern of state activity is the maintenance of the health and purity of the national body politic.

At the other end of the political scale are those strains of libertarianism for which the freedom of the individual is guaranteed only so long as he/she is able to have absolutely nothing to do with the state. Here citizenship may even be regarded as an unjust burden. This is a very English strain of political thinking, which still plays a part in the ideologies mixed up in the Tory Party. But such an ideology recognises that there may be threats to individual freedom, and so is not averse to advocating the deployment of state apparatuses to protect it. In England this too can tip over into a kind of nationalism, when the essence of the nation is identified with this kind of liberty, and the defence of national culture becomes identified with a struggle to maintain individual liberty. But more often libertarianism falls back on an appeal to the mythical, even mystical, 'invisible hand' that ensures that spontaneous order is the outcome of the combination of all our self-interested individual acts (this is the neo-liberal version of the spontaneous order anarchists imagine would come about if only the state were abolished).

It has been the task of forms of liberal thought (especially the socially oriented liberal thought to which Blair has expressed allegiance) to try and occupy this set of contradictions and hold the gap between republicanism and individualism. Here citizenship assumes a very special position. It is not just a legal condition or status, but a practice. The individual is a free citizen and able to act according to conscience, but it follows (in either Kantian or Hegelian fashion) that the conscience must work in ways that recognise the supremacy of universal over particular interests or identities. Thus, while classical liberalism rejects the strong communitarianism of the republican tradition (and, in any case, the vast scale of modern political communities makes such unity impossible to attain), the question of civic virtue is not ignored. Mandeville and Smith answered the problem by showing how the individual pursuit of self-interest could be a citizenly duty since, in the long run, it would produce collective benefits (so long as carried out within a reasonable framework of duties and bound by common law).[7] In the late nineteenth-century such thinking was revived in new ways suited to a new mass industrial society. For Durkheim, for example, the very division of labour could be the basis for generating the bonds of social solidarity, underpinned by a rational civil law and a professional ethical code of conduct.[8] Then, as patterns of class conflict and potential social disorder forced the growth of more interventionist and welfare oriented states, the question of citizenship and its practice became tied into the actions of this sort of state.

This brings us to the famous and influential narrative of citizenship developed by T.H Marshall.[9] Marshall divided citizenship into three components, which emerged over a long time-span: civil, political and social. Civil aspects of citizenship encompassed various forms of rights, such as those to speech, ownership, justice and so forth, protecting the individual from unjust despotism. Then the political aspects of citizenship grew, under which the citizen had the right to participate in political power (through voting for example). The third development was that of social rights. These were concerned not only with equality of income but with bringing about 'a general enrichment of the concrete substance of civilised life, a general reduction of risk and insecurity, an equalisation between the more and less fortunate ...'.[10] To these there corresponded institutions – courts, parliament and the educational and social welfare systems – such that the extension of the role of the state was part of the growth of citizenship into a guarantee of a certain level of dignity and status.

The context in which Marshall developed this analysis was, of course, that of post-war Keynesian Britain. As such his concept of citizenship was part of an attempt to combine amelioration of the corrosive effects of capitalism and inequality with maintenance of the basis to social unity: 'a direct sense of community membership based on loyalty to a civilisation which is a common possession'.[11] Social rights and the welfare state were part of a process of civilising society and its members, furthering their liberty, by enabling them to live secure lives, while tying them into a new kind of social contract that bonded citizens to each other as well as to the state. In this way the interests of individuals and of society could be understood as united.

New Labour finds itself living through the aftermath of the collapse of this settlement and at the present end of a long line of criticisms of state-led welfare systems that fed into the end of the Keynesian 'consensus'. In a way both left-wing and right-wing critiques of the welfare state in the post-war period agreed on the claim that it was incompatible with capitalism. For the neo-liberals, such as Hayek and Friedman, state provision of welfare undermined freedom, distorted markets and created a dependency in those who used it most. For left radicals it could also be seen as undermining capitalist growth, thus demonstrating the need for socialism; and for some it was seen as a compromise with capitalism allowing it to survive beyond its historically allotted life span. Other, more detached, analysts pointed to the way in which the welfare state undermined its own legitimacy by creating an expanded and better off middle class that no longer needed it and were thus less willing to pay for it. Meanwhile soft-left critiques drew attention to the ways in which welfare and social work could function as repressive state apparatuses practising techniques of normalisation.

By the time of the economic crises of the 1970s and 1980s, analysts such as Offe were pointing to the way in which crises of capitalism were becoming crises of the welfare state, causing the state in general to lose legitimacy. By the end of the 1980s analysts such as Lash and Urry could describe the growth of a 'less bureaucratic, more decentralised and in some cases more privatised form, as the welfare state of organised capitalism makes way for a much more varied and less centrally organised form of welfare provision in disorganised capitalism'.[12] Such analyses were matched in the real world by the reforms associated with the New Right and with Thatcherism in Britain. At the same time, in the workplace itself, analysts were claiming to observe increased individualisation in the relationship between employer and employee, with union activity and membership declining and 'an increased emphasis on individual mechanisms of control and monitoring, such as those inherent to systems of human resource management, total quality management and indeed many systems of employee involvement'.[13]

The development of New Labour took place against this backdrop: varying yet sometimes converging critiques of the welfare state; the reforms of the Thatcher years and the social changes that were put forward as the cause or effect of them; and changing workplace practices. By the time it took power, market mechanisms had already been introduced into welfare delivery, the role of the state was apparently being reduced and a general drive was underway (at the rhetorical level at least) to 'liberate' the voluntary impulse and to reconstitute 'community'. New Labour has interpreted such changes as not only irreversible but as the inevitable product of particular social transformations. It has also incorporated into its analysis the individualist critique of welfare advanced by sections of both the left and right, and added to it a contemporary human-resource management strategy, individualising mechanisms of monitoring and control. In the Blairite welfare state there will only be 'something for something'. Those who play by the rules will be rewarded and supported by the welfare state. At the same time criminal justice and policing are understood as a part of social welfare policy in the guise of, for example, anti-social behaviour orders, curfews, truancy arrests and so forth.[14] For some analysts this represents a sound basis for social policy because it is based on a clear picture of what human behaviour is really like,[15] while for others Blairism is not such a new and well thought out strategy, being based on bits of the old and, as one writer puts it, best described by the acronym PAP: pragmatism and populism.[16] For those more sympathetic to it, the New Labour reforms will make it possible to be more focused on the true requirements of those in need, opening the way to 'an approach to [social work] practice which goes to the heart of people's lived realities and attachments, which promotes effective life planning, enhances their mastery and ultimately their happiness'.[17]

We will make sense of New Labour's welfare reforms by understanding them as a way of reworking notions of citizenship in the context of the inability of the state to deliver social rights thanks to the legitimation crisis of the 1970s. Added to this are the effects of globalisation, which weaken the power of the nation-state to hold its citizens together and to maintain the conditions of nationally based socialisation. The proliferation of lifestyles to which Giddens points is also partly a result of the growth of social rights, and a subsequent rejection of the impositions of state-led bureaucratic welfare regimes that inevitably tried to standardise social norms and need. Rather than a uniform society of citizens with shared values and similar life experiences, we are increasingly a society of multiple identity claims, each of which expects special recognition and respect.

The makers of a new welfare state also have to contend with an unintentionally unruly population that is ageing wrongly and managing gender differences in increasingly problematic ways. In 1901 one in twenty of us was 65 years of age but in 1998 the figure was one in six. Between 1976 and 1996 the number of people aged over 85 trebled.[18] This ageing population poses a problem for systems of pension provision and geriatric care. Changes in family structure alter the nature of entitlement and need, as does transformation in the nature of work, which can no longer be relied on as lifelong and so productive of a communal identity.

All of these factors render the reconciliation of individual and collective even more difficult.

From welfare reform to social capital

The New Right made sense of such transformations via their critique of welfare as engendering moral degradation, expressed as a growth in idleness and scrounging, or dependency. The error of the welfare state, it was argued, lay in attempting to provide collectively, since this usurped the responsibility of the individual and encouraged people to make unreasonable claims upon society and state. The Thatcher governments tried to encourage free-market individualism in the belief that the renewed spirit of self-interest would, as Smith had seemed to suggest, lead to collective benefits. For the architects of New Labour and the third way, this approach underestimates the extent to which economic and market relations need to be underpinned by social and ethical bonds or frameworks. Thus, in contrast to the New Right, New Labour has tried to sustain an interest in citizenship. This is not only manifested in small but important policies such as the provision of citizenship education in schools, but in a general and extensive rhetoric of rights and responsibilities, combined with policies designed to induce self-regulating and pro-social behaviour that might obviate the need for extensive welfare provision. Potentially this represents a new sort of compact between state and citizens, and between citizens themselves. Keynesian social democracy sought to bring about social harmony by using the power of the state to incorporate (economically and socially) those otherwise likely to feel they had little stake in a society shaped in the interests of an elite few. The 'third way' seeks to apply policy mechanisms designed not to create the conditions for social inclusion but to create the sorts of citizens who will themselves create the conditions of their own inclusion. For this way of thinking to appear coherent a significant re-conceptualisation of the economy is necessary. Where part of the Keynesian conceptual structure was an implicit critique of the unchecked economy as causing conflict and social disintegration (that it was the task of the state to stave off), the third way has to imagine the economy as a force of integration.

But this is hard for New Labour and third way thinking to do. For in such thinking the economy occupies a particular place in the theoretical schema. It forms a pivot, a fixed point in relation to which other aspects of the overall philosophy are positioned. We have seen this already in our arguments about the meaning of modernisation and the nature of third way politics: the world has changed because of reconfigured economic processes and new technological capabilities, and it follows that we must modernise and change the way we do politics. We need, as Giddens does, to re-imagine the state, and redefine individuals and their capacities; but this is because the economy is already changing itself, independently of state action. The effect of this aspect of the New Labour solipsism is that, conceptually, individuality, state-hood and society are subordinated, and everything is understood in terms of its articulation with the economic. Economics does not rule over everything, but it is a privileged space within procedures of rule. Because the state can't or won't act on the economy directly, it must instead act on people in relation to their economic activities, attempting to create the conditions of conviviality.

This conceptual structure is very different from that of social democracy. In social democracy certain areas of social life were meant to be separated or protected from the influence of economic relations. Education and health, for example, were understood to be something other than tradable goods or commodities. They were ring-fenced and made available free of charge. The intention behind this was ethical and normative as well as practical and political. But the thinking of the third way, and the policy of New Labour, seems to reject this separa-tion. Indeed, it embraces the conjoining of all areas of social life with economic productivity, making this a central part of its philosophy, alongside the belief that it can square the circle of profitability and equality.

Thus Giddens argues that, while control of manufacturing capital and the regulation of financial markets remain important for centre left governments, the third way seeks priorities other than those suggested by Keynesian-inspired industrial policy and demand management, or market liberalisation. The new focus is on: 'education, incentives, entrepreneurial culture, flexibility, devolution, and the cultivation of social capital'.[19] There is to be a 'new mixed economy', with synergies between public and private, and a new balance of regulation and dereg-ulation. Culture thus becomes seen as an aspect of economic policy. This means culture in the 'concrete' sense of cultural products that can be traded, but also culture in general. Cultural values will sustain and grease the wheels of the knowledge economy, so part of economic policy must be engineering that culture. This links back to strategies found in contemporary management theory aimed at generating work-place cultures that ensure workers feel committed to their product. It also links to the kind of marketing strategies that predominate in New Labour's own branding, where having a presence in the market place is as important as having a product to sell there. As a result it is legitimate to see Britain itself as a commodity, a brand image, to be marketed abroad and believed in at home (and we also can conceive of ourselves as our own brand, designed to sell our unique portfolio of talents). Culture then becomes the terrain upon which citizen-subjects will be managed and produced, inducing a form of citizenship that is essen-tially in harmony with the economy. And it is at this point that the concept of social capital becomes very useful for New Labour thinking.

For most current users of the term, social capital means trust. According to Giddens, 'the cultivation of social capital is integral to the knowledge economy'. It balances individualism and co-operation, since it 'refers to trust networks that individuals can draw upon for social support just as financial capital can be drawn upon to be used for investment. Like financial capital, social capital can be expanded – invested and reinvested'.[20] So, the concept of social capital links directly to general network theories of society, but with the stress placed on the component of trust. It thus also refers us back to the question of how to develop the social relations that underpin a market society, but are also eroded by it. This all shades into attempts to rethink the role of the third or voluntary sector in delivering public services and, ultimately, to the social entrepreneur. The latter, according to Leadbeater, is 'a kind of research and development wing of the welfare system, innovating new solutions to intractable social problems ... they set in motion a virtuous circle of social capital accumulation ...'.[21] The concept of social capital is thus crucial to the third way. It is not so grand as to be New Labour's holy grail, but perhaps it could be described as their holy bracket, in that it links the dimensions of individual and state, society and economy. For one advocate, the integration of notions of social capital into those concerning the market will provide the third way 'with its own new, rigorous and *practical* analysis of the economy'.[22]

In its 'third way' usage the concept of social capital originates in economic analyses, particularly of the East Asian economies that grew rapidly in the 1980s (before they destroyed themselves); it was argued that in such economies certain kinds of social networks helped provide the underpinning of economic development.[23] It is part of a particular theoretical approach generated by the type of Anglo-American social science that turns on analyses of the interaction of acquisitive individuals in a complex environment and the sorts of social institutions they create.

It is nearly axiomatic for many that what characterises 'modernity' is the dis-embedding of economic activity from wider social networks. Where in 'primitive' societies exchange may occur within the context of kinship structures, religious rituals and so forth, modern and capitalist societies are notable for their conceptualisation of the economic sphere as formally autonomous. This underpins atomistic economic theories, such as those associated with classical utilitarianism. Economic structures can thus be imagined as self-regulating and independent from external influences. At the theoretical level competition can be conceived as taking place in an idealised sphere undistorted by exogenous social processes and interactions. The flipside of this sort of argument is that deriving from American functionalist sociology, in which social integration and order are emphasised, leading to a focus on the ways in which norms and routines are internalised by actors. This in turn generates regularity in the behaviours of social groups so allowing social structures to be conceived without reference to externalities.

Taking a cue from theoretical developments in economic sociology, James Coleman developed the notion of social capital in the context of marrying these kinds of sociological and economic analysis.[24] He took on board the principle of the purposive rational actor (so central to liberalism) and introduced social structure into it via the concept of social capital, to show how 'that principle, in conjunction with particular social contexts, can account not only for the actions of individuals in particular contexts but also for the development of social organisation'.[25] Coleman's theoretical agenda, then, was not to challenge approaches based on the assumption of rational actors by showing the importance of social structure and social relations, but to allow the introduction of the rational actor into the analysis of social systems while maintaining a grounding in organisational sociology. In this way, the domain over which economic concepts gain purchase was extended into social relations between people by comprehending them as resources used in the securing of individual interests:

> This conception is based on the notion of different actions (or, in some cases, different goods) having a particular utility for the actor and is accompanied by a principle of action which can be expressed by saying that the actor chooses the action which will maximise utility.[26]

From Coleman's elaboration the concept of social capital jumped into politics via a widely read article by Robert Putnam,[27] which reportedly inspired Clinton's State of the Union address in 1995. Here the concept of social capital became generalised into 'civic-ness' and applied not to low-level individual cases but to a large collective such as a nation. As Portes puts it: 'the journey was fast, explaining major social outcomes by re-labelling them with a novel term and then employing the same term to formulate sweeping policy prescriptions'.[28] Based on his research on regional government in Italy, Putnam came to the conclusion that:

> the quality of governance was determined by longstanding traditions of civic engagement (or its absence). Voter turnout, newspaper readership,

membership in choral societies and football clubs – these were the hall-marks of a successful region. In fact, historical analysis suggested that these networks of organised reciprocity and civic solidarity, far from being an epi-phenomenon of socio-economic modernisation, were a precondition for it.[29]

Social capital could thus refer to 'features of social organisation such as networks, norms, and social trust that facilitate co-ordination and co-operation for mutual benefit'.[30] In his article, Putnam aimed to 'use the central premise [of theories of social capital] that social connections and civic engagement pervasively influence our public life, as well as our private prospects – as the starting point for an empirical survey of trends in social capital in contemporary America'.[31] He duly noted the decline in political and public participation (from voting to the PTA, via unions and the Masons), and that while more Americans than ever before went bowling, fewer did so in organised leagues. Putnam corre-lated this decline in civic involvement with a decline in family, neighbourliness and general levels of trust as reported in surveys. The possible causes included all the familiar factors: women in the labour market; mobility and other demographic transformations such as changing family structures; divorce; lower wages; changes in social scale; the growth of supermarkets and decline of the corner shop; and the technological transformation of leisure that has increased the privatism of cultural life (which is to say we watch television when we should be at the PTA meeting).[32]

The concept of social capital has since become quite widespread. It is sufficiently fluid to be deployed by left, right and third way. For the right, 'the economic function of social capital is to reduce the transac-tion costs associated with formal co-ordination mechanisms like contracts, hierarchies, bureaucratic rules, and the like'.[33] In simple terms this just means that if people exchanging something know and respect each other it is not necessary for them to take account of every possible contingency in order to secure their transaction, just as the owner of a shop from which you regularly purchase things may take a cheque from you without a guarantee card.[34] For Fukuyama, the polit-ical meaning of all this is that norms derived from religion and shared historical experience can shape informal norms and produce social capital. This is far more important than any amount of state-led regu-lation. For the loose left the concept of social capital enables recognition of the necessary social dimension to economic activity, and could encourage corporations and companies to see their embedded-ness in cultural and communal contexts as a positive advantage. For the third way, social capital links corporate responsibility with economic gain by demonstrating how embeddedness in community is a sound investment strategy.

Besides such strategic-political concerns, what is important to us is that the concept of social capital facilitates the interpretation of social phenomena and problems in the language of economics. After all, the idea that social relations underpin strong social formations and facilitate social action is a banal tautology. But at a time when the capacity to interpret action socially is in decline, this re-description or translation of the social into the dominant language of individual, rational, utility maximisation is important and meaningful. The question answered by theories of social capital and trust is that of the structuring of a structure; of what it is that produces and reproduces a structure of economic exchange. Such a structure could be conceived of as entirely self-producing and self-regulating. Sometimes – in some forms of neo-liberal theory – it is: the many interactions of rational individuals seeking to maximise their utility will, thanks to an invisible hand, maintain the necessary structure, so long as nothing else interferes with it. On this analysis the structure is simply the expression of an innate rational acquisitiveness. In this sense there is nothing external to the structure of economic exchange, at least nothing external that is important for an understanding of its operations (other than the scarcity of certain natural resources). The economy can best be understood as simply the natural outcome of the otherwise unimpeded interactions of persons motivated by their rational acquisitiveness (i.e. their economic instincts) in the context of scarcity.

But the theory of social capital as developed by Coleman breaks this conceptual schema open. Here, that which structures the economic structure is not, strictly speaking, internal to it. Broader social structures and relationships need to be considered as part of general economic analysis. Furthermore, if we examine economic relations in their temporal context (rather than as static, synchronic, models) we will also have to analyse the ongoing social relations which structure economic activity even as they are themselves re-structured by it. This makes possible a certain sort of critique of neo-liberalism based on the recognition that the market is not self-structuring. Hence Coleman, for example, suggests that there may be a need to reconstitute lost forms of social capital at a public level. This can only mean public intervention of some kind, and as such it sounds like a way of re-conceiving and re-legitimating social democratic governance. But, since the concept of social capital provides a way of accounting for the external structuring of economic structure *within* the terms of economic behaviour, it makes it possible to begin conceiving the economic itself as a generalised sphere of governance: as if a pure neo-liberalism has been turned inside out; as if there is nothing external to the field of economic relations because there is nothing other than economic relations. Thus, that which was at the centre of the neo-liberal theory of the economy (relationships between rationally acquisitive and competing individuals) is now understood not as the force generating the conditions for economic activity but as a part of that activity. All social action is identified by its function in terms of furthering economic/instrumental ends. Erosion of social bonds and resources is not understood as an effect of economic activity, which clashes with it, but as a result of imperfect or improperly understood economic activity. The correct response is to begin accounting for social capital and auditing it. Consequently, social relations can once again become an object of government activity in a way they – formally – were not within neo-liberal frameworks of thought. However, in the process social relations undergo a relocation in the conceptual structure. Direct interference of the state into the field of social capital is believed to have the same deleterious impact as in the actual economy of money and goods. So, the state must stop providing social context directly, and turn instead to facilitating the supply side, as it were, encouraging the growth of social relations indirectly. If you can't actually produce the good society through intervention then you produce the good citizens who can. This is a reversal of the ancient Aristotelian approach to virtue, but absolutely at one with the organisation of contemporary liberalism. It allows social relations to be treated by policy-makers as on the same plane as all other matters of economy. Indeed the economic level becomes a generalised mode of governance applicable across policy areas. This in turn allows the welfare state to become, once again, a core area of governmental activity, but in a new form attached to a revised notion of citizenship aiming at the generation of a new sort of subject.

Because of their belief in and commitment to the knowledge economy, as well as their Thatcherite heritage, New Labour see all aspects of policy as economic in nature. Their conceptualisation of the economy as both a fixed point against which things change and as something that, in penetrating throughout social relations, redefines them in a way that is positive, means that more and more aspects of social life are seen by them as economic in nature. This necessitates and legitimates policies aimed at ensuring there is social capital out there and that people are not only able but willing to participate in the new knowledge economy. Thus, ultimately, policy (via a battery of techniques in various policy areas from education and health to social security) aims at the creation of a new subject: the good, self-governing, citizen.

This is how New Labour believes it can resolve the contradictions of political thought and practice that form the relationship between the state, society, economy and individuals. For an advanced economy to function, citizens must be educated, fed, reproduced and formed into autonomous rational citizens. Thus enhancing liberty and expanding social justice through wealth creation might be compatible. This entails a specific conception of the function of the state. Rather than an 'activist' state engaged in the political leadership of society, it is regarded as an organisation concerned with the management of society and ultimately with the delivery of certain social 'goods' and services in ways that maintain social harmony. The Thatcherite response to the crisis was to politicise the state, and to utilise its power for the completion of a particular project involving the undermining of the institutions that had been put in place to allow representatives of labour to make demands of the state, or to protest about the actions of their employers. This necessitated a rhetoric which downgraded the significance of society-wide systems of protection. But there was no corresponding attempt to increase the responsibilities taken on by employers. Indeed, quite the reverse argument was put forward, and the Hayekian claim that corporations should only take responsibility for maximising profits and returns to shareholders formed a central part of Conservative thinking. However another, newer, rationality of government also began to emerge under the Thatcher regime, which did not refuse to take any part in the moral governance of citizens. Indeed, the Thatcher era was marked by the uneasy combination of a reactionary rhetoric of nationhood, and exhortations as to the moral character of individuals who were encouraged to see themselves as singular self-interested agents. This led to particularly intense battles over those areas of state provision most involved with the induction of people into particular ethical orientations – education and welfare. There was an intrinsic instability in this attempt to marry a 'traditional' perspective on moral individualism with the encouragement of corporations to adopt only the morality of the market, where what makes money is taken to be good. Nevertheless a new rationality emerged by which social regulation could become even more focused on individuals rather than on social groups. The withdrawal of the state from the provision of certain services was intended to force individuals to take up responsibility for themselves, unleashing an entrepreneurial instinct that had hitherto been suppressed. As Rose argues:

> Within such rationalities, it appears that individuals can best fulfil their political obligations in relation to the wealth, health and happiness of the nation not when they are bound to relations of dependency and obligation, but when they seek to fulfil themselves as free individuals.

Individuals are now to be linked into a society thorough acts of socially
sanctioned consumption and responsible choice ...[35]

With the state 'downsized', responsibility was passed on to the individual, self-monitoring subject of community, acting on those nested
responsibilities that Blairism now likes to demonstrate in its rhetoric
and advertising (see Chapter One). Blairism takes up and continues this
rhetoric, which it sees as presenting the possibility for a re-moralising
of society in ways that will reinvent the virtuous circle whereby
economic growth and societal need complement rather than contradict
each other. Its innovation has been to link the whole into a specific
conception of the knowledge economy where being part of a creative
and supportive 'community' is essential for the entrepreneurial subject
to flourish.

New Labour's welfare policies are thus oriented towards the
production and regulation of this citizen-subject, immersed ever more
in the sphere of productive consumption; a self-governing individual
that must be so in order to contribute to a properly ethical communal
order. The state wants and needs people to engage in the activity that
keeps the weightless economy floating, but at the same time must
manage a society which is opening itself up to a proliferation of activities that cut across the very social and moral structures that constitute
it. The enabling state thus becomes also an 'exhortatory state', seeking
to change 'identities' and 'govern by culture' instead of direct regulation, aiming at the communal responsibility of the individual subject.
One is encouraged to be responsible for oneself not simply out of self-
interest, but because this is now part of our contribution to the social
whole. This is one reason why the third way embraces the shift from
the concept of equality to that of inclusion. It is not that the third way
is anti-equality, but that equality to be and live how we want to (as Mill
might have seen it) contradicts the demands of the economy and of
society. Thus we are *not* all equal in our rights to be 'old' labour or to
be inactive in the formal economy. We should all have free and equal
access to the labour market even if we have to be forced to make use of
it. The concept of inclusion assists in reducing a generalisable notion of
equality (in lifestyle, and in the ability to exercise our freedoms, to
make the 'constitutional illusions' real) to a specific kind of equality.
For though social inclusion is used to refer to membership of a wider
culture and to the exercise of citizenship, it is clear that these all derive
from inclusion within the workforce understood as a social and moral
as well as fiscal obligation.

In his 1999 conference speech Blair stressed that: 'We aren't just
workers. We are citizens proud to say there is such a thing as society

and proud to be part of it'. Where he spoke of 'the liberation of human potential not just as workers but as citizens', he was referring to the liberation of the hitherto wasted talents of 'the many'. This was allied to the argument that: 'Talent is twenty-first century wealth. Every person liberated to fulfil their potential adds to our wealth'. The citizen and the knowledge worker are one: liberty means employment. Blair's declaration of citizenship in this speech subsequently segued into a discussion on social values and respect and tackling crime.[36] Once again the liberty of the subject and his/her fulfilment is related to the fact that such liberty is now an economic necessity, since growth depends on 'creative investment', and citizenship is tied into a communitarian rather than republican imagination.

The policy areas where this sort of vision is particularly evident are those which most directly enter into the lives of citizens, primarily education and social security (though rhetoric around personal health is of interest here also). These two policy areas are closely linked in the minds of the present government. Education forms a central part of plans to tackle social exclusion, and is crucial to the welfare-to-work strategy. As the welfare green paper made clear: 'A skilled workforce is essential to a modern economy, and high educational standards offer people their best chance of a secure and prosperous life'.[37] So it is that the white paper on enterprise skills and innovation (jointly produced by the DTI and DfEE) stated that: 'we believe that Government has a crucial role in helping people develop the skills needed for economic prosperity and *social cohesion*' (emphasis added).[38] Elsewhere, David Blunkett has spelled out: 'The unique importance of DfEE's role ... [is] its responsibility for ensuring that the UK has a well-functioning labour market. It is here that we are clarifying the economic relationship between the citizen and the government – a relationship of rights and responsibility, with the goal of ensuring both economic efficiency and fairness for all'.[39]

New Labour's welfare strategy revolves around these core notions of work and social inclusion, with education as the hinge that links them. In the words of the Commission on Social Justice, welfare is to be productive of both social justice *and* economic efficiency. It is to be about promoting personal autonomy, choice and the 'confidence and capability' of people to 'manage their own lives'. For Giddens, we should shift from the redistribution of wealth to the redistribution of possibilities: 'The cultivation of human potential should as far as possible replace "after the event" redistribution'; or, in Blair's terms, we need 'the redistribution of opportunity'. Ruth Levitas describes this sort of welfare discourse as 'social integrationist' – the poor are seen to lack not power but work.[40] The emphasis of policy is on making people responsible for themselves through assisting them in getting into the labour force. Ruth Lister further describes it as the discourse of RIO (Rights, Inclusion, Opportunity).[41] To receive benefit, claimants must undergo an interview to discuss how they will find work. The 'something for nothing welfare state' will be ended and replaced by the balance of rights and responsibilities.[42] As Levitas also points out, the emphasis on 'employability over employment' is revealing. Because the new economy cannot itself be touched, so as to increase jobs available, policy must focus on the unemployed themselves in order to make them capable of working for it. The various New Deals are indicative of this (see Chapter 5).

Thus one of the key developments of New Labour welfare policy is an emphasis on the individualisation of service delivery, and with it the encouragement of responsibility for gearing up for the new economy. We have 'tailor-made packages' of help. Personal advisers can identify individual needs so that people may be 'empowered to seize the opportunities to lead independent lives' as they foster in themselves the skills that attract employers. Service will be 'customer-focused', and we can have things such as Individual Learning Accounts (see Chapter 5) to invest in that education, which is an investment in ourselves, while kiosk and other such technologies will make it possible (necessary) for people to find out information for themselves. It is up to individuals to find a role for themselves within the given of the economy (with some socially provided, yet individualised, assistance) and doing so is part of their obligation as citizens.

Education is taken to be the key route out of poverty or social exclusion. It is not seen primarily as an induction into the moral or traditional culture of the nation (much to the distress of traditional Tories), nor as a way of empowering individuals to think openly and freely (much to the distress of traditional academics). Primarily it is seen as the mechanism by which individuals can equip themselves, and by which the national economy can feed itself with the appropriate skills for the new economy.

Education was the key site for the production of economically usable individuals in the industrial revolution, disciplining them, ordering them, encouraging them to keep time and instilling in them the skills and knowledge necessary for worker efficiency. For Demos, however, this nineteenth-century approach is out-dated and unhelpful. In declaring that we need citizens who 'learn to learn' and do so across their lives they argue for something quite novel.[43] Knowledge, Demos say, has to be understood as open-ended and contextual. Education systems shouldn't aim to distil fixed blocks of information into their students, but to produce autonomy, responsibility and creativity.

Schools and universities should open up to 'the overlapping, mutual networks of community and economic life'. Funding should be individualised and parents enabled to claim it back if they educate children at home. This sounds like something completely different from the utilitarianism of much nineteenth-century educational thought. But this freeing up, decentralisation and diversification of education comes with its necessary corollary. In place of 'a single public education infrastructure, governments should concentrate on establishing the standards, outcomes and underlying bases needed to support learning opportunities'.[44] Parents' home-schooling should be supported 'as long as they can demonstrate their ability to achieve the outcomes and quality standards which governments must continue to set and monitor'.[45] Decentralisation is thus accompanied by a tightening up of what the newly freed can do and, once again, the underlying motive is the need for us to shape up for the new economy. The education system described by Demos writer Tom Bentley mirrors in its structure the shape of the knowledge economy. The manner of schooling is as important as its content and the opening up of schools to industry and business can become a way of tying the skills they teach back into the demands of economic 'necessity', making schools responsible not to society as a whole but to the demands of the economy, even those of particular firms. The extension of choice in education simply becomes an expansion of market choice, with parents empowered as consumers, offered choice via league tables of examination performance in their search for an entrepreneurial school that will train the next generation of entrepreneurs. Thus though the rhetoric is of liberty, the aim remains instrumental – our freedom is to be harnessed to the needs of the economy.

Educational and welfare policy can thus be seen as mechanisms through which the new subjects of the new economy are to be formed. They are to be individuated yet also habituated to the particular kind of autonomy that the knowledge industries can promote. They are subjects whose responsibilities for themselves and their communities must be borne through schooling themselves in permanent transformation and adaptation (modular learning), employing an individually focused form of natural selection upon themselves and their own attributes, preparing themselves to contribute to the new economy.

This discourse is found throughout New Labour rhetoric and policy. It is also there in the exhortations to new kinds of self-oriented moral construction that are intended to reawaken our desires for communality. Assisting the New Labour individual in this endeavour is the notion that s/he is also part of a community to which s/he owes obligations, and within which the key characteristics of trust and cohesion can be developed. This is New Labour's 'break' with Thatcherism, but also a part of its continuity with that project, reworking collectivism into 'governance by community'.[46] New Labour's vision of the ideal subject is that of the reflexive individual who regards his/her self as a form of capital to be processed, refined and invested, and who does this within the context of an obligation to the community to be productive. Being so will contribute to that community, which in turn contributes to the well-being and prospects for self-capitalisation of that individual. Naturally the whole is contained within the all-embracing economy. Once again we see that the innovation of New Labour is to deal with the dominance by the field of the economic over other spheres of social life by rendering everything a branch of economic policy and producing subjects for whom everything is an economic calculation.

The effective power of concepts of subjectivity resides precisely in their generally 'un-thought' nature. We take for granted some conception of who or what we are, derive judgements and generalisations from it, and place the whole beyond question because doing so seems to be essential for continuing to be and act. This is even more the case when self-hood is believed to be the object of continual invention and creation. Ideas of the 'social construction' of self are not indicative of the end of regimes of control. Rather they turn self-hood into a permanent endeavour operating across many levels of our existence (from our diet, bodily shape and close relationships to our general philosophy of life, ambitions and successes), intensifying the powers of subjection. New Labour works with a renewed notion of the subject and bases policies upon that notion in order both to reflect its 'given' nature and to produce it.

Conclusion

At one level the emergence and meaning of a movement such as New Labour (and it is not a unique development for it is mirrored across western capitalist democracies) is really quite simple. Under Capitalism, as we know, 'all fixed fast-frozen relations with their train of ancient and venerable prejudices and opinions, are swept away, all new formed ones become antiquated before they can ossify'.[47] Such an effect has been intensified by electronic media and communications systems which allow capitalism to function faster, as well as enabling the direct transmission of varied visions and expectations. Under these conditions, the moral orders of tradition, as Giddens knows, begin to collapse, exposing us to an ever greater sense of uncertainty yet also an increasing freedom from the weight of the past. But the lack of shared, binding principles undermines capitalism itself. And as a result, the acts of 'committee management' that used to define the bourgeois state become less feasible. Pluralisation of values and lifestyle demands new kinds of governmental strategy, oriented towards facilitating the fast flow of capital and goods while developing new kinds of self-governing individuals who can exist in the new environment.

Addressing the relative absence of the idea of liberty in third way thinking, Ralf Dahrendorf has argued that it seems to reject traditional democratic institutions, supplanting parliament with referenda and focus groups.[48] It makes saving for pensions compulsory, insists we must work regardless of family commitments, advocating a state that 'will no longer pay for things, but tell people what to do'. The advocates of New Labour would no doubt reject such a charge of illiberality, pointing out that they are enabling people to be free by educating, training and exhorting them to make the most of, and to be responsible for, their liberty. For Foucault, however, liberty and liberalism were never to be understood through such straightforward claims about the presence or absence of freedom. In analysing the developments of nineteenth-century political economy and the growth of the modern state, he argued that liberty came to be seen 'not only as the right of individuals legitimately to oppose the power, the abuses and usurpations of the sovereign, but also now as an indispensable element of governmental rationality itself'.[49] Security and cohesion are maintained through liberty and not despite it. The activity of government is oriented towards a continual preoccupation with how it is possible to govern a society and an economy, to relate them to each other, and to maintain security within the social itself, through developing forms of liberty. Where it cedes power to non-governmental agencies, the state is not giving up on governing them, but introducing different ways of managing the population. The entry of things into the market from the state is not a liberalisation so much as subjection to other forms of discipline.

Third way theorists believe in a renewed social democracy, operating on a terrain in which the capacity of the market is taken as proven. But they argue that it is still social democracy, in that it advocates a state form with a clearly interventionist role. That is 'to promote a go-ahead mentality and a new entrepreneurial spirit at all levels of society', 'a competent and well-trained workforce eager and ready to take on new responsibilities', and a welfare system that 'opens up new opportunities and encourages initiative, creativity and readiness to take on new challenges'.[50] In this way supply and demand side economics are presumed to be united. Social democracy will manage the transition 'from industrial production to the knowledge based service economy of the future',[51] reducing regulation, and shifting the state from administration and investment in productivity, to administration and investment in people: 'the top priority must be investment in human and social capital'.

For Blair, the national economy rests on 'people' being encouraged to fulfil and manifest their potential. This of course fits into the new language of human and social capital, the notion that everyday interactions, relations and deeds can be something which we account for, foster, develop and invest. Citizens' rights, roles and responsibilities all cohere (economically, morally, politically and psychically) around this commitment to what Jack Straw calls 'active community', a strategy of 'social intervention' rather than 'social engineering'. Clearly there is something of a paradox in the idea of a state that because it can't really take on any major role in directing society will reduce its function to that of creating the sorts of people who will volunteer for good causes, look after themselves and eagerly develop their entrepreneurial skills. In order to be the kinds of people we are supposed to be, responsible for ourselves and not mediated by the state, that very same state has to act so as to make it so. This clears the ground for a changed conception of the form and function of the state.

Notes

1. G.W.F. Hegel (1995) [1892], *Lectures on the History of Philosophy: Greek Philosophy to Plato*, London, University of Nebraska Press, pp48-9.
2. Etienne Balibar (1994), 'Subjection and Subjectivation' in Joan Copjec (ed.) *Supposing the Subject*, London, Verso.
3. See Stephen Mulhall and Adam Swift (1992), *Liberals and Communitarians*, Oxford, Blackwell.
4. Colin Gordon (1991) 'Governmental Rationality: an introduction' in Graham Burchell, Colin Gordon and Peter Miller (eds.) *The Foucault Effect: Studies in Governmentality*, Hemel Hempstead, Harvester Wheatsheaf, p3.
5. Nikolas Rose and Peter Miller (1992), 'Political Power Beyond the State: problematics of government', *British Journal of Sociology*, Vol. 43, No. 2, p175.
6. Ibid. p174.
7. See Bernard Mandeville (1989) [1728], *The fable of the bees, or, Private vices, publick benefits*, Indianapolis: Liberty Classics; Adam Smith (1977) *The Wealth of Nations*, London, Dent.
8. See Emile Durkheim (1933) *The Division of Labour in Society*, Glencoe, Illinois, The Free Press; and (1957) *Professional Ethics and Civic Morals*, London, Routledge and Kegan Paul.
9. T.H. Marshall (1992) *Citizenship and Social Class*, London, Pluto Press.
10. Ibid. p33.

11. Ibid. p24.
12. Scott Lash and John Urry (1987) *The End of Organised Capitalism*, Cambridge, Polity, pp230-1.
13. Louise Amoore (2000), 'International Political Economy and the Contested Firm', *New Political Economy*, Vol. 5, No. 2, p197.
14. Ian Butler and Mark Drakeford (2001) 'Which Blair Project? Communitarianism, Social Authoritarianism and Social Work', *Journal of Social Work*, Vol. 1, No. 1, pp7-19.
15. Julian Le Grand, 'Knights, Knaves and Pawns: Human Behaviour and Social Policy', *Journal of Social Policy*, Vol. 26, No. 2, pp749-70.
16. Martin Powell (2000) 'New Labour and the third way in the British Welfare State: a new and distinctive approach?', *Critical Social Policy*, 62, p53.
17. Harry Ferguson (2001), 'Social Work, Individualisation and Life Politics', *British Journal of Social Work*, 31, pp41-55.
18. Bryan S. Turner (2000) 'The Erosion of Citizenship', *British Journal of Sociology*, Vol. 53, No. 2, pp189-209.
19. Anthony Giddens (2000), *The Third Way and Its Critics*, Cambridge, Polity, p73.
20. Ibid. p78.
21. Charles Leadbeater (1997) *The Rise of the Social Entrepreneur*, London, Demos, pp9-10, quoted in Anthony Giddens (1998), *The Third Way*, Cambridge, Polity, p82.
22. Simon Szretzer (2001) 'A New Political Economy: The Importance of Social Capital' in Anthony Giddens (ed.) (2001), *The Global Third Way Debate*, Cambridge, Polity, p291.
23. There are other sources to the concept, and conceptualising non-economic aspects of social life in economic terms is not a practice confined to North American positivists and their British followers. Sometimes the concept of social capital is related to the work of the radical French sociologist Pierre Bourdieu. Certainly Bourdieu coined concepts such as cultural and social capital to refer to the ways in which attributes (accent, dress, taste, etc), and locations in social structure, can function not only as markers of class differentiation but as resources deployed in maintaining hierarchical status. But here one feels that Bourdieu's use of the term has a poetic as well as scientific licence. It makes apparent how the bourgeois renders everything a resource, an instrument for the maintenance of power and distinction. It is thus not only an analytical category but a critical one. I am not sure the same can be said for the concept of social capital.
24. See for example, Mark Granovetter, (1985) 'Economic Action and Social Structure: The Problem of Embeddedness', *American Journal of Sociology*, Vol. 91, No. 3, pp481-510.
25. James Coleman (1988), 'Social Capital in the Creation of Human Capital',

American Journal of Sociology, Vol. 94, Supplement, p96.

26. James Coleman (1990) *Foundations of Social Theory*, Cambridge Mass., Harvard University Press, pp13-14. Coleman's purpose is not, however, narrowly reactionary, and the phenomena on which it is focused are small in scale. He uses it to argue, for example, that single parent families lack social capital in the absence of a second parent. Similarly moving house can lead to a depletion in resources. These factors can help explain why children from single parent or peripatetic families have children more likely to truant. His approach to social capital explicitly stands opposed to what he terms the 'fiction' associated with natural rights theory and neo-classical economics theory, that society consists of individuals acting to achieve independently formed goals. For him 'individuals do not act independently, goals are not independently arrived at, and interests are not wholly selfish'.

27. Robert D. Putnam (1995), 'Bowling Alone: America's Declining Social Capital', *Journal of Democracy*, Vol. 6, No. ?, pp65-78.

28. See Alejandro Portes (1998), 'Social Capital: Its Origins and Applications in Modern Sociology', *Annual Review of Sociology*, Vol. 24, p19.

29. Putnam (1995) p68.

30. Ibid. p67.

31. Ibid. p67.

32. This last being a situation for which I can personally provide ample anecdotal evidence.

33. Francis Fukuyama (1999), 'Social Capital and Civil Society', paper delivered at the IMF Conference on Second Generation Reforms, The Institute of Public Policy, George Mason University, October 1. http://www.imf.org/external/pubs/ft/seminar/1999/reforms/fukuyama.htm

34. Fukuyama (ibid) makes sense of it thus: 'If we define social capital as instantiated, informal norms that produce cooperation, economists have a straightforward explanation of where it comes from: social capital arises spontaneously as a product of iterated Prisoners Dilemma (PD) games. A one-shot PD game does not lead to a cooperative outcome because defection constitutes a Nash equilibrium for both players; if the game is iterated, however, a simple strategy like tit-for-tat (playing cooperation for cooperation and defection for defection) leads both players to a cooperative outcome. In non-game theoretic turns, if individuals interact with each other repeatedly over time, they develop a stake in a reputation for honesty and reliability'.

35. Nikolas Rose (1999) *Powers of Freedom: Reframing Political Thought*, Cambridge, Cambridge University Press, p166.

36. Tony Blair (1999) Speech to Labour Party Conference, Bournemouth, pp3-4; 11.

37. DSS (1998) *New Ambitions for Our Country: A New Contract for Welfare*, Green Paper, Cm 3805, DSS, London.

38. DTI (1998) *Opportunity for All in a World of Change: A White paper on Enterprise Skills and Innovation*, Section 2.4.
39. David Blunkett (2001), *Education Into Employability: The role of the DfEE in the Economy*, Speech to the Institute of Economic Affairs, 24 January 2001.
40. Ruth Levitas (1998) *The Inclusive Society? Social Exclusion and New Labour*, Basingstoke, Macmillan.
41. Ruth Lister (1999) *To RIO via the Third Way*, Paper presented to ESRC Research Seminar on New Labour and the Third Way in Public Services, London, 22 April.
42. Tony Blair, quoted in Levitas (1998) p6.
43. Tom Bentley (1998) 'Learning Beyond the Classroom', in Ian Hargreaves and Ian Christie (eds.), *Tomorrow's Politics: The Third Way and Beyond*, London, Demos, pp80-95.
44. Ibid. p91.
45. Ibid. p92.
46. See Rose (1999).
47. Karl Marx (1988) 'The Communist Manifesto' in David McLellan (ed.), *Selected Writings*, Oxford, Oxford University Press, p224.
48. Ralf Dahrendorf (1999) 'Whatever happened to liberty', *New Statesman*, 6.9.99, pp25-27.
49. Cited in Colin Gordon (1991), 'Governmental Rationality: An introduction' in Graham Burchell, Colin Gordon, Peter Miller (eds.) *The Foucault effect: studies in governmentality*, London, Harvester Wheatsheaf.
50. Tony Blair and Gerhard Schroder (1999) *Europe: The Third Way – Die Neue Mitte*, London, Labour Party and SPD, p5.
51. Ibid. p8.

CHAPTER SIX

Culture and the State

Introduction

The state is not an easy phenomenon to understand despite its absolute centrality to politics and political studies. It is not only an organisation that formulates and enacts laws. It is also a range of institutions that are (by definition) separated from the immediate function of formulating laws – the judiciary, military and police force for example – but enforce or enact them. Then there are all the state (or state-related) agencies of social welfare and regulation concerned with matters ranging from trading standards and food hygiene to adoption and mental health management. This diversity of function and formation makes the state hard to pin down, define and explain. There are few areas of life that are not in some way touched upon by the state, which regulates so many aspects of social life and the things that we consume within it and as a result the boundary of public and private or state and non-state is somewhat unclear. This is only to consider the state in terms of its domestic role. The state is also some sort of actor on the international stage and thus has relationships of various kinds with other states, and with a growing number of non-state, inter-state and supra-state institutions and organisations.

Because of this empirical plenitude, talk of the state must also always be theoretical and is often ideological. When we talk about the state, when we define it, we are also making a political decision of some sort. To define the state as the body charged with manifesting and executing the common will of the people, or as that agency charged with establishing and implementing the common good, is to make a normative political statement. So is the claim that the state is a committee to manage the affairs of the bourgeoisie, as is the suggestion that it is a body whose function is to ensure morality and stability in society. Finally, the question of the state is also always the question of sovereignty – of who should rule, but also of where power should lie and its exercise take place. Historically, the notion of national sovereignty helped to define limits to the state by tying it to a territory, while locating the source of authority in a people (or some people) who afforded it legitimacy.

All these notions from the smallest to the largest are under pressure at the present time. It is now a banal axiom to claim that the age of the nation-state is in decline, or even over, and that the state can no longer effectively monopolise power over its own territory. It is under threat from 'above', where larger and more powerful organisations are taking shape, be they public-political such as the EU, UN, WTO and IMF or private-economic (BP, BAT etc). It is also under threat from 'below', as people's expectations of the state change, and no longer (it is said) feel that the state can express or manage their common interests or common will. On the international arena, actions such as the Gulf War and the Kosovo conflict (the latter a military action in which Blair and New Labour played an important if not central role) put into question fundamental notions of national sovereignty. Added to recent events centred on Iraq these would seem to, at the very least, suggest that the principle associated with the Treaty of Westphalia, that no state would interfere in the sovereign affairs of another, is manifestly no more.

However, what we are interested in here is not how to theorise the state in the context of all these changes and challenges. We are interested in how New Labour conceives the state, responding to these challenges and formulating a role for it in the 'new' environment. One way into this is to begin by thinking of the state as a way in which power is organised. It is certainly part of the tradition of thinking about the state and government to see them as a centre of power and much analysis and theory of the state has been given over to considering the limits to such power and the legitimate scope for its exercise.

With regard to New Labour we can identity a number of 'ideal type' analyses of the way in which it exercises power. From a (broadly speaking) liberal or pluralist perspective, the questions asked of New Labour would concern how it uses state power, whether it seeks to centralise it and hold it ever tighter, or whether it is prepared to relinquish powers of state and devolve control to other bodies or to individuals. The presumption here is that power is a resource that can be shared or hoarded. From this perspective there is a mixed assessment of how New Labour views the state. It has devolved some power to Scotland, Wales and Northern Ireland and, in a limited way, to London. Perhaps in future it will do so for other cities building on direct mayoral election. It has begun reform of the House of Lords in ways that may serve in the end to balance the power of the House of Commons, and by extension that of the core executive. But at the same time as this decentralisation has occurred the office of Prime Minister has taken on a much more direct role in day-to-day government, especially because of the need to maintain a certain front for the media. Under Blair, New Labour has shown little interest in electoral reform for the House of Commons (though the introduction of proportional representation for the European elections may suggest otherwise). Moves to 'modernise' local authorities with cabinet style executives have also received mixed responses, in that the attempt to introduce professionalism may allow councils to be more important centres of power, but may also remove them from local control. Then there is the granting to the Bank of England of 'operational independence', and the involvement of private organisations in public services through PPP and PFI. This last may be seen as a ceding of power, but it also prompts concerns that former areas of public service, once under the control of private organisations, will be less accountable to the electorate or community at large.

Allied to these sorts of critiques is the – loosely termed – Conservative view, which focuses on the abuse of power by New Labour, represented by their apparent wilful rejection of certain traditions of parliament. Blair has reduced the number of times he has to face questions in the House, and has on more than one occasion appeared to brief the media before parliament about aspects of policy change. Such things anger Conservatives, some of whom like to see power as residing in the traditions and customs of British politics, which, consequently, are sacred.

The Marxist tradition has bequeathed a wealth of sophisticated theories of the state to us. These can be detected (though often in residual form) in the analyses of New Labour in power that come from some parts of the left. Classically, Marxist theories see the state in terms of the dynamics of capitalist accumulation. It has the function of compensating for market failures at both the economic and political levels. It manages exploitation, as it were, while ensuring consent or hegemony. Hence, New Labour may be understood to be acting in the interests of capitalist corporations to whom it is beholden, or which need it to intervene in society in order to secure conditions for further profit. This may be analysed at an abstract level as a structural feature, or in a more concrete way by showing the links between big business and New Labour.[1] This links into looser instrumentalist theories of the state which see it as a tool seized by certain interests who want to use it to advance their own cause.[2] It is certainly true that New Labour's personnel are deeply entwined with leading figures in business, and that they have adapted the conduct of government in ways that have allowed them to further those links and to give people from the private sector positions of power and authority.

All these political positions do catch hold of part of the way in which New Labour operates. But here we are interested in the sort of state or mode of government New Labour thinks itself to be developing. This may not always be related to the operations of government itself. In its rhetoric of pragmatism and de-politicisation, and in maintaining that it is non-ideological, New Labour expresses a kind of truth about the self-conception of liberal government: that it is concerned only with the management of the affairs of the population in ways that are to the good of society. Of course the management of a population is not solely carried out by agencies of the state. It is carried out in sub-state organisations such as schools and also by the legal, financial and medical professions (for example), whose concern is with the conduct of personal affairs and with the care of the self. New Labour makes use of these and other such mechanisms, and in hiving-off certain state activities or privatising them it is simply trying a different way of making them work to this end. As Barry Hindess points out, freedom is not a limit of government but a mechanism of it.[3] In ceding power and pushing responsibilities onto individuals (for their education, health, financial future, etc), the government is employing a particular mechanism in order to induce them to behave in particular ways, and subjecting them to the power of medical, financial, legal administrators and so on (which is why it is also trying to work on these professions and modernise them).

So, in order to get a sense of how New Labour views or operates the state, we must not proceed by first establishing a definition of the essence of the state, and from there mapping out the way in which New Labour is conditioned by it. But neither should we attempt to divine what essence New Labour ascribes to the state. Rather, we want to see what system of government is being made possible by its reforms. This need not be understood by means of an essentially voluntaristic analysis of government. New Labour is conditioned by prior modes of government and ways of understanding it, as well as restricted by the immediate context in which it found itself upon taking power in Britain. We will see how the term 'Schumpeterian Workfare Regime' is a useful description of part of that larger context, and how this links into a particular aspect of social management that we will describe as government by culture. In order to understand that, we will have to dwell a little on New Labour economics, but first we will fill in a little of the immediate historical and theoretical context of contemporary governance in Britain.

The changing context of government

Throughout the 1980s, Thatcherite reforms of the institutions of government (scaling down the civil service, privatising industries but introducing new forms of regulation, and 'rolling back' the state) began to reduce the function of government to that of central co-ordination within a network of institutions. Government was replaced by governance: the management of policy sectors and networks, inducing actors to follow ministerial strategy.[4] Using financial incentives and the power that comes from holding purse strings, institutions and organisations can run things at arms-length, through demands for business plans and the imposition of methods of performance assessment. For example, the Department of Culture, Media and Sport does not directly interfere in the running of many cultural institutions, yet it is in a position to act in ways that manifestly do alter them. As core funder, it can demand that policy actors behave in circumscribed ways. Government becomes like a head office, franchising out its standardised operations, allowing individual units to operate independently but subject to rules and procedures formulated from above.

This is an increasingly widespread pattern of what Rhodes has called 'governing without government'.[5] The state manages through a range of institutions, exercising control rather than command, steering without hierarchy. It is a sound hegemonic strategy for a state in flux, requiring it to build and sustain strategic alliances. In combination with the dissipation of the power of national governments to control the flow of trade, or to regulate the practices of commercial companies that transcend borders, and the growth of international and supra-national state institutions, this leaves us with what Jessop has described as the 'hollowing out' of the nation-state.[6] In the 1980s the discourse of the new public management, NHS reorganisation, and the creation of grant maintained schools and the Next Steps Agency (to list but a few 'innovations'), built on these trends and transformed key organisations of the state.

New Labour has inherited this hollowed out state model, and in this sense it undeniably operates on a terrain set by Thatcherism, even if it has not become comprehensively Thatcherite.[7] But Thatcherism did not entirely succeed in securing its neo-liberal project of state 'withdrawal', partly because its mistrust of collective or state institutions and its hostility to the notion of society prevented it from understanding the communal and cultural underpinnings of market relations.[8] By contrast New Labour believes in the need to generate the relations of mutual obligation and trust that underpin the contract society, and in a new kind of role for the state in their production (see Chapter 5).

The legacy of the Thatcherite reforms is a set of state institutions that cannot expect automatic approval on the basis of deference to authority, or the belief that 'they' know what they are doing. They must justify themselves through their 'market' performance, their efficiency, value-for-money, quality of service, and so forth, and are made accountable through the publication of their achievements and failures. New Labour's 'modernisation' entails an extension of this logic. Schools are being encouraged to diversify more, and to reach their attainment targets or face direct intervention. Universities, perhaps, will eventually set differential rates for fees, leading to a premiere league of super-funded institutions and a range of competitive options for students.[9] Performance related pay, pledges and quality commitments form the framework of accountability.

But there is a contradiction in a government committing itself to this consumerist logic of judgement. Although there is competition for the contract to govern us, the rules of that competition are quite different from those of the market. Only the very rich and multi-national corporations can exercise a meaningful choice as to which state they are to live under. Certainly governments now market themselves as offering attractive regimes, and territories ripe for good investment, but this does not constitute much of a basis for the relationship between the state and its citizens. If we are reduced to mere consumers of the state and of democracy, then social relations will remain anomic and privatised, undermining the very things – the shared framework of values and mutual responsibilities – that make even the most liberal of liberal free markets function.

As a result, in order to pursue a substantial market-based reform of the state-society relationship, it becomes necessary to find new ways of building consensus and legitimacy for the state and for society. The specific benefits of the state, or of a commitment to sociality, can no longer be the source of this legitimacy, for they are exactly what has been hived-off to bodies judged on the grounds of pure efficacy. Thus it is the state *as such* and sociality *as such* that must find a new ground on which to stand. That they are failing to do so is clear from the fact that political criticism has become increasingly pre-occupied with finding reasons to question the honesty or propriety of politicians, their managerial competence or the quality of their hairdressing rather than their political and economic ideas.

New Labour clearly does believe in a role for the state and for a public political life, but it does not conceive of it in terms of blunt intervention. Instead it is prone to exhortation and the employment of policies that function to exhort. As Blair put it in his foreword to the competitiveness White Paper in 1998: 'Old-fashioned state intervention did not and cannot work. But neither does naive reliance on markets. The Government must promote competition, stimulating enterprise, flexibility and innovation by opening markets ... In

Government, in business, in our universities and throughout society we must do much more to foster a new entrepreneurial spirit: equipping ourselves for the long term, prepared to seize opportunities, committed to constant innovation and enhanced performance'. And this entrepreneurial spirit is not limited to economic activity. Citizens are instructed to care for their own health, to develop within themselves the skills necessary to find work and to take more of an interest in the education of their children rather than expect the state to do it all for them. They are to recognise their responsibilities as well as exercise their rights. Simultaneously, as we have also seen, it becomes quite logical for government to develop a deep interest in its media representation. The people need to be reminded of what government does for (or to) them and informed (through advertising for example) about what they can get from it.

Thus, slowly, a new sort of relationship between government and people evolves. One in which the state regards its citizens as separated, individuated units, not to be represented by sectional institutions. For New Labour contemporary 'subjectivity' is an ever changing, self-creating, reflexive entity (see Chapter 5). Society can no longer be conceived as any sort of homogenous mass or bloc, best analysed along one axis, such as class. Rather notions of plurality are emphasised. And it should be noted that this plurality is not seen as emerging from forms of difference embedded in the varied historical and cultural experiences of different groups of people. Plurality for New Labour goes all the way down, and becomes the difference of individuation. The task of government is to enhance and increase that individuation as part of the conditions for the structural competitiveness of the nation.

This individuation is the logic behind popular control that takes the form of market choice (OMOV in the party, direct management of schools accompanied by free choice and league tables, doctors who don't intervene between 'customer' and 'service provider', mayors directly elected without boroughs getting in the way and so forth). As we have seen, this goes along with the simultaneous simplification of that which is chosen – parties narrow down the choice of candidates for election, schools are restricted in what they can teach and when, and so on. And in the absence of any social intermediaries, government must speak directly to the people through the media, and it must attempt to embody the values and aspirations which we now lack. These are the processes at work within the ideology and policy of New Labour. But these have not occurred in a vacuum, produced from the whims of political leaders. They have emerged from a background of social and economic change, and the interpretation of that change.

Where dogma-driven neo-liberals sought to liberate the market from the state, New Labour seeks to deploy that state in the name of the market, because it sees that the market itself has changed. To facilitate that change, only the state, with its virtual monopoly of education and its key role in social security, can assist. Thatcherism foundered because it could not see the contradiction between valorising tradition while advocating an economy that, by its very nature, destroyed tradition. New Labour seeks out ways to ground a new kind of social and economic order, developing a political ethic of open-ended democracy, and of governance oriented towards encouraging risk and the entrepreneurial life-style. Its programme is based on the necessity, as New Labour sees it, of managing the completion of a transition from one mode of capital accumulation to another. Such a programme requires more than policies that alter the way governments interfere with the economy. It requires, so the argument runs, a restructuring of the relationship between the state, the economy and citizens. But states must act not only to reproduce the economic conditions essential to continued capital accumulation; they must also secure the conditions for its social and ideological reproduction. The Thatcherite rhetoric of nationhood, self-reliance and moral authoritarianism failed to do this because it required practices deemed to be at odds with neo-liberal orthodoxy. New Labour's 'historic mission' is to secure the conditions for the radical restructuring of the state-citizen relationship in ways that permit the creation of the conditions for the expansion of a particular form of economic accumulation. As a result the economic philosophy and policy of New Labour is far wider than usually assumed.

New Labour economics

The simplest way to explain New Labour's economic theory is to see it as nothing more than political expedience. The Labour Party in Britain, until 2001, had consistently failed to secure long-term electoral success because of a failure (both perceived and actual) to manage the economy competently. What this means more precisely is that it had not been able to win the confidence of business (otherwise known as the capitalist class), which, in turn, precipitated economic crises that brought down Labour governments. Thus the Treasury's overwhelming stress on stability or prudence stems from electoral-political anxiety given previous failures. New Labour regards it as necessary to maintain the confidence of the financial sectors and to secure the consent of those rich and powerful in business in order to stay in government.

Such an interpretation is appealing but insufficient. Just like theories of New Labour's general re-branding, this thesis can be equivalent to a simple assumption of cynicism on the part of politicians. While there is certainly truth in the claim that New Labour has adjusted economic policy as a response to electoral pressures, and that it does see a need to win over high profile business leaders, this does not of itself explain the what or the why of current economic policy. Politicians are not wholly or purely cynical, and New Labour has not enacted policies that are solely in the short-term interests of a business elite.

A more sophisticated version of this argument attributes the accommodation of New Labour to business interests to structural rather than Machiavellian causes. Here the argument is that in a capitalist context no government can attain all its goals without winning over the power of capital. Because it is structurally dependent on capital, the state must act to secure the conditions favourable to continued accumulation.[10] Therefore social democratic parties serious about attaining power have little choice but to tailor their policies accordingly.

This view also has a certain amount of truth in it. Clearly, in a capitalist society capitalists are, by definition, a powerful interest group whose consent may well be needed if a party is to secure even limited hegemony. But this too is insufficient as an explanation since it is really only a description. As Hay makes clear, the thesis of 'structural dependence' implies that social democratic policies must necessarily be against the interests of capital, that capital itself is capable of knowing where its long term interests lie, and that capital has a single unified interest. As such, the thesis depoliticises capitalist economics and poses a static, non-historical model of the relationship between the state and the economy, failing to take full account of the fact that at any one time the interests of capital and the interests of the state (not to mention the interests of the people) are far from clear, and are established only on the basis of ongoing political argument and struggle. That is to say, the interests of each of these sectors are not objectively given and made available to us. Even if one accepts that the interest of capital indisputably lies in rapid and continuing accumulation, the best way in which to achieve such a goal is not clear outside of particular ideological perspectives. The very notion that social democratic governments have no useful part to play in the reproduction of capital is itself the outcome of recent political disputes and failures. The threat of capital flight if a government looks likely to impose any burden at all on multi-national companies is based on particular beliefs, attitudes and practices, and not on any undisputed maxim of capitalist management. This strategy is based on particular attachments to quick profit, immediate shareholder return and the maximising of income through worker degradation, rather than on, for example, increased quality of product and therefore better sales. As such, a tendency towards capital flight may have been a class-based political response by capitalism to the crises of the 1970s, but it was not the only possible response, nor was it intrinsically necessary. It may not even have been in the interests of capitalists.

So, whatever, 'natural' pressures the frameworks of electoral competition and the claims of capital may exert upon a social democratic party, they are articulated with other sorts of ideological pressure and with past political choices, convictions and decisions. Simple expediency may lie behind some changes of economic policy, but this doesn't explain either what they are or where they came from. Political decisions were made (influenced by the differentials of power possessed by differing portions of the political and economic elite), and those decisions were based on assumptions about the nature of capitalist economics. It follows that the interpretation of New Labour economics has to include some reference to this wider dimension of political practices and intellectual beliefs.

Of course, much turns, then, on arguments about the actual state of the UK economy, its position in the world, reasons for its relative decline and so forth. It is widely argued on the British left (with varying inflections) that the British problem lies in an over emphasis on capital markets, combined with the tendency of British capital not to invest inwardly, and to operate on the basis of general short-termism. Hence there has been a lack of industrial modernisation and strategic planning for growth. An exemplar and symbol of this is the historic and oft-bemoaned domination of economic policy (and of government in general) by the Treasury, to the detriment of those departments concerned with industrial development. One popular recent version of this argument is that developed by Hutton.[11] For the right, Thatcherism was a modernising strategy that cleared out the dead and dying institutions which slowed down capital (such as government subsidy and management, as well as trade unions) and exposed British firms to the bracingly healthy air of competition. But for the left this approach simply exacerbated the problem, supporting mobile capital in the acquisition of quick profit and failing to address the deeper underlying difficulties.[12]

It is possible to interpret New Labour's economics as an attempt to solve these long term problems (as understood by the left), but in the context of a state that has been dramatically weakened by the years of Tory rule and shifts in global economics. Thus, Andrew Gamble and Gavin Kelly, while accepting that New Labour has generally adopted a supply-side approach, draw attention to the way the Department for Trade and Industry is beginning to look at problems of productivity, the supply of capital and the need to finance research. They stress that 'there remains a sharp contrast between Labour and the Conservative governments of the 1980s and 1990s ... Labour retains a much stronger belief in the role of an active state in promoting a fairer and more prosperous society'. Labour's 'linking of a commitment to macro-economic stability with an active policy to increase employment opportunity, redistribute resources and find ways to combat social exclusion ... places [them] squarely in the long tradition of economic revisionism which has been such a distinctive feature of the evolution of the party in the last fifty years'.[13]

New Labour, from this point of view, is attempting to forge a new version of social democracy in the post-Thatcher/Reagan period, and in the context of evolving post-cold war globalisation. But how social democratic is it? As two reasonably sympathetic but generally objective analysts, answering this very question, argue: 'Preoccupation with the supply side is the most distinctive aspect of Labour policy, combining a wholesale reorientation of the welfare state towards encouraging work, with abandonment of both the interventionist policies towards industry and the collaboration with trade unions so characteristic of social democracy in the 1960s and 1970s'.[14] While spending on health and education is increasing quicker than under the Conservatives, the overall proportion of GDP spent by government is falling, and high spending in one area is matched by cuts elsewhere. In attempting to target certain kinds of welfare provision towards those at the very bottom, New Labour does seem to show more interest in poverty (if not inequality) than Tory governments. Yet it clearly subordinates this to the need to maintain business confidence. In terms of stimulating growth or managing the economy, the New Labour approach seems decidedly non-social democratic and certainly post-Keynesian. It attempts to keep intervention and regulation to a minimum, and has pursued further privatisations of state monopolies (such as the Post Office) while favouring the Private Finance Initiative and Public Private Partnerships over direct subsidy. Despite some representations to the contrary the formation of the Strategic Rail Authority does not reverse this trend.

In terms of competitiveness New Labour seems, at least rhetorically, to be determined to steer a middle course, rejecting both state intervention (of the non-modernised old-fashioned form) and pure reliance on markets. In this respect, despite much criticism, the New Labour approach may indeed be an attempt to break away from the debilitating British pattern of low-investment and short-termism. It has increased investment in science and technology and encourages the private sector to do likewise. Education Action Zones are intended to promote links between education and industry, a policy also encouraged in the universities. Indeed, the basis of New Labour economic policy is (as in other areas of policy) the need for companies to respond to the knowledge economy, and it seems to be interested in helping them to do it. So, while New Labour seems to be moving away from the traditional tools of social democratic economic policy, and to be very focused on the supply side, it retains an interest in some kind of role for the state in generating the conditions for the growth of the (knowledge) economy. Maybe it is indeed a case of traditional values in modern setting.

In complete contrast, Arestis and Sawyer describe third way economic policy as 'new monetarism' or 'interventionist neo-classical economics of a new Keynesian variety'.[15] They argue that third way economics clearly holds it as axiomatic that markets are in essence good, and market actors rational (that markets are essentially stable but macro-economic policy can destabilise them). Third way economics also argues that markets may fail and that governments should compensate for imperfect information and remedy some externalities. The economy is imperfectly competitive, and dependent on 'public goods' (such as knowledge and information) which will not be provided by the private sector. With globalisation making things harder for governments, the creation of favourable conditions is the priority for policy, and this includes the condition for such endogenous growth. Therefore the third way sees a role here for the state.[16] Furthermore, growth may depend on the presence of a skilled and properly trained workforce. Thus: 'long-run growth in income per head depends on investment decisions rather than, as in traditional growth theory, resulting from unexplained or exogenous improvements in technology ... government policy can influence these decisions both directly through taxes and subsidies and indirectly via reform of institutional arrangements ... intervention might in principle be used to raise investment and hence the long-run growth rate'.[17]

Thus New Labour employment policy, for example, has shifted away from an emphasis on state intervention and investment stimulation, to a focus on the labour market itself, which is understood as the source and location of employment problems. The government's approach to unemployment seems to be aimed at the securing of stability, with an attempt to square the circle by arguing that bringing people back into the labour market through training policies and making work pay, through the minimum wage and tax credits, will lead to an increase in tax revenue; and this will then enable the balance between spending and income to be maintained while not endangering growth through inflation. Thus growth and social security can be made friends not enemies. As Arestis and Sawyer conclude, the notable feature of the New Labour approach to inequality is: 'first, the continuing emphasis on changes relating to the labour market as a means of reducing unemployment and inequality rather than any emphasis on capacity and demand; and, second, the emphasis on reduction of inequality of opportunity and what may be termed pre-market inequality, rather than on the reduction of inequality of outcomes and post-market inequality'.[18] Third way macroeconomic policy, they conclude, is marked by a:

> rejection of Keynesianism, an emphasis on control of inflation rather than the reduction of unemployment and a perceived need to acquire credibility in the financial markets ... microeconomic policy [is] concerned with the correction of 'market failures' ... a policy which accepts the beneficial operation of markets, albeit one that can be improved by appropriate government action [and to] equip individuals to compete in the market e.g. through training and education.

This is 'neo-liberalism with a human face'.[19]

In a sense then, these critics of New Labour concur with sympathisers in terms of analysis if not in terms of evaluation. But in these and other analyses[20] evaluation is often based on an assessment of how close or distant current New Labour policy is to that of both Tory and Labour predecessors. Are their policies a capitulation to Thatcherism (a simple continuation of neo-liberalism), a continuation of trends within social democracy and rooted in the Smith and Kinnock years, a capitulation to the interests of capital or an attempt to redirect it during a period of transformation? Yet the general nature of New Labour economics is quite clear and straightforward, and is expressed in numerous comments by Tony Blair, including some already quoted. For Blair: 'To succeed as an economy we develop the talents of all. To be a fair society, we give opportunity to all. The political consequences are historic; self-interest and the common good are at long last in alliance ...'.[21] New Labour sees its economic policy as ending the short-termism of traditional British economic policy and as absolutely emblematic of modernisation. It consists of targeting modest, but not insignificant, benefits at the very poor, raising money and investment through the inclusion of the private sector in the business of the state (thus heralding a new form of government-economy relationship, the consequences of which we have all barely begun to think about) and concentrating on the improvement of the workforce as an all round panacea to the problems of unemployment, poverty, growth and investment. The shell within which all this is expressed is that of absolute conviction in the newness of the new world of new things.

As far as New Labour are concerned there is little point interpreting this economic approach in terms of previous or other approaches. Where analysis is concerned to locate it somewhere among the complex phyla of economic thought, the ideology of New Labour sees economics in a different light. This is a government where a minister is prepared to cite Manuel Castells in outlining her business philosophy.[22] They believe themselves to be thinking in a holistic or joined-up and rather grand way that responds to the challenges of the present. Colin Hay roundly criticises New Labour for blowing the opportunity to enter office and develop a new economic paradigm able to combat the deep-rooted weaknesses of the economy. He blames the party and its think tanks (IPPR, IFS, DEMOS) for 'consigning their creativity to the parameters of a market liberalism whose ascendancy they refuse to challenge'.[23] But the failure of New Labour to advance a new paradigm with which Hay agrees is not the same as a failure to have a paradigm at all. Because he is unable to identify a project from New Labour that would be an adequate response to the diagnosis he has made of the economic problems of the UK, Hay interprets what they do have by way of policy as a capitulation to the Thatcherite legacy. Meanwhile, sympathisers such as Gamble and Kelly or Glyn and Wood try to show that New Labour economics exhibits signs of continuity of some sort with the social democratic tradition. But New Labour is not really interested in these sorts of interpretation or debate. It has developed a paradigm for economic interpretation and policy formation. This picks up and moves on from the Thatcherite legacy and is believed to be a genuine modernisation of the economy. That paradigm, as we keep stressing, is that of 'post-fordism' and of the 'new' knowledge economy, and within this the domain of economic policy is reconfigured.

Almost all of the policies of New Labour are economic policies. Reforms of welfare, health, education and cultural policy are, in essence, economically motivated. The state is charged with the role of creating an environment conducive to economic success and this means education and training policies that produce a skilled workforce. It means a tax and regulation system that encourages investment. But it also means the creation of the correct social conditions – the right 'hubs' in the forms of 'science parks' and new silicon valleys. Charles Leadbeater (a central author of the *Manifesto for New Times*, discussed in Chapter 4, and now a government adviser) argues that 'the unit of competitiveness in the modern economy should be the network, not the company or the sector' and government should act to foster the co-operative and competitive nature of such networks by stimulating and encouraging their development around key sites such as universities.[24] In turn this means that government must be in partnership with regional authorities and local businesses to help create that 'world-class' environment. It must act to foster the human or social capital 'on the ground' that helps secure the foundations for business success. This sort of thinking then allows New Labour to differentiate itself from pure neo-liberalism in that it can claim to recognise that the market only functions because of non-market institutions and a social environment that is favourable to it. For these reasons New Labour can (and does) point to constitutional reform, the Scottish Parliament, Welsh Assembly and Northern Irish legislative assembly as part of its economic policy. Similarly, the Regional Development Agencies, Learning and Skills Councils, New Deal for Communities, Single Regeneration Budget and Sure Start for families can be sold as new partnerships in the creation of social capital.[25]

For this reason we need to develop a slightly different way of making sense of New Labour economics, premised on taking them seriously and on seeing such policies as symptomatic expressions of our present condition. For it may be that New Labour does not interpret the economic problems of the UK in the way implied by many scholars. Indeed, it may not even understand economics in quite the same way.

The term or concept of 'the economy' is not fixed. Its meaning is itself an object of political contestation. One of the most pernicious of modern intellectual developments has been the narrowing down of the reference of economics such that it can often appear to be the preserve of a small and very skilled elite accompanied by complex mathematical calculations designed to allow a 'guru' to divine the future movements of the mysteries of consumer desire. But what counts as economic and what doesn't, what may be made the object of economic policy or not, what is to be seen as an economic relation and what not, and what it means to call any of these things 'economic', are highly important philosophical and ethical questions.

For example, in his book *Living on Thin Air* (praised by Tony Blair), Leadbeater declares that the knowledge economy must lead to a re-fashioning of government policies and of the theories about what such policies are for and can do. His proposed refashioning, an 'economic constitution', involves re-addressing issues of innovation, investment, ownership, security and the sources of value. It also means altering tax and regulation policies to cope with a situation where goods are easily transferred across borders, and where earnings do not necessarily derive from a simple wage or salary. His mission is to convince everyone that the new economy is in their interests. Since nothing can be done to alter it, it is incumbent on those who understand the situation to help those who don't, or those who feel threatened by it. In other words the primary political task is to bring the aspirations of people into harmony with the needs of the economy.

For him, as for New Labour, economics is not simply a matter of the management of the UK household budget. Firstly, it specifically means wealth creation, which means an increase in the overall growth of tradable goods. This is so obvious (and not unique to Labour) that it is not often remarked upon, but it has a bearing. Secondly, the economy primarily consists of people selling things, as opposed to making them, and the market is thus of immense, primary, importance. The economy, for New Labour, is primarily a commodity economy in which what the classical economists saw as unproductive labour is now understood as the key source of 'added value'.[26] New Labour likes this because commodities are free, they flow, they move, they combine and recombine. Things that enter the market therefore become free and so, it follows, things should be encouraged to enter that market, especially workers, because if they do so, they will be free. Keeping them out of the market (as old-style social democracy did) is tantamount to imprisoning them.[27] Thirdly, the crucial component of the economy is knowledge. The knowledge revolution means that so much more than we ever thought can now be traded. As Leadbeater puts it: 'Knowledge empowers people to take charge of their lives ... The more an economy promotes the production and spread of knowledge, rather than just the exchange of goods and services, the better-off we become'.[28] Fourthly, this breaks down old divisions between social sectors, such that the economic impulse is free to roam throughout the social organism. This means that lots more things can be capitalised. So, for example, we refer now, routinely, to human capital and to social capital (see Chapter 5). This concept of the economy is fundamental to New Labour thinking. It is the place where the solipsism of their argumentation can appear to have found solid ground outside of itself, the Archimedean position of judgement. But this has effects on all other aspects of New Labour thinking. If, under Keynesianism, the economy was understood in terms of the relations of demand and supply – as a chain of production and consumption – this constituted a clear domain of action and set of potential policy instruments. But for New Labour the economy is broader and flatter than that; it is a different regime requiring a different state.

The 'Schumpeterian Workfare Regime'

New Labour does not primarily understand state power in traditional behavioural, institutional or constitutional terms, but works on the basis of multi-dimensional assumptions.[29] It sees political and governmental power in far broader terms, at the same time as believing this capacity to be heavily circumscribed. This is part of the reason for conflict between New Labour and those Tories who repeatedly accuse them of ignoring parliamentary protocol and procedure. New Labour does not understand the state simply in terms of governmental practices, and does not recognise itself as limited by the Palace of Westminster. Instead government is conceived as an enabling institution and as the centre of a variety of networks of policy formulation and implementation. This affords it the indirect form of power that sets agendas and leads policy by inducement rather than direct intervention. But more than this, Labour recognises the overall power of government to shape perceptions and set frames for all of those working within state- based institutions, and potentially those beyond it. This perspective underpins attitudes to the reform of education and welfare, where the emphasis is not only on exposing the welfare system to cold winds but the claimant as well. The options by which the claimant can shelter from such blasts are then set by government enforced procedures. As the House of Commons select committee has recognised, 'the notion of a service-wide system appropriate to everyone is becoming increasingly a fiction'.[30] Hence the system is reoriented towards more nuanced forms of relationship with 'clients', shifting from the imposition of certain kinds of state support to the inducement of certain kinds of choice. From a monolithic Fordist system where pay-outs and treatment are uniform, we move to a post-fordist one where standardised packages are given a – not insignificant – gloss of pseudo-individuation, with tailored 'care-packages' and a focus not on keeping citizens or claimants in their place, but on re-shaping their place and their perceptions of it.

Welfare-to-work is not a new policy. It builds on various training schemes developed in the 1970s and re-worked by the Tories in the 1980s into programmes such as the Youth Training Scheme and Youth Opportunities Programme.[31] It also has precursors in schemes developed by the 'new' Democrats in the United States.[32] What is new for Britain is the wholesale development and extension of the policy. At one level it is open-ended, with employment options for work in the voluntary sector, or with the environmental task force, or involvement in education or training. Furthermore it seems also to involve an explicit role for government in employment creation – something of a novelty after such a long period of purely neo-liberal rule. Employers are given a subsidy to give full-time work to the long-term unemployed, and there are national insurance exemptions for those employing the low-paid. This combines with the rhetoric of a new contract between the state and citizens, in which the return for being flexible enough to take work where it is available is the guarantee of state assistance in finding it and the assurance that work will pay. But there is also a strong element of compulsion. While there is a choice between forms of work and forms of training staying on benefit is an option available to fewer and fewer people. Where Conservative governments moved towards various schemes in order to reduce the statistics of unemployment, New Labour is committed to this version of 'workfare' as a way of actually reducing unemployment, and thus, by extension, as a way of providing particular sorts of workers for the new economy. While the rhetoric is that of active government, intervening to achieve full employment, the practice, with its orientation towards training and flexibility, is clearly supply-side. Social inclusion requires the willingness to be fit for the labour market, and hence allows the combination of compulsion with claims about social justice. It is clearly not the intention to tackle employment policy through Keynesian procedures of macro-economic management, but rather to facilitate the individual in becoming ready to face an unmanaged and unmanageable economy. Thus: 'the government is determined to build an active welfare system which helps people to help themselves and ensures a proper level of support in times of need'.[33] Such an approach emerges in part out of a communitarian interpretation of the causes of decline, in which they are found to reside in inappropriate moral attitudes. The response is to try and foster a sense of individual responsibility and duty balanced by an acknowledgement of the responsibilities of the government and of society.[34] But this approach also emerges from the desire to generate new kinds of active welfare recipient, who are clear that ultimate responsibility for their self-improvement rests on their obtaining the right skills and capacities for entering the flexible labour market, on being an ideal citizen. Underlying such proposals is a clear moralisation, but one that can be understood as feeding into a strategy of governance aiming to change the culture and outlook of those it touches. Similar motivations can be seen in the way the government is developing a generalisable discourse of community and partnership to displace that of market and contract.

This is an intriguing strategy of governance. Where that term is usually used to describe the relationship between government and the agencies with which, or through which, it operates, one can see a form of governance behind welfare to work that aims at the individual claimant. A 'work ethic' is encouraged, and the claimant individualised, so as to regard him or herself less as an object of state policy and more as a subject who must take on the responsibility for change and development. A number of analysts have opted to describe the sort of state/society relationship under development here (which also seems to be emerging out of post-fordism in Europe) as a 'Schumpeterian Workfare Regime'.[35]

The aims of the Keynesian welfare state were to secure full employment through policies formulated on the basis of managing a national economy. Given that the mode of mass production was somewhat inflexible, the emphasis of economic policy could be on the demand side and achieved through the alliance of the state with key social and economic corporations. This involved a degree of collectivism and the provision of a large-scale system of welfare support. But we are now witnessing the shift from welfare to workfare. With the Tories the motivation behind such policy shifts had more to do with cutting welfare expenditure than reforming the nature of the labour market itself.[36] But New Labour has entered into the wholesale reform of the social security system through the development of welfare-to-work schemes. It has rejected ideologically driven neo-liberalism, while endorsing the supposedly 'pragmatic' aspects of Thatcherite change. It is thus developing a version of the 'Schumpeterian' state.

The Austrian economist Joseph Schumpeter was concerned to develop a theory of economic development, as opposed to the static models of idealised economic processes that tended to dominate neo-classical economic theory. Schumpeter placed special emphasis on the role of entrepreneurs, and began to describe economic transformation in terms of endogenous factors as opposed to the effects of external 'contingencies' (among which he counted population change). He focused on the question of how 'the economic system generates the force which incessantly transforms it ... a source of energy within the economic system which would, of itself, disrupt any equilibrium that might be attained',[37] and he argued that:

> the essence of economic development lies in the fact that the means of production, which hitherto have been put to certain static uses, are being deflected from this course and are devoted to new purposes ... these new combinations are not carried through on their own accord ... but for their realisation are in need of a kind of intelligence and energy which inhere only in a minority of economic agents. The intrinsic function of the entrepreneur consists in carrying out these new combinations.[38]

From this perspective economic growth occurs because of changes in the supply side as opposed to that of demand. It is driven by entrepreneurial innovation, such as the creation of new goods, or their better deployment, new techniques of production or marketing, the establishment of new markets or new sources of supply and so forth. Inventions may make possible new developments, but they require entrepreneurial innovation to be deployed. This means that the availability of investment capital (through banks and other credit sources for example) is crucial to economic development. Where neo-classicists had sought for the way towards a state of economic equilibrium, Schumpeter pronounced 'stationary capitalism' a contradiction in terms, and found the core characteristic of capitalism to be its changeability, its 'creative destruction'.[39] Thus economic management is not about steering the economy towards a notional point of stability; it is about managing change and promoting it.

Innovation comes from knowledge. Economic processes cannot be understood in terms of the rational calculation of essentially utilitarian agents. Rationality proceeds on the basis of fixed routines, whereas innovation consists in departing from the tried and tested ways of making economic decisions. Factors such as consumer taste or want are thus not external to the economy but endogenous: 'It is the producer who as a rule initiates economic change, and consumers are educated by him if necessary; they are, as it were, taught to want new things, or things which differ in some respect or other from those which they have been in the habit of using.'[40]

In sum, this is a supply side approach, but one that sees the capacities for rationally predicting what will happen in the future as limited, since innovation, by definition, is not explicable from within the confines of the present routines. It follows that the way to manage an economy is to ensure the flexibility to take up new innovations and to encourage their development; that governments can't plan ahead but can create conditions for the circulation of knowledge and the continued supply of entrepreneurs to innovate. One could extend this logic into other areas of social organisation, such as the public services and, when combined with the interpretations of 'New Times' and 'reflexive modernity', one has a vision of a permanently evolving social order, the enemy of which is any kind of conservatism, since the future depends on our 'permanent revision' and open embrace of change.

The 'Schumpeterian Workfare Regime' thus represents an attempt to promote a kind of permanent innovation as the way to enhance structural competitiveness. The role of the state is greater than with a neo-liberal system, since it must work to move the national economy into the international arena, and to ensure that the conditions are there for permanent innovation. It is a supply-side strategy, where it seeks to ensure a sufficient skills–base in the workforce, and can encourage investment in, for example, research and development and in small firms with an innovative strategy. The state arenas of social security and education thus become central, since both can be used to enhance the competitiveness of the supply side, not least in the creation of the entrepreneurial subject.

Jessop summarises the role of such a state, in terms of economic and social reproduction, as: 'to promote product, process, organisational and market innovation in open economies in order to strengthen as far as possible the structural competitiveness of the national economy by intervening on the supply side; and to subordinate social policy to the needs of labour market flexibility and/or to the constraints of international competition'.[41] As Torfing points out, and as we have seen, this is more appropriately termed a regime than a state as such, since, while 'the state may retain the overall responsibility for the formulation, legitimisation and outcome of different policies ... the responsibility for operationalising and implementing these policies is to an increasing extent shared with different non-state actors with self-organised policy networks.'[42]

As Torfing shows, the forms taken by any particular SWR will vary in different countries depending on the strategies employed. He identifies neo-liberal, neo-statist and neo-corporatist versions. The neo-liberal version seeks to reduce the role of the state and to privilege the market, though it may use the state in order to secure that freedom for markets. The neo-statist version employs the state to re-organise the economy and society through developing competitive management in the public sector and new forms of multi-faceted governance. With the neo-corporatist strategy there is greater integration, but in a more open framework of policy networks. He further distinguishes between offensive and defensive strategies. The offensive aims to be pro-active, perhaps utilising workfare schemes to offer empowering education and training within a universalist system, while the defensive strategy prioritises punitive policies towards the unemployed.[43]

Torfing argues that reforms to the Danish welfare state have proceeded on the basis of an offensive neo-statist strategy. They have been able to do so because of specific features of Danish society, such as a strong tradition of universalist welfare provision, a labour movement that has been closely involved in active labour market policies and their regional implementation, and the separation of the benefits system from that involved with the offering of employment. By contrast, he argues, in Britain there is not such a strong commitment to universalism, the union movement is fragmented and confrontational, while the linking of the benefits payments system with job centres intensifies claimants' hostility to the finding of work.[44] As a result Britain has tended to pursue more neo-liberal strategies, operating on a defensive, punitive, basis.

But these 'deficiencies' of the British system are not simply inherent in British life, though their embeddedness in social and state institutions makes change difficult. They are also the result of many years of Conservative hegemony. The task of a government, committed to a 'post-fordist' kind of analysis, and to developing a welfare system involved in the active creation of workers and employment, is to break these habits and 'traditions', to defy these 'forces of conservatism'. Thus the managerialism of New Labour includes a political task, aimed at encouraging people to embrace change, to alter their outlook on what work means and how work is to be found, and to shift their perceptions of what they can expect out of life for themselves and their children. Much New Labour and third way discussion is, as a consequence, quite explicitly concerned with how to do this, how to tell what Charles Leadbeater calls an 'economy story' that would 'show why it [New Labour] is uniquely well-placed to tap the knowledge economy's potential for growth, innovation and productivity'; it would be 'a story about how the economy will develop, that will help people to make sense of how they and their children will make their living, what sort of companies they will be working for, making what sorts of products and using what sorts of skills'.[45] The dilemma for New Labour is that of finding ways to justify change to politics, work-life and social life, in a situation where people in their public, private and financial lives are dispersed and suspicious of state action. It consequently pursues something between a neo-statist and neo-corporatist approach, following British traditions of state-centralism while linking into private corporations and interest groups, extending the practice of governance beyond the state. In his analysis of the Schumpeterian Workfare Regime, Jessop includes a fourth ideal- type strategy, the neo-communitarian; in place of the active labour market policy and state sponsorship associated with statism, this emphasises the third sector and the social economy.[46] New Labour, while hanging on to some degree of faith in state-based mechanisms, and remaining interested in developing some partners for its policy of change, tries to square yet more circles through this (occasionally populist) attachment to community, and so extends governance into these realms, trying to govern through culture.

Culture as a strategy of governance

Thus far we have been concerned with changes in institutional structure and procedure, but the underlying theme has been the question of how New Labour can maintain legitimacy and coherence within the conditions it identifies as characterising our present. So, we need to think more specifically about its practice of government or governance. But this is not just the process by which, as we have seen, the state creates the subject of the economy through exhortation, expressed via new education and welfare policies. The 'knowledge economy' presents a strategic opportunity by which government can maintain and extend itself. Seeking to change 'identities' and 'govern by culture', instead of direct regulation, is not simply an appropriate way of governing in order to meet the needs of the knowledge economy. It is also itself a mechanism by which we are governed, demanding a new order of ceaseless movement and innovation. As Stephen Byers suggests: 'The answer must lie in the modernisation of all our social and political institutions. We must look at everything afresh, from the detail of individual policies down to how we develop policy, communicate and deliver it ... The more creative you are, the more dynamic and enterprising, the more you stand to benefit'.[47] Or, as Blair puts it: 'There will be no slowing down in the pace of change ... the speed of our modernisation programme will be accelerated. By definition modernisation has to be a continuous process ... Modernisation and improvement have to be a permanent drive to ensure that things really are getting better'.[48]

This endless reinvention necessitates new ways of governing and ordering, targeted at new objects. Where once the state had to intervene to make society and its citizens fit for the new industrial economy (by forcing people off land and into cities, developing disciplinary education systems to train them and so forth), now the state must intervene to bring about the people of the knowledge economy: the true reflexive individual, possessing a kind of permanently revisionist self; an empowered and mobile subject (geographically, economically and psychically) who is his/her own entrepreneur of selfhood. As a corollary the state will cease to be a tool of direct intervention. It will merely be an 'enabler', while those individuals, and the associations of which they may be part, move into fill the space left by the state. People and organisations are set free yet they must take on the burden of establishing moral direction and exercising responsibility.[49]

In New Labour speak this mutates into attempts to govern through exhortations to community and responsibility. Community becomes for the government both a problem and a solution; something it must revitalise, through which it can reach individuals and re-orient them, but at the same time something into which it cannot fully go. As Rose points out, 'community, rather than society, is the new territorialisation of political thought, the new way in which conduct is collectivised'.[50] In New Labour's discourse of community, questions of moralisation, individualism, citizenship, responsibility and adaptability all find a presumed answer. The management and refinement of 'communities' becomes the procedure by which security and legitimacy can be attained in the 'fast-forward future'. This also means that everything can become understood as a community. In the mobile world, only a few types of community are tied to anything so twentieth-century as a place. There are work-based communities, communities built around certain types of people or types of labourer, national and international communities, and so on. Anything can be seen as a community, since the meaningfulness of the word does not entail satisfying some basic definitional criteria. Rather, it requires a reorientation of our perception in order to see that we were always looking at a community. Reconceived as being part of a community, relationships and a variety of social phenomena can be grasped in the terms of government practice.

This new mode of governance cannot operate through the supposedly 'old' ways of government intervention, legislation or anything so crude as taxing people. For Perri 6:

> Culture is now the centre of the agenda for government reform, because we now know from the findings of a wide range of recent research that culture is perhaps the most important determinant of a combination of long-run economic success and social cohesion. The mistake of both statist left and laissez-faire right was to ignore this fact.

Educational achievement cannot be enhanced without 'a shift in the mentalities of parents and children towards valuing education and investing time and energy into it'; law and order requires changing the cultures of the people who live in areas with high crime rates; environmental improvement rests on changing attitudes to energy efficiency, and unemployment requires addressing not only economic barriers to the long-term unemployed, 'but also their own cultural and attitudinal handicaps'.[51] This, in Nikolas Rose's phrase, is an 'etho-politics', which 'seeks to act upon conduct by acting upon the forces thought to shape the values, beliefs, moralities that themselves are thought to determine the everyday mundane choices that human beings make as to how they lead their lives'.[52]

This is the context within which we can make sense of a variety of government initiatives. Let us take Individual Learning Accounts as an example. These were conceived as a different way of offering what used to be called student or educational grants. The difference lay in their being targeted at those seeking supplementary, skills-based learning and they took the form not of a grant but of an account (with the trainee eligible for various 'discounts' on their education), of which the individual could feel 'ownership'. The ILA was a fully branded product of New Labour plc, and as much attention was paid to the presentation of the policy as to its functioning. According to the DfES 'style guide': 'Our overall brand proposition to individuals can be summarised as follows: "Individual Learning Accounts make it easier to pay for your own learning and training, putting you in control of realising your potential"'. The 'brand proposition' came complete with four supporting pillars, 'that will convert the brand proposition into reality for our customers and partners'. These were Flexibility, Simplicity, Self-Empowerment and Stature. The schemes would help individuals 'feel in control of their destiny and enriched through their experience', while stature 'ensures that participants feel part of a national movement which has status'.[53] As we noted in Chapter Two, this marketing is not to be understood as a distraction from, or substitution for, real policy. It was a vital component of the policy itself, in that the target was not simply employment or the workforce. Nor was it only training centres. It was not even just the individual in search of work and skills. The target of the policy was the individual's sense of self and of 'well-being'. For New Labour there is no point being part of a top-class training scheme if this does not translate into cultural and psychological 'capital'. The values of the would-be trainee were the true object of the policy.

In October of 2001 the Individual Learning Accounts were suspended. Badly designed and insufficiently audited the scheme became prey to fraudsters claiming to have provided training when they hadn't and thereby gaining illegal access to the available funds. The attempt to design a brand and to induce a new sense of self in those desiring training neglected to consider a culture of greed and corruption which can easily be the flipside of Schumpeterian 'creative destruction'. 'Governing by culture' has not been a way in which the values of society are challenged and transformed but an extended terrain for contemporary welfare intervention targeted at individual claimants. Schemes such as the National Strategy for Neighbourhood Renewal (which draws on the various New Deals, the child-care strategy, Sure Start schemes and so forth), along with punitive measures in the form of laws against anti-social behaviour, can be understood as 'generative', in Giddens's sense, since their intention is to facilitate the adaptation of geographically located communities to the 'new' world. From the Keynesian approach of influencing the 'external' conditions of existence of such communities (by trying to create jobs and so forth), we have moved to attempts at altering the orientation of the people in these communities to the world. It follows that the justification of such policies is the erroneous or damaged culture they currently manifest – welfare dependency, habits of crime and so forth. As David Blunkett argued in 1999, explaining the purpose of the 'Single Work-Focused Gateway': 'It's about saying to anyone who seeks help through the benefits system … You will be given guidance as to what makes it possible for you to actually earn your own living. To be able to restore your own dignity. To give you aspiration and expectation that you can be part of the solution'.[54] The rhetoric of inclusion/exclusion is also relevant here, in that it implies a process of bringing 'them' back into line with 'us', of introducing them to a normal life, inside mainstream society and culture.[55]

What we see, then, is the emergence of a framework of governmental activity at the level of 'culture'. This applies across fields of state action, from the economy, where the 'social embeddedness' of markets necessitates attention to the generation of social networks that produce trust, to welfare reform where the culture and values of the claimant are the object. These are, naturally, not disconnected. The state is 're-engineering' itself, changing the goals, values and aspirations of workers in the public and civil services. In the kind of management theories discussed earlier in this book (see Chapter Three), managers are, as Rose puts it: 'to live as if running a *project* of themselves: they are to *work* on their emotional world, their domestic and conjugal arrangements, their relations of employment ... to develop a style of being that will maximise the worth of their existence to themselves'.[56] There is really no distance between this procedure and the positive arguments of Giddens for a life politics in which freedom is reinterpreted as the capacity to manage one's own life projects, and through them to maximise potential in the globalised brave new world.

When knowledge is understood as the central commodity flowing in the economy, it is a short step to such a cultural mode of governance. After all a culture can, at one level, be understood as a set of shared knowledges. As such the analysis of economic production and the analysis of culture begin to fuse, and they do so in the form of management theories about how to generate the right workplace culture. This has spread out and affected government, which is also now 're-engineering' itself. Furthermore, in a context where 'everything' is now 'cultural' everything becomes available as an object of government policy. Precisely because it is believed that government can now not do very much, the range of potential government activities becomes both more focused and much broader than ever before. This is reflected across aspects of the New Labour programme from the smallest to the largest, affecting not only policies but the presentation of the government and its actions. For example, the introduction of Annual Reports is indicative of an attempt to situate government on the terrain of culture, but in ways shaped by contemporary management theory and practice. The latter operates in a financial world where firms may be open, and flexible workers may suddenly find themselves working for a newly merged corporation and workplace colleagues may change depending on the project to be realised: how then can one maintain some sense of belonging and corporate loyalty? Human resource management has thus found it needs to pay attention to corporate identities and cultures, in order to generate such belonging and homogeneity, through the construction of values and meanings, most obviously – and crudely – in the mission statement. Efficiency in the workplace is established not through simple command but through the installation of self-discipline in workers via the creation of commonly shared values and a 'corporate culture'. Taylorism is replaced by the attempt to regard the firm as a kind of collective intelligence where improvement rests on the managed unity of aspirations for all workers. Such management strategies are also pursued by the government which seeks to secure a similar kind of identification with the business endeavours of the nation. In this way signing up to the 'brand' of the Individual Learning Accounts (or whatever) is a mechanism through which citizens will find security and prosperity, their goals for themselves becoming one with the cultural aspirations of the country. This is a novel conception of citizenship.

Conclusion

The New Labour political project emerges from quite definite intellectual and political trends within western capitalist economies. It takes these trends and makes them into the foundation of a programme for the continued transformation of the practices of political, economic and personal existence. As such it can be made sense of by reference to all the debates and discussions on explicating the nature of current transformations; it is on the basis of these that New Labour tries to construct a response in specific ways (specific to the UK, specific to the context of the Labour Party). Crucial to this is the underlying desire to govern through changing the culture of people, government and communities, in order to develop a way in which wealth creation and moral cohesion can be combined. In fact these two are found to now be as one – an historic opportunity thrown up for 'socialists', which New Labour believes it has grasped. The lines then become drawn between the 'conservatives' who resist change and those who embrace 'modernity and justice' with 'the courage to change'. Ultimately this means that the direction and conscious object of New Labour's state practice is different from that of previous UK governments. Where some have tried to manage economies, to organise and mediate the interests of trade unions and employers, and to administer state-wide systems of delivery, New Labour's object is quite explicitly different. The twenty-first century nation needs a knowledge economy and strong civic ties. How is it to obtain these? 'The answer is people. The future is people.'[57] So they must be made.

Notes

1. This was the form of analysis carried out by, for example, Ralph Miliband in (1969) *The State in Capitalist Society*, London, Weidenfeld and Nicolson.
2. Such would be the sort of analysis advanced by, for example, George Monbiot, in his critique of the state as captured by certain business interests. See Monbiot (2000) *Captive State: The Corporate Takeover of Britain*, Basingstoke, Macmillan.
3. Barry Hindess (2001) 'Power, Government, Politics', in Kate Nash and Alan Scott (eds.), *The Blackwell Companion to Political Sociology*, Oxford, Blackwell, p44.
4. For a good illustration see Andrew Taylor (1998) '"Arm's Length But Hands On". Mapping the New Governance: The Department of National Heritage and Cultural Politics in Britain', *Public Administration*, 75, pp441-466.
5. R.A.W. Rhodes (1996), 'The New Governance: Governing Without Government', *Political Studies*, 44, 652-67.
6. See Bob Jessop (1994) 'The transition to Post-Fordism and the Schumpeterian Workfare State', in Brian Loader and Roger Burrows (eds.), *Towards a Post-Fordist Welfare State?*, London, Routledge.
7. See Stephen Driver and Luke Martell (1997) *New Labour: The Politics of Post-Thatcherism*, Cambridge, Polity.
8. Hence the recantation of figures such as John Gray; see Gray (1998) *False Dawn*, London, Granta.
9. As advocated in Elspeth Johnson and Rana Mitter (1998) *Students as Citizens: Focusing and Widening Access to Higher Education*, London, The Fabian Society.
10. The thesis of structural dependency is well summarised in terms of its relation to New Labour in Colin Hay (1999) *The Political Economy of New Labour*, Manchester, Manchester University Press, Chapter 5.
11. See Will Hutton (1995) *The State We're In*, London, Jonathan Cape; also Colin Hay (1999) pp165-67.
12. See Will Hutton (1995); Colin Hay (1999); and sections in Paul Hirst (1994) *Associative Democracy: new forms of economic and social governance*, Cambridge, Polity.
13. Andrew Gamble and Gavin Kelly (2001) 'New Labour's Economics', in Steve Ludlam and Martin J. Smith (eds.) *New Labour in Government*, Basingstoke, Macmillan, p183.
14. Andrew Glyn and Stewart Wood (2001) 'Economic Policy under New Labour: How Social Democratic is the Blair Government?' *Political Quarterly*, Vol. 72, No.1, p50.
15. Philip Arestis and Malcolm Sawyer (2001) 'The Economic Analysis Underlying the Third Way', *New Political Economy*, Vol. 6, No. 2, p259.
16. Ibid. p259.
17. Crafts cited in Arrestis and Sawyer (2001) p260.

18. Ibid. p273.
19. Ibid. p275.
20. See also Noel Thompson (1996) *Political Economy and the Labour Party: the economics of democratic socialism, 1884-1995*, London, UCL Press; and Eric Shaw (1996) *The Labour Party Since 1945*, Oxford, Blackwell.
21. Tony Blair (1999), Speech to Labour Party Conference, p13.
22. See Patricia Hewitt (2000), Speech to Said Business School, Oxford, 21 November (www.dti.gov.uk/ministers/speeches/hewitt211100.html). Of course this might say more about Castells than about Hewitt or it might mean only that Anthony Giddens provides ministers with a reading list.
23. Hay (1999) p168.
24. Charles Leadbeater (1998) 'Welcome to the Knowledge Economy', in Ian Hargreaves and Ian Christie (eds.) *Tomorrow's Politics: The Third Way and Beyond*, London, Demos, p20.
25. See Hewitt (2000).
26. On the distinction of productive and unproductive labour in classical economics see, Adam Smith (1977) *The Wealth of Nations*, London, Dent, Book 2, Chapter 3.
27. This view was also important for Thatcherism of course.
28. Leadbeater (1999) p33.
29. See Martin Smith (1998) 'Reconceptualizing the British State: Theoretical and Empirical Challenges to Central Government', *Public Administration*, 76 (Spring), pp45-72.
30. Cited in Smith (1998) p62.
31. On this question of continuity see Jonathon Tonge (1999) 'New Packaging, old deal? New Labour and employment policy innovation', *Critical Social Policy*, 59, Vol. 19, No. 2, pp217-232.
32. See Desmond King and Mark Wickham–Jones (1999) 'From Clinton to Blair: The Democratic (Party) Origins of Welfare to Work', *Political Quarterly*, 70(1), pp62-74.
33. DSS (1998), *New Ambitions for Our Country: A new Contract for welfare* (summary), p16.
34. On the influence of communitarianism see Stephen Driver and Luke Martell (1997) 'New Labour's Communitarianisms', *Critical Social Policy*, 17(3), pp27-46. On communitarianism and stakeholding in welfare see Emma Heron and Peter Dwyer, 'Doing the Right Thing: Labour's attempt to forge a new welfare deal between the individual and the state', *Social Policy and Administration*, Vol. 33, No.11, pp91-104.
35. See Bob Jessop (1994); Jacob Torfing (1999) 'Workfare with Welfare: Recent Reforms of the Danish Welfare State', *Journal of European Social Policy*, 9(1), pp5-28.
36. See Colin Hay (1996) *Re-Stating Social and Political Change*, Buckingham, Open University Press.

37. Joseph Schumpeter, 'Preface to Japanese edition of The Theory of Economic Development', cited in Nathan Rosenberg (1994), *The Emergence of Economic Ideas*, London, Edward Elgar, p156.

38. Joseph Schumpeter, 'On the Nature of Economic Crises', cited in Erich Schneider (1975), *Joseph Schumpeter: Life and Work of a Great Social Scientist*, Bureau of Business Research, University of Nebraska.

39. Joseph Schumpeter (1992) *Capitalism, Socialism and Democracy*, London, Routledge.

40. Joseph Schumpeter (1961) *The theory of economic development*, Oxford, Oxford University Press.

41. Jessop (1994).

42. See Torfing (1999).

43. Ibid. p9.

44. Ibid. pp24-5.

45. Charles Leadbeater (1998) 'Welcome to the Knowledge Economy', in Ian Hargreaves and Ian Christie, *Tomorrow's Politics: The Third Way and Beyond*, Demos, pp12-13.

46. See Bob Jessop (2000) 'From the KWS to the SWPR', in Gail Lewis, Sharon Gewirth and John Clarke (eds.) *Rethinking Social Policy*, Buckingham, Open University Press.

47. Stephen Byers (1999) 'People and Knowledge: towards a new industrial policy for the 21st century', in *Is Labour Working*, London, Fabian Society, p45.

48. Tony Blair (1999), 'Foreword' in *Is Labour Working*, London, Fabian Society.

49. Nikolas Rose (1999) 'Inventiveness in Politics', *Economy and Society*, Vol. 28 (3), p476.

50. Ibid. p475.

51. Perri 6 (1997) 'Governance by Culture', in Geoff Mulgan (ed.), *Life After Politics*, London, Fontana, 1997, p273.

52. Rose (1999).

53. See http://www.dfes.gov.uk/ila/styleguide/index.stml.

54. David Blunkett (1999) *The Welfare Society*, Speech to Demos, 19 May, Demos London. Quoted in Chris Haylett (2001) 'Modernization, Welfare and "third way" politics: limits to theorizing in "thirds"', *Transactions of the Institute of British Geographers*, Vol. 26, pp43-56.

55. See Haylett (2001) p49.

56. Nikolas Rose (1996) *Inventing Our Selves: Psychology, Power and Personhood*, Cambridge, Cambridge University Press. Cited in Nigel Thrift (2000) 'The Rise of Soft Capitalism', in David Marsh and Colin Hay (eds.) (2000) *Demystifying Globalisation*, Basingstoke, Macmillan, pp71-102.

57. Tony Blair, Speech to Labour Party Conference, p3.

CONCLUSION
The Need for Politics

In this book I have tried to make sense of New Labour. To do so I have focused, primarily, on what those connected with it say and do. I have tried to work back from this to construct something like a social or political theory that could be said to underpin the sayings and the doings of New Labour. A brief summary of the conclusions I have come to is this: New Labour is developing a form of state practice centred on a particular method of media management and on 'culture', oriented towards the production of consuming and self-capitalising subjects, able reflexively to integrate themselves into a modernised economy/society; the latter, by definition, being centred on information technology and participation in the productive network – as opposed to the non-productive political-communal bloc.

Of course this summary involves a singular definition of what is, in reality, a more discontinuous and mediated project. But that more nuanced approach is for another time and place. My concern has been to ask (and answer) a narrow question. All along I have been implicitly asking of New Labour: 'what are they thinking of?'. The result is the beginnings of a picture of what can be called a conceptual structure.

But I have also been careful to note the context within which New Labour says and does. New Labour philosophy is not an invention *ex nihilo*. It has been built out of, and in response to, prior and concurrent political, social and economic discourses, not the least of which are the ideologies of public and rational choice, and the discourses of contemporary management theory. I have not explored all of the further constraints and influences that might be said to shape New Labour, but I have tried to show that it needs to be understood as a symptom of some kind, a reflection of present conditions. I have not tried simply to provide a map of New Labour; I have also tried to see what sort of map they are using, and which way round they hold it up.

Central to the conceptual structure of New Labourism is a kind of latent vanguardism. In as much as it believes itself to have seized an historic opportunity to transform the ideological landscape of British (perhaps world) politics, and to make the most of certain social changes, New Labour thinks of itself as a movement leading Britain out of the 'old ways' of hierarchy, tradition and entrenched power, and into a new fluid world of networks and opportunity for all. This gives to the party an almost cultic aspect; it is possessed of a certain truth which only it and a select few can fully understand, and this leaves them charged with the responsibility of taking us all to a land of properly marketed milk and honey, where capitalist accumulation and social justice will be synonymous.

This is also a self-supporting, solipsistic form of thinking. New Labour does what it does because of what is already happening, and must do what it does because only it understands what is happening. Perhaps because of the legacy of a certain kind of misunderstood Marxism (which, however buried, is there in the 'collective unconscious' of the labour movement), certain perceived changes in the organisation of the economy are understood as the underlying motor of social transformation. They are then understood as both the cause and effect of New Labour. Opponents or enemies stand as evidence of how right the party is, as exemplars of the backwardness of all other positions.

As we have seen, this is a problematic strategy. It reduces politics to the management of state and society in the interests of a development of the world economy which is presumed to be given. Political actions thus become justified as resulting from the inevitable pressures of this irreversible economic logic. As Chantal Mouffe noted early in the governmental career of New Labour: 'The usual justification for the "there is no alternative" dogma is globalisation ... This kind of argument takes for granted the ideological terrain which has been established as a result of years of neo-liberal hegemony, and transforms what is a conjunctural state of affairs into an historical necessity'.[1] Similarly, Doreen Massey points out that the term 'globalisation' has become a 'de-politicised, unexamined, assumption', spoken of as if it is inevitable, and in such generalisable terms that its 'politico-economic specificity' is obscured. Globalisation is a politically motivated neo-liberal globalisation, but is treated as if it is 'a *deus-ex-machina* that we had just better get used to'.[2] This is why New Labour doesn't like politics very much. As we saw in Chapter 4, it tends to subordinate political choice to the exigencies of the present, and to seek a mode of governance focused on the management of individuals rather than the construction of coalitions of varied interest groups and social blocs.

In a thought-provoking argument, political scientist Peter Mair has argued that New Labour is attempting to create a 'partyless democracy'.

He describes this as an almost Madisonian system, designed to prevent the rise of faction – a consensual and 'depoliticised democracy'.[3] Writing of the reforms within the Labour Party itself, he notes that the centralisation of party discipline might seem like a way to make the party stronger after the weakness of division but '… it may also be seen as a means by which the party itself may be taken out of the equation … [the reforms] may not in fact be intended to strengthen the party, but instead to marginalise it'. He goes on: 'The point is to take "politics", especially when understood as partisan politics, out of the governing process and to institute a system of good governance in which the people voice their plebiscitary approval of policy decisions, based on the pledge or contract – an output oriented democracy'. New Labour's presupposition is that everyone really has the same interests in the end (and – according to Blair's 2001 'Leadership' party political broadcast – knowing what people want and need is not 'rocket science'), and that these interests can be objectively determined, and policy for them instituted. Everything is a matter of competence and of what works.

This rejection of, or hostility to, politics is multiply debilitating. For one thing it stands in contradiction to any commitment to increase 'social capital' and active citizenship. People participate in political parties because they believe it gives them some input into the political process. If they do not feel this they are less likely to participate. Civic engagement comes about not simply when there is a need for it but when there is a possibility for it to be meaningful and effective. The rhetoric of New Labour, its presentation of the inevitability of very specific kinds of change, and its close control of what happens in the party and in government, are a contributory factor to a declining interest in politics at all levels.

The need for democracy
There are other reasons why the anti-political aspect of New Labour is damaging. A political approach is essential to the reform of the public services. But, as we saw, the tendency, taking off from versions of public choice theory, is to try and initiate change through fixing incentive structures. In an important piece of work, Peter Taylor-Gooby conducted survey research into the attitudes of the public sector salariat, to establish why they sometimes seem 'conservative' in the face of government initiated reforms. Public choice theory might suggest that the reason for inertia is that the cosy interests of such workers are being threatened. But Taylor-Gooby shows that these are not conservative, idle, self-interested and inert people. Quite simply they have an intellectual difference of opinion with the government.[4] They do not

regard the problems of welfare claimants as their individual failure, but endorse the 'traditional' view that welfare polices should be directed towards structural or systemic disadvantage. To put it simply, the government has not won the argument with them. If the government wants to transform public services it needs to do so not only through instituting certain systems of management, but by campaigning for its programme, by taking the workers in the public sector to be a particular constituency in need of, as it were, 'political' management. This is not to advocate a more sophisticated degree of opinion manipulation. Winning people over politically means forging a coalition with them. It also means making use of one of the key benefits of democracy. If people feel they have participated fairly in the shaping and taking of a decision they are more likely to pursue and act on it even if it was not their original first choice. Just as we accept governments we do not support, because we feel we played a part in their selection and were fairly defeated, so people who work in large organisations (state or private) will work better for them if they feel they have some power or control over what it is they are doing. If they experience change as something imposed on them from above (and so cannot see the reasons for it or feel 'ownership' over it), they may comply but will not endorse and, as every management theorist knows, compliance is not enough. One needs the employee to feel committed to the project of the enterprise.

This brings us to one of the sad ironies within the rhetoric of management theory. The talk is all about freeing up the worker, giving them control over their skills and labour, allowing them to be creative and so forth – all sounding very democratic and emancipatory. But such liberty does not necessarily imply democracy: they are not the same thing. While you cannot have democracy without liberty, you can have liberty without democracy. It is quite possible formally to be free, to do as you please as far as able, without being attached to a social group in which decisions are made collectively and openly. This is the ideal state for libertarian ideology but that is quite different to democracy. The ideal of democracy (as opposed to that of pure liberty) is that one is attached to a social group (a collective of some kind) within which decisions are taken (collectively and openly) as to the ordering of relations within that group. While this entails certain restrictions on the absolute liberty of each individual it also means that they are better placed to take some control over the sorts of choices that are put before them. The libertarian individual can only respond with freedom to that which is put before them. He or she is still constrained by the structure of the society in which he or she lives. The democratic individual is able to have some say over that structure. This is why (as every true liberal knows and as John Stuart Mill made plain) democracy is to be understood as a transformatory system: it changes the individuals who participate in it and they in turn change the kind of society in which they live. Thus, when liberty and democracy are conjoined they produce great benefits. We are free to make and act on decisions, but that freedom is usefully constrained by our participation in a wider social group. We can escape that group if we find it stifling, but we might well find it to be a useful way in which to advance our liberty and our understanding of ourselves. Furthermore, we do not have all the answers to all the problems we face, and we need to be in a position to have our ideas, our preferences, shaped and re-shaped in the encounter, in the dialogue, with others. In the Kantian ideal we exercise our public reason, which is not only reasoning in or by a public, but also an attempt to think at the public level, to think about what is best for all as well as for ourselves.

As we have seen, in current management theory, 'freeing' the corporate worker is just a different strategy of control. Risk and the threat of redundancy can be more effective disciplinary tools than time and motion studies; taking away a particular system of power is not the same as giving power. But this is what people need, especially in public services: power to come to decisions, in concert, about how to organise things. New Labour appears at times to want to give workers in public services a bit of room to 'innovate', but this is usually within narrow parameters. Incentives and charter marks may help, a little, in the breaking down of bureaucracy. But history teaches us that the only way to really break away from stultifying absolutism and centralisation is to have a democratic revolution, and let power go to the subjects of rule. Perhaps it is finally time for democracy to penetrate the firm and the large-scale public enterprise.

Within society generally there is a pluralisation of politics underway. This is not simply a pluralisation of the different views or positions people hold and take, but of the sites and forms of political activity. Much attention is paid to the spectacular and headline-getting 'New Social Movements', but there are also many lower level and local campaigns, often involving developments in schools, hospitals, in streets and parks and, crucially, in the workplace. If democracy is to spread and deepen, it will not do so simply in the form of increased liberty (the removal of power), but in the form of increased capacity to take control of different spheres of our lives (the increase and spread of power). Democracy emerged as opposition to absolutist forms of rule. It was thus often conceived in terms of limiting the power of authorities to interfere in the lives of citizens. But as the democratic revolution spread and developed, it became clear that the absence of restraint was not enough. Democratic practice came not only to define the relationship of state to citizen, but also of citizens to each other, of citizens to themselves and of citizens to their world. Consequently it meant the getting and using of power and not just its evasion.

As we saw in Chapter Five, the spheres of state, individual, society and economy have become more complex, blurred and inter-related. This does not make politics less important but more. Pick your metaphor, but politics is the glue that binds them, the oil that keeps their relationship smooth. When contradictions arise (as they often do) between the different dimensions of our lives (as citizens, as private people, as social beings, as workers), it is politics that can articulate them and establish a new way of ordering. Politics needs to be understood as the sphere of life where we decide on how to order these relationships and set goals for ourselves, and this can only be done in concert with others. Here the democratisation of work is crucial. As we spend more of our time in work, and as systems of management become more extensive or all encompassing, then we need to have some sort of reconfigured relationship between worker and corporation. It is now not enough simply to have legal protections for workers, procedures by which grievances and disputes are resolved. It is also vital to have political systems that open up and democratise the workplace. Such would be an important step towards putting the economy back in touch with the world from whence it came and making a reality of that which certain management theories pretend to be the case.

But we should also keep hold of the vision of a society that fulfils the promise of our technology and our fantastic productive capacity. There is a rich heritage in left-wing thinking that can fill out such a vision with a commitment to freeing societies from the despotism of the economic, and the reduction of everything to the price it reaches at market. New forms of technology very probably do possess the capacity to improve aspects of the lives of many millions. But they will not do so of themselves, since technologies possess no capacity for self-direction. The political question concerns how we are to envisage these new forms of social and economic potential. What is to be the focus that guides their implementation, so that we can benefit from their capacity to liberate us from old forms of futile desire and helpless drudgery, and from the necessity that we attune ourselves to the economy as the price of inclusion? After all, work in a telephone call centre is no less sweatshop drudgery for the fact that it is high-tech.[5] The blurring of blue collar and white collar work, seen by some as evidence of the democratising effects of new modes of labour, can easily be achieved by pushing everyone down rather than lifting everyone up. Momentous transformations cannot be ignored or refused, but they should be treated as transformations that we are bringing about, whose direction will derive from the decisions we take. This is also why democratisation cannot be equated with marketisation. We need to be empowered not simply to say yes or no, buy or sell, but to question the terms of debates, invent new choices and feel they belong to us.

Globalisation, the knowledge economy and the spread of commodification

Of course, we can hear the argument that such things are not possible, that the organisation of the globalised knowledge economy is such that any attempt to impose democratisation on the firm or the public service will slow it down, act as a disincentive to investment and so forth. So let us be clear about what globalisation and the knowledge economy are. This is not the place to attempt a summary of debates about globalisation,[6] but it is clear that there is a debate to be had, and it is not all settled and clear. Some see globalisation as an unstoppable force, undermining the capacity of national states to look after themselves and their citizens. Others believe it is possible to introduce new forms of regulation (perhaps at supranational levels). There are also a number of perspectives that doubt either the extent of globalisation, or the newness of it.[7] Data seems to suggest that the extent of openness to trade is not as great as is often assumed, and that convergence of economies is occurring more at a regional than global level (as with the EU). This suggests that what marks globalisation is as much the increasing disparity between an integrated part of the economic world and a subordinate, not integrated, part. Furthermore, the extent of what integration there is has not come about in a linear fashion. Globalisation has not been a smooth or unidirectional phenomena. The biggest recent change in global economic exchange has been in the financial markets. Here technology and policy liberalisation have permitted an expansion in the range and types of global financial transaction, as well as their speed and, consequently, volume. It is this that has furthered a heavy rhetoric of globalisation more than anything else. The power of financial markets, well documented early on by Susan Strange,[8] has shifted the balance of power in global trading and become something to which national states have to respond. Realising this is important in clarifying the fact that 'globalisation is not only a new mythology but being such it is neither historically inevitable nor technologically predetermined. It is ... an historically open, indeterminate and, above all, thoroughly political process, and therefore subject to human action and potential transformation'.[9]

Whatever it is and whatever its extent, globalisation is neither a given process nor a unitary one. But the way globalisation is usually conceptualised goes a long way to making it seem so, and part of the point of the concept is to allow people to think through a range of changes (in media, in culture, in governmental structures, in trade) as if they were clearly and easily related. But the form these changes take is not inevitable or given and it is not universal. Different regions develop different forms of capitalism and different forms of economic or industrial organisation. Forms of organisation are dependent on social and cultural relations within a given region, which are external to the narrowly defined realm of the economy. Consequently political questions should not be about how we respond to globalisation or deal with it, but about what sort of globalisation we want. To be sure this is often implicit in arguments about globalisation, and it is implicit in New Labour's own rhetoric – and in its attempts to reform the structures of world debt, and preparedness to talk about ways of bringing stability back to financial markets. The globalisation debate only really takes off when economic processes are treated not as constraints but opportunities. They are not there only to further accumulation, but to transform the way the world deals with social and political problems. That is to say the debate becomes interesting when it is what globalisation means, or can mean, that becomes the subject of dispute.

In the same way as the concept of globalisation helps provide apparent unity to changes in global economics, the concept of the knowledge economy also has determinate effects. Scepticism about the extent to which we really are in a new knowledge economy need not entail that we reject any suggestion that the economy might have been changed somewhat by new technologies and techniques of production and exchange. But it is worth thinking through the implications of the fact that enthusiasts of the knowledge economy tend to emphasise the newness of it, the discontinuity rather than the continuity. On inspection many such enthusiasts seem to be engaging not so much in the elaboration of something entirely novel as re-describing what is already there (though this can sometimes be useful). Re-description can be an extremely significant form of intellectual, cultural and ideological work. Leadbeater, for example, chooses to describe Princess Diana as a brand. She was 'one of the world's leading practitioners of thin-air economics'. In the royalty market she was 'an entrepreneur who used new technology to outmanoeuvre the established but tired incumbent'.[10] Similarly, it turns out that Delia Smith is an example of thin-air and knowledge economics. Her recipe books are a form of knowledge that, in the form of cookbooks, we download into our kitchens so we can draw on her knowledge in creating our own culinary environment. This is just re-description. Obviously, royals existed and manoeuvred for power, cooks made up and passed on recipes long before Diana or Delia were around. Leadbeater is taking an old phenomenon and describing it with a new vocabulary, with the intention of making us think about, and understand it, differently. Indeed, at this level it is hard to see what is new about the knowledge economy other than this shift in our perspective. Surely when George Stephenson built his Rocket steam train this was knowledge-based innovation. Presumably many of the people who worked in steel factories had acquired what used to be called skill, craft or experience, but could just as easily be described as knowledge. So what is new? There are perhaps two new things worth noting, though they can be reduced to just one. Clearly the expansion of high-tech industries and the increased reliance of most us on high-tech equipment which we do not actually understand makes us need more people whose essential trade is their specialised knowledge. In the 'age of industry' we would not have called directly on a steelworker to help us but now (in the 'information age') we may well have to call on a computer engineer. Secondly, the expansion of electronic technologies such as computers and broadcasting platforms leads to an expansion in creative types needed to create things to put out on those computers and television screens. Innovation not only comes in the making of the machines but in the things that make people want to use those machines. After all, who would want a home computer if there wasn't a range of useful and entertaining things for all the family to do on it?

Both of these aspects, the need for technical support and for content, are symptomatic of contemporary commodification. Leadbeater himself points out that 'Knowledge about how to cook food, once a craft skill, has become a commodity'.[11] This is the key to discourses about the knowledge economy. It is not primarily about analysis or description of a substantially new form of economic activity; it is more about the re-description of aspects of activity in terms of commodification. We have seen how this has affected New Labour in as much as it forms part of a broader movement of the capitalisation of everything. Within this context the discourse of the knowledge economy helps the formulation of new ways of thinking about the managing of both workers and consumers. For social democracy the subject was a producer, a worker. But, as Leadbeater repeatedly points out, consumption in the knowledge economy is part of the process of production. In buying access to Microsoft products, to the ideas the new technologists provide for us, we buy the right to make things with them and in turn market them (such as the words I am writing now).[12]

Capitalist markets have always needed to train their consumers, to generate individuals who recognise their need for a new product and are capable of using it. Such innovation is central to Schumpeter's theory of economic development. He writes: 'innovations in the economic system do not as a rule take place in such a way that first new wants arise spontaneously in consumers and then the productive apparatus swings round through their pressure ... It is ... the producer who as a rule initiates economic change, and consumers are educated by him if necessary; they are, as it were, taught to want new things, or things which differ in some respect or other from those which they have been in the habit of using'.[13] Advertising, especially in the post-war period, has gone to great lengths to educate consumers not only about what is available but about why new goods are worthwhile and how they can be used. In a hyper-commodified society, where the weightless predominates over the solid, this becomes an even greater requirement, and one which the New Labour state is helping with. Many of the new technologies do not offer anything that will, strictly speaking, improve the material quality of life, or that we would have thought we needed before they were made known to us. Luxuries are no doubt welcome, but they are in an important sense superfluous. This is why we require some training in order properly to recognise our new needs. The 'creative industries', such as advertising but also software design, and the horizontal integration of markets in, for example, entertainment, are increasingly important as a way of ensuring that I do want that video, that particular shirt or that particular video game (and that I want it now, in this financial year). The thrust of innovation is shifting from refining productive or carrier technologies to designing the mechanisms that sell the content to us, that teach us how attractive and desirable a product really is and reassure us that we are capable of using it – the mechanisms that train me in my job as consumer where in turn I can produce more. All of which links in to discourses of a 'postmodern', ever-developing subjectivity, and the 'fusion' of 'the aim of manufacturers to sell products and increase market share with the identity experiments of consumers'.[14]

Simultaneously, many of the things that we used to do routinely have become far from routine. People no longer have to wash all their clothes by hand, prepare all their own food and make their own entertainment. Machines can do it for us. As such, these otherwise everyday acts cease being part of the private or household economy and become part of the mainstream, weightless, economy. Thus, there is work for the inventor of a new flavouring, a new ready-meal, a new soap powder, a bag-less vacuum cleaner or another sit-com. And there is work for the people who sell these things to us. The concept of the knowledge economy is part of a process whereby a variety of activities, capacities and skills become translated into things understood as tradable commodities of fundamental significance in the organisation of economic life. It is a short step from such a recognition to the introduction of commercial sponsorship in schools, the better to ensure that the young are trained early in their socio-economic obligation to consume.

Markets are liberating but they are also disciplinary. They free us to make our own choices about what we want to do and what we want to achieve, but they demand that we make those choices within the parameters set by the market. At certain points in our lives we may have the opportunity to be successful entrepreneurs marketing our skills and wares to those that want them. But most of us, and for most of our lives, are only consumers with a passive choice of to buy or not to buy from what is made available to us. And the decision about what is available is made by sellers. Being a consumer is not all about autonomy. If we are forced to be only producer-consumers (and never anything else) we will suffer further from the erosion of other kinds of social relationship. Demand is becoming implicitly understood as a part of supply. In the commodity-led society our 'job' is to buy and there is never any free time from work.

The public sphere

This brings us back to civic-ness and politics. As we saw, New Labour continues the Thatcherite trend of understanding the public as equivalent to a mass of consumers whose interest lies in the smooth running of the consumer economy. For New Labour, employee interests are trumped by those of consumers (though these are in reality the same people just at different moments), and the sphere of consumption is treated in such a way as to serve finance and the market, whose interest lies in the continuing and increased circulation of money at a velocity high enough to ensure rising profits. Thus the sorts of social relationships formed by commodification increasingly outweigh all others. But commodity relations are relations between things and not between people. They are antithetical to civic relationships and renaming the latter as social capital will not change this.

As an example of what happens when commodity and consumption relations are substituted for public, civic and political ones, we can consider culture and cultural policy. Back in 1996 Geoff Mulgan, now an adviser to the Prime Minister, argued for the marketisation of public culture in the name of democratisation and liberty. He wrote: 'the consistent theme about Britain's cultural policy not only since 1945, but probably long before, has been its exclusivity: the overwhelming skew of funding to the pleasures of the elite, to London and to traditional art forms, and the deep hostility to any kind of democratisation'.[15] The post-war systems of cultural policy, Mulgan argued, were wedded to pre-twentieth century forms of culture; their purpose was to improve the spirituality and values of the nation, and they were focused on giving grants to centres of excellence rather than to the increasingly important forms of popular culture. As such, cultural policy could not but be class-biased and privileged in its outlook and activities. It saw the arts as an alternative to everyday life rather than as part of it: 'As a result, where the redistributive state was meant to take from the rich and give to the poor, in arts it did the opposite, using general taxation to subsidise the leisure pursuits of the relatively prosperous'.[16] Thatcherite reforms challenged the professionals in the arts, but carried on making some of the same mistakes in failing to take on board how culture has changed thanks to the emergence of electronic transmission and the commercialisation of culture. Cinema, theatre, local civic culture – in each case: 'the problem with cultural policy was that it came to be much more about preservation and heritage than about influencing real life'. These are the bad guys in Mulgan's story: patrician arts funders, Reithian snobs in the BBC, left-wing intellectuals who think they can speak for the people. The good guys are in the market. Commercial television decreased audiences for the BBC and 'had positive effects ... It forced the BBC to be popular'. As a result we were almost saved by Radio Caroline, Z Cars and That Was the Week That Was: 'For the BBC, the pressure of ratings, and the direct political pressure of having to justify a licence fee, has helped it steadily evolve, not too far behind public values. It has had to develop popular genres of entertainment, soap operas and dramas, game shows and documentaries.'[17] Mulgan's narrative is a smaller version of the standard critique of social democracy – that it was a top-down model of organisation and as such gave power to bureaucrats, who were, by definition, out of touch with the needs and interests of the real people. Thus, for him, the high arts of political theatre and music achieved little in the way of liberating people, since true liberation, 'everyday, prosaic, about fun and pleasure and intimate passions', is despised by the elite. This liberatory popular culture 'achieved its influence not through the state, but through the market – through Hollywood cinema, cheap magazines, Sky Television and the Sun, through Zoot suits and Mohicans, Northern Soul and rave ... it subtly called into question the social democratic project which took its culture from the elite and became its most ardent defender, usually against both the interests and the arguments of its working class supporters'.[18] Mulgan concludes by saying: 'in culture more than anywhere else, the social democratic rhetoric was in time unravelled, as it transpired that public service was for the public, not of the public, for professionals not amateurs or volunteers and for balance and sobriety, not pleasure and risk'. [19]

Such an analysis is not without merit. Mulgan is certainly right to point to the ways in which the management of social democracy, by those unable or unwilling to recognise the needs and interests of the rest of the population, contributed to its weakness in maintaining legitimacy. He is also right to point out that the organisation of support for the arts and culture did reflect the interests and tastes of only a part of the population, and allowed power to be held by sections of a profession exercising it in what they perceived as the interests of that profession. A shorthand way of putting it is that the institutions of culture were not especially democratic in their structure. But Mulgan's solution is absolutely typical of New Labour thinking, and yet again indicative of the tendency of New Labour intellectuals to take 'the present' at face value and so subordinate themselves to it. After all there is not really a common thread between 'Hollywood cinema, cheap magazines, Sky Television and the *Sun*, through Zoot suits and Mohicans, Northern Soul and rave'. These are not equivalent forms of cultural expression in their content, purpose, audience or organisation. A television station owned by one of the largest global media corporations is not the same sort of phenomenon as dance nights organised in Wigan by devoted followers of rare soul. Mulgan takes the market to be the only way in which pressure can be exerted on the managers of cultural institutions. Certainly it is necessary, if we want such institutions to be more responsive to the demands of citizens, to introduce some mechanism by which those demands are translated into pressure upon them. And the market is an obvious way of doing so. But it is not the only way and not necessarily the best one. Cultural institutions can also be opened up through democratic means that connect them to a public eager and willing to make decisions not just about their own taste but about the way these institutions should serve us socially as well as culturally. Hollywood cinema may be demotic but it is not democratic. The same is true of *The Sun* and Sky television. Not everything about these cultural 'institutions' is bad, but neither are they good simply because they sell well. They do not only respond to tastes; they foster them, promote other products through them and are primarily interested in attaining a mass audience to sell to advertisers. This is not the role of public services such as the BBC.

While the government, in its Draft Communications Bill, does claim to recognise the importance of public service broadcasting and plurality of ownership, it is clear that the Bill is primarily shaped by the Department of Trade and Industry, and its guiding intentions are market oriented. It is not at all clear that they understand the distinction between being responsive to consumers and being responsive to a public. Consumers are individuals acting on individual preference. A public is something else entirely. Being part of a public means being part of a collective group of some kind, and precisely not thinking only of individual preference but of what might be good for the whole public. In order to service that public, but also to bring it into being, an institution such as the BBC needs to be capable of being democratically responsive. The world is not the same as it was when the BBC was founded. We cannot now fool ourselves into thinking that there is only one public and that it can be fully represented, even less so by the narrow and self-referential group of North Londoners that runs the BBC. The insight of the New Labour 'postmodernists' that social life is more varied and open-ended can be put to use here. The public service media needs to be diverse, but not because it needs to suit varied consumer tastes. Rather it needs to serve the varied publics it can represent and call into being. Regional and local bodies need to be linked into the media, but also non-geographically-based constituencies. It is precisely the capacity of the non-commercial BBC to take risks, to run programmes at a loss and to respond to the democratic pressures of the public, that is its strength. It needs not to be marketised but to be democratised, and forced to consult and work with as many representative local, regional and national 'stakeholders' as possible. This is a model that can be extended throughout other public services and actions of government, as well as to the relationship of corporations to the society of which they are part. In our complex societies power and politics are everywhere. Our institutions do indeed need to be reshaped to fit a different world in which our loyalties and interests are multiple and not limited to geographic location. But this would not be modernisation along New Labour lines.

What kind of modernisation?

As we saw in Chapter Three, the discourse of modernisation serves a number of functions: rhetorical, ideological and governmental. We also saw that the way in which this discourse has developed has led it to draw on a range of themes from within management theory. As such New Labour modernisation can fairly be said to mean the introduction of currently fashionable business ideas about the restructuring or reengineering of the firm into the management of state services and even the state-society relationship. But can the idea of modernisation mean only this? There is an important and obvious sense in which modernisation ought to be endorsed by everyone. Change and development in western countries have occurred unevenly across societal sectors. Our institutions are not able to cope and there is a mismatch between the way we live and the services we have to help us. A good example of the sense behind modernisation is provided by the proposal of the government to change the arrangements for school terms. At present, the timing of the school year is organised the way it is simply because that is the way it has always been organised. It is meant to fit in with the vagaries of the religious calendar (a floating Easter) and to keep children free for labour in the fields. Since we are neither predominantly agricultural nor mostly Christian this may not be the best way to organise the school year. As it is, with many families consisting of two parents working full-time, the long summer holiday presents a range of problems for parents and families and introduces a hiatus into learning that can be detrimental to educational progress. In this sense the need for 'modernisation', for reforming the practices of such central public institutions in the light of overall changes in social life, is clear. Indeed, one could extend this. The whole school timetable, from the time of starting to ending, the common habit of beginning with whole school assemblies and breaking lessons up into chunks of a fixed length may be worth reconsidering. And this is exactly what some of those schools which have already been taken over by private companies are doing; and they do it not because they are private and have a profit incentive (not all are profit-seeking), but because they are free and able to enthuse and work with local people. We could go a lot further. Our schools are essentially nineteenth-century in their design. Their purpose was not to produce autonomous citizens but to produce people capable of taking on certain kinds of labour. We have a legacy of crumbling schools whose very architecture and scale contradict the demands of contemporary education. If we were to imagine without reference to the present the best way of educating our children I am sure we would never come up with anything as daft as the idea of putting one and a half thousand of them together in a vast flat roofed building on the edge of town and forcing them all to shuttle from geography to history via chemistry, without much regard for the specific abilities and interests of the individual pupils. Similarly, our hospitals are an old design, operating a system devised for the remedy of present illnesses, when many contemporary health problems are better treated through their prevention rather than cure. We could continue with the examples, but such observations are not new. The point is that there is a sensible truth behind the notion of modernisation. But at the same time we are afraid of responding to this mismatch by digging up the old and imposing a new design on everything. This kind of approach was partly responsible for the post-war (especially 1960s) vision of development, which ended in tower blocks being exploded on *Jim'll Fix It* in the 1970s. But this is a fear we must get over. The error of such post-war planning was neither the notion of planning itself nor the vision which informed it. The problem was the imposition of such planning without thought for those on whom it was imposed, and doing things on the cheap. Our current lack of faith in 'experts', a welcome rejection of deference and paternalism, should not be transformed into an equally debilitating populist consumerism. Rather, both need to be replaced by an attempt to abide by the principles of democracy and 'political' management. 'Post-traditional' society does not make politics and ideology less important but more so. It does not simply entail us pursuing our ends with greater independence than before, free of the shackles of old habits and routines. It means that we do not take authority or right for granted. Things must be demonstrated to us as acceptable and agreeable. That means ideological visions and political strategies become more significant than in a context where attitudes were taken as given. There is no evidence to suggest that New Labour understand this.

A return to utopianism

A crucial aspect of a renewed rhetoric of modernisation, aiming to liberate public sector workers to do the jobs they want to do, has to be a vision of the future. Most visions of the future are really visions of the present, which is by definition really a product of the immediate past. We are full of the hubris that tells us that our time is the most important of times and that we see things much more clearly than our predecessors. We never do. In fact political visions of the future must have absolutely no basis whatsoever in reality. That is their point. In this sense it might be time to reverse a wrong in the trajectory of the left created by one aspect of Marxism – the rejection of utopianism in the Communist Manifesto. We need a vision of how the future could be and we should not subordinate this aspect of the symbolism and imagery of politics to a notion about the scientific way forward. (In any case, Marx and Engels's critique of utopian socialism was aimed at strategies of transformation that made little attempt to understand the political and social visions of the present. Both, but especially Marx, were well aware of the symbolic and rhetorical aspects of politics.) So we should not be afraid of putting forward bold and admittedly unrealistic visions of how things ought to be, not least to combat the fatalism of the present. Who would object to a description of a future world free of poverty, hunger, hopelessness and war? Who is prepared to stand up and say that they really want the world to be organised in such a way that the United States becomes unfeasibly rich at the expense of everybody else? Neoliberals have their vision of a utopian future, and their left-wing critics need to be quite vocal in insisting that the point of economic development should always be to get us nearer to an ideal of abundance and liberty for all. Then we can argue about the ethics of each of our ideological options.

There is another reason why we need this return to utopianism. We need inspiration because underlying many of our present uncertainties in the West is what I think we can justly call a crisis of faith. Not of faith in God or fate but in collective action. God died a long time ago – at least a century. In the place of religion we in the west put collective action and rational planning. We believed that we could overcome the problems of the world not by following the right religious rituals but by thinking about them hard enough, forming a plan and then mobilising mass action to achieve it. This brought us welfare states, improved health and literacy, eradicated diseases, created wealth that a century ago would have been unimaginable, and even put Americans on the moon. But it also brought us the repressive total mobilisation of society in the form of Fascism and Stalinism. And in the social democratic states collective organisation came to feel like an imposition and restraint, a harbinger of repression not liberation. So we lost faith in collective action. As the problems we faced became more subtle and intractable (problems of how to cope with scientific advance, ethical uncertainty, the clashes of diverse groups in society, internationalisation), we lost faith in our capacity to deal collectively with problems and retreated to the safety of consumption. Thus the sense of communality, of being part of a public, is the most crucial thing we need to reinvent for our times. The reactions to the death of Princess Diana or to the bombings of the World Trade Centre, and to other, lesser, events, suggest that we almost relish times of crisis – when we can feel sure that what we are seeing, doing and thinking about is also being experienced by others simultaneously, even if we do not share the mood imputed to the majority of us by the media. We want to know there is something bigger than ourselves of which we are a part. But the apparent unity of grief created by the simultaneity of mass media consumption is a poor substitute for an ongoing sharing of aspects of life. This is why many are drawn to the internet as a way of forming communities, of singling out amongst the anomic crowd those who share a passion or an interest. Despite the fact that we organise our lives in ways that undermine sociality, the urge to commune will out, and will always exceed the capacities of others to make money from it.

But we cannot pretend that we are part of a unified community of homogenous peoples. Rather we need to be able to generate a sense of unity in difference, forged out of the sharing of certain common projects. And this is why the public services matter so much. Their reform and their continued existence is not only a good thing in its own right. It is a good thing because it is important to have in existence institutions that speak of the fact that we live together and depend on each other. Our social problems (from health to crime) can only be solved by political action in the broadest sense, by the mobilisation of people to achieve ends on which they have managed to reach agreement. Here is a role for government. New Labour is creating a state that acts as the disseminator of best practice. It acts as personnel manager, sending us memos to update us on procedure. But the state needs to return to politics. Parties occupy government so that they can continue to campaign, building alliances and coalitions for change. The state needs to be a campaigning hub, assisting political actors to establish the points of power within a given context (a hospital, a local community, a housing estate, an educational network), and assisting them in generating the capacity for change. This is not as top-down as it may at first sound. Indeed, to be successful (and to repeat the point) such change needs to be based on the consent and support of those participating in it. We know that what is successful about private initiatives in, for example, schools, or in public initiatives such as those that sometimes emanate from social work departments, depend on mobilising the support of the people, parents or residents concerned and drawing on their energy. It takes a different form in each place because each place and each institution is different. Only actors on the ground can be sensitive to this specificity. So we need dedicated, committed and, yes, charismatic people. New Labour likes to call such people social entrepreneurs, so that it can pretend that this is a non-ideological phenomenon. But it is not. For such activity to come about there needs to be a prior commitment to the collective self-organisation of people even where that means the taking of decisions with which central government disagrees. But this cannot occur spontaneously. To achieve anything requires cajoling, the employment of power, and the taking away of it from others; and the outcome of such strategies cannot always be predicted or defined in advance by bureaucrats and policy specialists. This is the sort of idea still buried somewhere in New Labour: that modernisation really means a kind of decentralised, future-oriented and open-ended way of organising society, and that the role of government is not only to withdraw from direct involvement and become 'generative', but also to ensure that other powerful institutions do not interfere with this autonomy. That is to say, autonomy can only be enhanced through the extension of politics, and not through its reduction or withdrawal. In this sense, modernisation can almost be made equivalent to democratisation – a process that entails a certain labour on behalf of all of us, a ceding of purely individual autonomy in the name of a collective freedom that is for all and guaranteed by all, and in which there are no special provisions on the grounds of high opportunity cost.

It is only with such autonomy that we will 'unleash our potential', a potential that cannot be confined in the small box of the tradable. Then we can see what excellence we really possess, and we will not be able to count it on an audit report or a balance sheet.

Notes

1. Chantal Mouffe (1997) 'Politics without Adversary', *Soundings*, 9.
2. Doreen Massey (1997) 'Problems with Globalisation', *Soundings*, 7, p9.
3. Peter Mair, *Partyless democracy and the 'paradox' of New Labour*, http://www.fsw.leidenuniv.nl/www/w3_pol/MEDEWERK/MEDEWRK S/MAIR/Mairp.htm.
4. Peter Taylor-Gooby (2000) 'Blair's Scars', *Critical Social Policy*, 64, 20: 3, pp331-348.
5. See Sue Fernie (1998) *(Not) hanging on the telephone: payment systems in the new sweatshops*, London, Centre for Economic Performance, London School of Economics and Political Science.
6. See Andreas Busch (2000) 'Unpacking the Globalisation Debate: Approaches, Evidence, Data', in Colin Hay and David Marsh (eds.), *Demystifying Globalization*, Basingstoke, Macmillan.
7. See Paul Hirst and Grahame Thompson (1999) *Globalization in question: the international economy and the possibilities of governance*, Cambridge, Polity (2nd edn.).
8. Susan Strange (1997) [1986] *Casino Capitalism*, Manchester, Manchester University Press.
9. Barry K. Gills (2001) 'Re-orienting the New (International) Political Economy', *New Political Economy*, 6, 2, p242.
10. Charles Leadbeater (1999) *Living on Thin Air*, London, Viking, pp18-19.
11. Ibid. p31.
12. Charles Leadbeater (1998) 'Welcome to the Knowledge Economy', in Ian Hargreaves and Ian Christie (eds.), *Tomorrow's Politics: The Third Way and Beyond*, London, Demos.
13. Joseph Schumpeter (1961) *The Theory of Economic Development*, Oxford, Oxford University Press, p65.
14. Nikolas Rose (1999) 'Inventiveness in Politics', *Economy and Society*, Vol. 28 (3), p477.
15. Geoff Mulgan (1996) 'Culture', in David Marquand and Anthony Seldon (eds.), *The Ideas that Shaped Post-War Britain*, London, Fontana, p196.
16. Ibid. p201.
17. Ibid. p206.
18. Ibid. p212.
19. Ibid. p213.

Index